STREET FOOD DIARIES

STREET FOOD DIARIES

IRRESISTIBLE
RECIPES INSPIRED
BY THE STREET

MATT BASILE

PHOTOGRAPHY BY **KYLA ZANARDI**

PENGUIN

an imprint of Penguin Canada Books Inc.

Published by the Penguin Group

Penguin Canada Books Inc., 90 Eglinton Avenue East, Suite 700, Toronto, Ontario,
   Canada M4P 2Y3

Penguin Group (USA) Inc., 375 Hudson Street, New York, New York 10014, U.S.A.

Penguin Books Ltd, 80 Strand, London WC2R 0RL, England

Penguin Ireland, 25 St Stephen's Green, Dublin 2, Ireland (a division of Penguin Books Ltd)

Penguin Group (Australia), 707 Collins Street, Melbourne, Victoria 3008, Australia
   (a division of Pearson Australia Group Pty Ltd)

Penguin Books India Pvt Ltd, 11 Community Centre, Panchsheel Park,
   New Delhi – 110 017, India

Penguin Group (NZ), 67 Apollo Drive, Rosedale, Auckland 0632, New Zealand
   (a division of Pearson New Zealand Ltd)

Penguin Books (South Africa) (Pty) Ltd, 24 Sturdee Avenue, Rosebank,
   Johannesburg 2196, South Africa

Penguin Books Ltd, Registered Offices: 80 Strand, London WC2R 0RL, England

First published 2014

1 2 3 4 5 6 7 8 9 10

Copyright © Matt Basile and Kyla Zanardi, 2014

Photography by Kyla Zanardi

Manufactured in the U.S.A.

LIBRARY AND ARCHIVES CANADA CATALOGUING IN PUBLICATION

Basile, Matt, author

Street food diaries : irresistible recipes inspired by the street /
Matt Basile ; photography by Kyla Zanardi.

Includes index.
ISBN 978-0-14-319130-8 (pbk.)

1. Street food. 2. Food trucks. 3. International cooking.
4. Cookbooks. I. Zanardi, Kyla, illustrator II. Title.

TX368.B37 2014   641.59   C2014-904060-1

Visit the Penguin Canada website at **www.penguin.ca**

Special and corporate bulk purchase rates available; please see **www.penguin.ca/corporatesales**
or call 1-800-810-3104, ext. 2477.

IN LOVING MEMORY

IN LOVING MEMORY OF CARLA ZANARDI AND ALBINO PALLIDINI,
TWO PEOPLE WHO TAUGHT US THE MEANING OF LIFE AND FOOD.

CONTENTS

INTRODUCTION

I remember being a little boy and watching my nonno cook. Sometimes putting a meal together was a two- or three-hour process. Tomato sauce was made every fall in his garage and stored in mason jars in the basement. I'm talking a year's worth of sauce. Bread was made from scratch every week. It was normal to see fresh pasta hung from every apparatus in the spare bedroom. I remember watching all of this thinking this was how you cooked food. This is how people eat all the time.

I remember certain times I wouldn't want to finish something on my plate. He would always say to me, "Matteo, *mangia* ... that's the best part." Somehow the part I left was always the best part. Sometimes I just wouldn't eat things to see if that would be the new best part. But he was right. It was the best part. It was all the best part. All food handmade with love was and is the best part.

When I was growing up, I had no desire to go to culinary school and model my technique on things done by some French chef who lived in the 1500s and who I had never met before (not that there's anything wrong with that, but it wasn't for me). I wanted to create something from scratch, just like my nonno had taught me, and I wanted the meals that I created for other people to be the very thing that defined me, that made me who I was.

Street food is as much about roots and stories as it is about recipes and ingredients. The act of cooking isn't about technical skill, but about falling in love with feeding people.

The whole street food movement really does epitomize this. It's the perfect combination of home-cooked meals and homemade stories. It can be the hotdog empire that started off as a cart 90 years earlier. It can be a family moving to a new part of the world and bringing with them a piece of their past. It can be a little park where people meet by the hundreds around 8 a.m. and buy you out of every last ounce of BBQ you smoked. It can be a kid from Toronto (cough, cough) who quit his cubicle job to start a pop-up, a food truck, a restaurant ... a street food revolution.

Street food is my life. It's how I connect with food, and in turn connect with people through food. When I first came up with the idea for Fidel Gastro's, my only aim was to open up a sandwich shop. That was my end goal. Open up one shop. It was my now business partner and girlfriend, Ky, who insisted I think bigger. Very quickly, though, thinking bigger ultimately became smaller in reality. I had a meeting with the bank, and once they discovered I had no experience and no money they very quickly told me I had no business. I was crushed. To the point where I didn't even want to hear the word *sandwich*. And then something happened. I stopped working toward something finite and just started cooking again.

I was at a party with some friends, and instead of ordering in food, a bunch of them asked me to cook. So I did. But I didn't just cook, I brought some energy and fun to it. To the point where cooking food at the party was a part of the party, just like music, shots of tequila ... and then boom! The next night I wrote on a

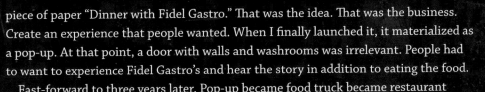

piece of paper "Dinner with Fidel Gastro." That was the idea. That was the business. Create an experience that people wanted. When I finally launched it, it materialized as a pop-up. At that point, a door with walls and washrooms was irrelevant. People had to want to experience Fidel Gastro's and hear the story in addition to eating the food.

Fast-forward to three years later. Pop-up became food truck became restaurant became catering company became reality television became this cookbook — and on and on and on and on. Ky was right, Fidel Gastro's wasn't about opening up a sandwich place, it was about connecting with people through fun food and taking that principle as far as it can go.

Creating this cookbook has been a journey for both me and my partner, Kyla (Ky) Zanardi, who is also the book's photographer. She would capture moments with street food vendors and restaurant chefs, even pit masters, while I would scribble notes down on a napkin ... the same one that had sauce on it. Together we chronicled food stories and the recipes they inspired. This is a book about the people we met, the stories we heard, and the food we ate across North America's incredibly close street food community. Now, although some of the stories aren't necessarily from street food vendors, their food still inspired us to create street food for this book. They all represent fun food like bacon and deep-fried things, but they also make telling a story through a meal that much easier. They are the core of street food's roots — inspired by others and created to bring people together by sharing a meal.

I never wanted to just write a cookbook. Neither did Ky. So we didn't. We haven't given you cookie-cutter recipes and fluffy over-exposed photos of staged, plastic food. This is a cookbook about street food. It's gritty and unapologetic. I hope you change things around and make each recipe your own. I want you to get creative with some of these recipes. Don't feel you have to follow my instructions to the letter, instead see them as a guide to street food creativity.

I hope this cookbook inspires you to travel across North America or the world or your own city, to eat amazing street food and be inspired by it as well. I hope you look at these recipes and say, "Ya, I love that, but what if we did this ..." I hope you embrace street food for what it is: an opportunity to tell someone a bit about yourself by the food you make.

This is a cookbook inspired by stories, smells, that perfect dish, something clever written on a chalkboard, a loved one, a desire to be more than just a food trucker or restaurateur. Ultimately, inspired by everything and anything.

VIVA LA STREET FOOD REVOLUCIÓN
MATT BASILE

STUFF IN BUNS

THERE'S SOMETHING ABOUT PUTTING STUFF IN BUNS THAT JUST EPITOMIZES STREET FOOD FOR ME. IT'S MOBILE, IT'S FUN, AND IT'S NOT REALLY SPECIFIC TO ONE TYPE OF CULTURE. IF YOU THINK ABOUT IT, SAYING YOU LIKE SANDWICHES OR BURGERS IS KIND OF LIKE SAYING YOU LIKE TV. I MEAN, THAT'S JUST SO BROAD. THERE ARE SO MANY GENRES AND SUB-GENRES OF FOODS THAT GO IN BUNS, MAKING IT IMPOSSIBLE TO JUST LABEL IT SO ARBITRARILY. I MEAN, YOU CAN HAVE VIETNAMESE SUBS, JAPANESE INTERPRETATIONS OF A 90-YEAR-OLD HOTDOG RECIPE, OR YOUR FAVORITE MEAL REMIXED TO FIT IN A BUN. THE OPTIONS REALLY ARE ENDLESS WHEN IT COMES TO PUTTING STUFF IN BUNS.

STUFF IN BUNS WAS MY FIRST ATTEMPT AT BREAKING INTO THE WORLD OF STREET FOOD. IT WASN'T ABOUT JUST MAKING A GENERIC SANDWICH THAT PEOPLE HAD SEEN A MILLION TIMES BEFORE, BUT INSTEAD ABOUT TAKING UNIQUE APPROACHES TO CLASSIC DISHES AND STUFFING THEM INTO BUNS. THE MEAT, THE BREAD, THE TOPPINGS, AND THE SAUCES ARE ALL EQUALLY IMPORTANT TO MAKING SURE THE "BUNNED" VISION IS COMPLETE — AND DESPITE IT COMING UNDER THE UMBRELLA OF "STREET FOOD," THESE STUFF IN BUN CREATIONS ARE THE RESULT OF A TRUE CULINARY PROCESS.

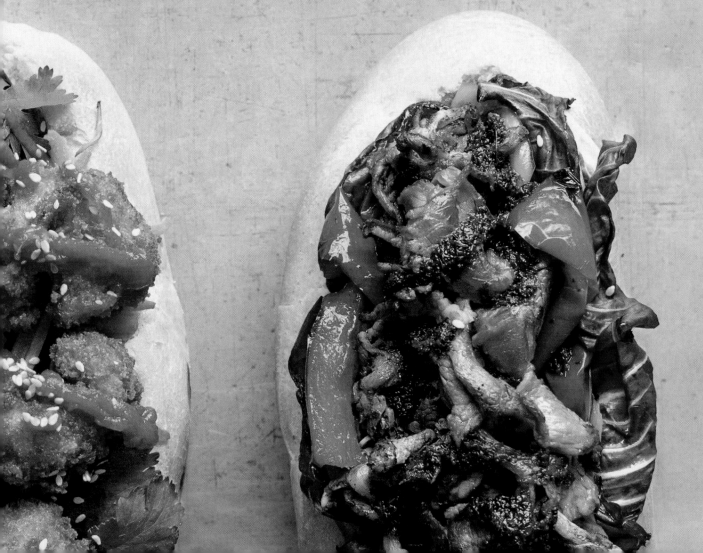

AMERICANA BURGER

A GREAT BURGER GOES A LONG WAY. I MEAN, IF YOU CAN MAKE A STANDOUT BURGER, THEN PEOPLE RESPECT YOUR CULINARY ABILITIES A LITTLE MORE. IF YOU HAVE TO MAKE JUST ONE KIND OF BURGER, MAKE THIS ONE.

SERVES 4

THE MEAT

In a big bowl, mix the ground beef with the salt, pepper, and paprika. Make sure the spices have been mixed really well into the meat so that there aren't any little pockets of them hiding behind a nice chunk of fat. Form the meat into four evenly sized patties, but instead of making them incredibly thick, try flattening them a little so they appear much wider than thicker. The beef patty is less likely to cook unevenly and will actually turn out juicier because you're not constantly flipping it and not pressing it down while it's cooking. A wise burger man once told me that pressing is for pants, not burgers.

THE TOPPINGS

Thinly slice the tomato and chiffonade the romaine lettuce. "Chiffonade" is a very fancy term for cutting the lettuce so thin that it looks like it was shredded.

There are two ways to prepare the bacon: either cook it in a skillet over high heat for approximately 4 minutes per side or place it on a grill pan and cook it in the oven at 350°F (180°C) for 7 minutes per side. Take the bacon to the next level by basting it with honey while it's cooking, and then hit it with bourbon to deglaze the pan. Believe it or not, I learned this technique while at university — not culinary school — but literally at university, hungover from the night before. The thick-cut bacon is already cured, so now you're just trying to bring out the crispiness of the fatty piece of meat. ❯❯❯

2 lb (1 kg) coarse ground chuck (ground beef)

1 tablespoon (15 mL) kosher salt

1 tablespoon (15 mL) black pepper

1 tablespoon (15 mL) smoked paprika

1 Roma tomato

1 heart romaine lettuce

4 slices extra-thick-cut bacon

1 tablespoon (15 mL) unsalted butter

4 eggs

4 burger buns

4 slices processed American cheese

A GREAT BURGER

GOES A LONG WAY

>>> BUILDING THE BURGER

Heat the butter in a grill pan or skillet over high heat. Place the meat patties in it, and sear the burgers for approximately 2 minutes per side. Turn down the heat to medium-low, and cook the burgers for approximately 4 minutes per side.

In a separate, nonstick pan, either cook one egg at a time or find a pan that's big enough to cook multiple eggs. Personally I would never cook more than two or three eggs in one pan. Cook the eggs, sunny-side up, over medium heat for approximately 5 minutes. If you like your egg yolks a little less runny, over-easy is the way to go. If you don't like a runny yolk, scrap the egg altogether as this yolk is going to get all over the burger.

Place the cooked bacon on the bun bottom. Top with a burger, followed by a slice of cheese, then a fried egg, and then some lettuce and tomato slices. Press the bun top down to complete the delicious burger. People often ask me why I use American cheese for burgers. To be honest, I find that nothing melts over hot ground beef quite like processed cheese. Normally I don't use any sauce for this burger because that ooey-gooey egg yolk becomes sauce the very second you press that top bun down on your Americana burger.

A WISE BURGER MAN ONCE TOLD ME THAT PRESSING IS FOR PANTS, NOT BURGERS

CHIMICHURRI STEAK SANDWICH

SERVES 4

NORMALLY I WOULD ALWAYS SAY THAT THE MEAT IS THE MOST IMPORTANT ITEM IN A SANDWICH. IN THIS CASE, THE SAUCE MAKES IT A TIE. THIS SANDWICH IS A MUST-EAT.

1 bunch green onions

1 bunch cilantro

1 bunch basil

Kosher salt

2 cups (500 mL) canola oil, divided

10 cloves garlic

Juice from 6 lemons

Black pepper

4 thin striploin steaks (6 oz/185 g each)

2 jalapeño peppers

⅔ cup (150 mL) red wine vinegar

Splash white wine, light beer, or lemon juice

4 ciabatta buns or rustic baguette

1 red onion, thinly sliced

THE CHIMICHURRI SAUCE AND THE BEEF

Wash the green onions, cilantro, and basil. Cut off the roots of the green onions, but leave the majority of the stems on the herbs and green onions. Throw the green onions and herbs into a blender with 1 teaspoon (5 mL) salt and 1 cup (250 mL) of the canola oil. Then add the garlic and the lemon juice (reserving a little bit of juice). Blend well but keep it chunky. Taste the mixture and add an additional 1 teaspoon (5 mL) salt and a little more canola oil if the sauce seems too thick or you want to adjust the flavor.

Lightly salt and pepper the steaks, place them in a large resealable plastic bag, and pour in the chimichurri sauce. Save 2 tablespoons (30 mL) of the sauce to drizzle on the steaks after they have been cooked. Let the meat marinate in the fridge for at least 1 hour.

Meanwhile, prepare the peppers.

THE PEPPERS

Preheat the oven broiler. Cut each pepper in half and remove the seeds. Lightly salt the peppers, and toss them into a bowl with the remaining 1 cup (250 mL) of canola oil. Place the peppers under the broiler, skin side up, for approximately 5 minutes, or until lightly toasted. Remove the peppers from the oven and slice them into thin strips. Place them in a small bowl, cover with the red wine vinegar, and transfer to the fridge. After an hour or so the peppers will have sucked up most of the red wine vinegar flavor.

THE SANDWICH

Grab a skillet or a searing pan or a griddle and add a little bit of canola oil. Turn the heat to high, and when the oil starts to smoke a little bit place the steaks in the pan. The light smoke means the oil and pan are hot enough to sear the steaks perfectly. Because you are a sensible human being, you recognize that the steaks will taste best when cooked to medium-rare. Sear the steaks for approximately 3 minutes on each side, or until a nice crust has formed. Remove the steaks from the pan, and let the meat rest for approximately 5 minutes. While the meat rests, add the white wine, light beer, or lemon juice to the pan to deglaze it.

Spread the reserved chimichurri sauce inside a bun, and stuff the bun with one of the steaks, some vinegar peppers, and slices of red onion. Repeat with the remaining ingredients and drizzle the deglazing liquid over top.

KOREAN FRITA

A FRITA IS ESSENTIALLY A CUBAN BURGER. IT IS USUALLY ON THE SMALLER SIDE AND OFFERS A MILLION DIFFERENT FLAVORS AND TEXTURES IN JUST A FEW BITES: SMOKINESS, SPICE, CRUNCH, COOL, AND ACID. THIS VERSION OF A FRITA PUSHES THOSE EXTREME CONTRASTING FLAVORS EVEN FURTHER. I'VE GIVEN YOU A RECIPE THAT ALLOWS YOU TO MAKE MORE SAUCE THAN YOU NEED FOR JUST ONE BATCH OF FRITAS. THAT WAY YOU HAVE EXTRA SAUCE IN THE FRIDGE FOR UP TO TWO WEEKS IF YOU WANT TO MAKE MORE OR JUST HAVE SOMETHING DIFFERENT HANDY.

THE TOPPINGS

Slice the cucumber into very thin rounds. Soak the cucumber rounds in the sauce from the kimchi at room temperature for approximately 1 hour (or in the fridge overnight). Discard the leafy top and the root stem of the leek. Slice the meat of the leek in half lengthwise, then cut each half into long strips and soak in cold water for about 30 minutes to remove any hidden dirt. Add canola oil to a skillet to a depth of ¼ inch (0.5 cm), and warm it to 350°F (180°C). Toss the leek slices in the flour, and fry for approximately 4 minutes, or until the leek pieces are golden brown. Once cooked, remove them from the oil, place them on some paper towels to soak up the excess grease, and then lightly salt them. The leek and pickles give this frita its crunch factor.

THE SAUCES

You have two sauces for the recipe, both of which are very easy to make. To make the first sauce, blitz the garlic and Greek yogurt in a blender or processor to combine well. To make the second sauce, mix the ketchup, 1 tablespoon (15 mL) of the cayenne pepper, and the soy sauce in a bowl. Combining the ketchup and the garlic sauces will give the little burger two very distinct flavors; one adds an intense cooling flavor and the other a smoky, spice flavor.

Ingredients:

- 1 large English cucumber, skin on
- ½ cup (125 mL) kimchi sauce (see page 118)
- 1 leek
- 1 cup (250 mL) all-purpose flour
- 4 cloves garlic
- 2 cups (500 mL) plain Greek yogurt
- 2 cups (500 mL) ketchup
- 2 tablespoons (30 mL) cayenne pepper, divided
- ½ cup (125 mL) soy sauce
- 1 lb (500 g) coarsely ground beef
- 1 tablespoon (15 mL) kosher salt
- 1 tablespoon (15 mL) black pepper
- 4 slider buns

BUILDING THE LITTLE PATTY

In a big bowl, combine the ground beef, salt, black pepper, and remaining 1 tablespoon (15 mL) of cayenne pepper. Form the seasoned beef into four evenly sized patties. Throw a little bit of vegetable oil into a nonstick skillet and cook the patties for approximately 3 minutes per side over high heat. Spread the smoky ketchup sauce on the top and bottom of a bun. Add a patty and top with kimchi pickles, garlic yogurt sauce, and crispy leek. If you're feeling extra adventurous, throw a second little patty on top.

SUGO BURGER

IF YOU CALL YOUR GRANDPARENTS *NONNO* AND *NONNA* THEN YOU'LL KNOW WHAT SUGO IS. MEAT SAUCE. HEAVENLY SUNDAY AFTERNOON SUGO. YOU WILL LOVE THIS RECIPE.

20–30 1-inch (2.5 cm) pieces boneless beef short ribs

2 tablespoons (30 mL) kosher salt, divided

2 tablespoons (30 mL) black pepper, divided

2 teaspoons (10 mL) olive oil

2 Spanish onions, diced small

6 cloves garlic

1 cup (250 mL) unsalted butter

2 cans (28 oz/796 mL each) chopped San Marzano tomatoes

2 lb (1 kg) coarsely ground chuck beef

1 tablespoon (15 mL) smoked paprika

4 crusty kaiser buns or burger buns

1 piece (3 ½ oz/100 g) Parmesan cheese

1 bunch basil

THE SUGO

Lightly season the pieces of short rib with 1 tablespoon (15 mL) each of the salt and pepper. Heat the olive oil in a large skillet over high heat, throw in the beef pieces, and begin to stir. Once the meat gains a little bit of color, add some of the diced onion and the garlic. Continue to stir the meat and add the butter. Once the butter has fully melted and coated everything in the skillet, add the canned tomatoes with their juice. Turn down the heat to medium-low, and let it cook, uncovered, for approximately 3 to 4 hours, occasionally stirring to remind the sugo that you love it. Check the sauce after 3 hours. If it's nice and thick, it's ready. If not, keep going for up to 4 hours, checking regularly.

THE BEEF PATTY

Place the beef in a bowl and add the remaining 1 tablespoon (15 mL) of both salt and pepper with the smoked paprika. Mix well until the seasoning has been evenly distributed through the meat. Form into four wide beef patties. Place them in a large skillet with a little bit of vegetable oil over medium-high heat and cook for approximately 4 to 6 minutes per side. Now, I'm not telling you to cook your burger to medium, I'm just saying, if you trust the quality of the meat your butcher ground for you, then … Well, you know, medium is best.

THE BURGER

Place the beef burger on the bun and top with a mountain of sugo. Grate Parmesan cheese all over the sugo and top with fresh basil leaves. Repeat using the remaining ingredients.

SWEET 'N' SOUR BEEF STEAK SANDWICHES

SERVES 4 TO 6

I CAME UP WITH THIS RECIPE WHILE DOING A POP-UP EVENT IN THE WORLD'S SANDWICH CAPITAL, PHILADELPHIA. AFTER EATING MY BODY WEIGHT IN PHILLY CHEESESTEAKS, I THOUGHT IT WOULD BE GREAT TO PAY HOMAGE TO SAUCY, JUICY BEEF WHILE EMBRACING OTHER FOOD COMMUNITIES WITHIN PHILLY. THE BREAD WE USED WAS STRAIGHT FROM PHILLY'S PICTURESQUE GERMANTOWN AND THE SEASONING AND TOPPINGS RIGHT FROM CHINATOWN. TO ME, THIS SANDWICH IS ABOUT LOOKING AT THE ENTIRE STREET FOOD SCENE OF A CITY AND BRINGING IT ALL TOGETHER IN ONE DISH.

ANY REAL BUTCHER SHOP, ESPECIALLY ONE THAT ALREADY SLICES CARPACCIO, WILL BE ABLE TO SELL YOU SLICED BEEF FOR THIS RECIPE. THE TRICK IS TO ORDER IT AT LEAST ONE DAY IN ADVANCE SO THAT THE BUTCHER CAN PARTIALLY FREEZE THE MEAT SO IT SLICES MORE EASILY. SIRLOIN IS THE LEANEST OF THE CUTS OF MEAT AND THE LEAST EXPENSIVE. RIBEYE IS THE FATTIEST AND MOST EXPENSIVE. BECAUSE THE MEAT NEEDS TO BE SLICED SO THINLY, THE FAT CONTENT SHOULDN'T MATTER AS MUCH BECAUSE MOST MEAT FROM A QUALITY BUTCHER SHOP SHOULD BE TENDER WHEN CUT SLICED THIS THINLY VERSUS WHEN AT THAT THICKNESS.

8 oz (225 g) piece fresh ginger

4 cups (1 L) soy sauce, divided

1 cup (250 mL) ginger beer

2 cups (500 mL) honey

Juice from 3 lemons

2 lb (1 kg) beef sirloin, striploin, or ribeye, thinly sliced (Note: keep meat cold)

4 large carrots

1 large daikon radish

3 jalapeño peppers (optional)

Kosher salt

8 cups (2 L) rice wine vinegar

1 lb (500 g) baby bok choy

1 bunch cilantro

1 tablespoon (15 mL) sesame oil

1 ½ tablespoons (22 mL) olive oil

5 cloves garlic, finely chopped

1 cup (250 mL) ketchup

4–6 hoagie-style buns

MARINATING THE MEAT!

Peel the ginger, cut it into chunks, and place it in a blender or processor. Blend until it is almost a purée but still has some small chunks in it. Transfer the blended ginger to a large bowl, and add 2 cups (500 mL) of the soy sauce and all of the ginger beer. Add the honey and lemon juice to the bowl, and lightly whisk to prevent the honey from clumping. Add the cold slices of beef to the marinade. Be sure to pull the meat apart as you place it in the bowl so that all the meat slices are coated evenly. If your marinade requires more liquid, add a little more soy sauce. ⟩ ⟩ ⟩

>>> THE SLAW

Peel the carrots and the radish, and discard the tips and bottoms. Cut the carrots in half and the radish in thirds. Use a mandolin to cut them into matchstick pieces. If you're using a knife to do this, first cut lengthwise into the carrots and radish so you have flat pieces of veg. Then julienne the pieces to the thickness you prefer. Slice the jalapeño peppers as thinly as possible. Only use all of the jalapeño peppers if you want your slaw to have some serious kick, or use no jalapeño peppers if you want zero kick. Mix all the cut-up veg in a container together, and lightly salt the entire mixture — no more than 2 teaspoons (10 mL). Add enough rice wine vinegar to the container to cover half the slaw. Add up to 8 cups (2 L) of water to the container. The slaw should be fully covered. Normally I will use equal volumes of vinegar and water and let the slaw sit in the fridge overnight to pickle. If you want a quicker process, use four parts vinegar to one part water so the slaw will be ready in approximately 1 hour. Whichever way you do it, don't discard the pickling liquid. Put the liquid into a jar and keep it in the fridge for the next time you want to pickle some veg.

MAKING THE SANDWICH

First bring 4 cups (1 L) of water to a boil in a medium pot. Flash cook the bok choy for 5 minutes, or until its color has brightened.

Pick and clean as much cilantro as you desire. Take the slaw out of the vinegar solution, draining as much of the liquid as possible. The easiest way to do this is to put the slaw in a pasta strainer and gently press the excess liquid out. Place the slaw in a clean, dry bowl, and toss with the sesame oil and cilantro. Season to taste with salt if needed.

Throw the olive oil in a wok or skillet over high heat, and add the finely chopped garlic, marinated meat, and marinade. I would cook the meat in three stages or so. If you put all the meat into the skillet at one time, it will cool down the contents and will prevent the meat from having a nice sear. Sear the meat for approximately 2 minutes. Add the bok choy, ketchup, and the remaining 2 cups (500 mL) soy sauce, dividing it all between each batch of meat, and toss to coat everything evenly. Because of the quality of meat and the acid in the marinade, you can cook it from rare to well done — it's entirely your call.

Grab a hoagie bun, fill it with the saucy meat and bok choy, and top it off with the slaw. Repeat with the remaining ingredients.

THE OPTIONS REALLY ARE ENDLESS WHEN IT COMES TO PUTTING STUFF IN BUNS

CUBAN SANDWICH

THIS WAS THE FIRST SANDWICH I STARTED MAKING UNDER THE FIDEL GASTRO BRAND. AT THE TIME, I WAS FAMILIAR WITH PULLED PORK SANDWICHES BUT HAD ONLY HEARD OF TRADITIONAL CUBANO SANDWICHES. WHEN I FIRST STARTED MAKING THEM MY GOAL WAS TO JUST MAKE SOMETHING FAMILIAR (PULLED PORK) A LITTLE BIT DIFFERENT BY GIVING IT SOME NEW LIFE AND SPICE (CUBANO). IT'S A GREAT ALTERNATIVE TO THE TYPICAL BBQ VERSION OF PULLED PORK — NOT THAT THERE'S ANYTHING WRONG WITH THE TYPICAL VERSION. THIS SANDWICH GETS A TREMENDOUS AMOUNT OF FLAVOR FROM THE MEAT, PICKLES, HAM, AND CHEESE, AS WELL AS THE CARAMELIZED ONIONS AND CHILI AIOLI.

PLASTIC WRAP IN THE OVEN? NOPE, YOU'RE NOT SEEING THINGS. IT'S PERFECTLY SAFE AT LOW TEMPERATURES.

3 tablespoons (45 mL) kosher salt

2 tablespoons (30 mL) black pepper

2 tablespoons (30 mL) smoked paprika

1 tablespoon (15 mL) cayenne pepper

1 bunch cilantro, stems removed

2 cups (500 mL) Dijon mustard

5 lb (2.5 kg) boneless pork shoulder

2 pints (16 oz/470 mL each) light beer

2 Spanish onions

2 eggs

6 cloves garlic

4 cups (1 L) canola oil (approx)

2 cups (500 mL) Sriracha sauce

8–12 light and airy submarine-style buns

1 jar (17 oz/500 mL) kosher dill pickles

8–12 slices cooked ham

8–12 slices Havarti cheese

2 cups (500 mL) salted butter

BRAISING THE PORK SHOULDER

Preheat the oven to 275°F (135°C). Mix the salt, black pepper, paprika, and cayenne pepper together in a medium bowl. Make sure everything is evenly mixed without any spice clumps. Wash the cilantro and finely chop it. Mix the finely chopped cilantro into the spice bowl, and add the Dijon mustard. Rub this marinade all over the pork shoulder. Place the pork shoulder in a deep roasting pan, and add the beer. Tightly cover the pan with a layer of plastic wrap followed by a layer of aluminum foil. Place the pork in the oven for approximately 6 hours.

THE CUBANO TOPPINGS

Slice the onions into small, thin pieces. Place them in a large pan with a little bit of canola oil over high heat. Cook without stirring for 5 to 6 minutes. You will notice the onions start to char. Hit them with ¼ cup (60 mL) of water, and start to stir them. You will see them start to pick up all the char off the bottom of the pan. Feel free to add a little more water if it looks like they could use it. Turn down the heat to medium-low and allow the onions to cook slowly. Continue to stir them so they pick up all those beautiful caramelized sugar colors (and don't burn on you). They should be fully caramelized after approximately 20 minutes. ❯❯❯

PULL THAT MEAT APART!

››› The chili aioli for this recipe has a little bit of heat but isn't meant to be insanely hot. It's supposed to just balance the acid from the pickles and the fattiness of the meat.

Crack the eggs into a blender or food processor, add the garlic, and blend. Slowly add the canola oil while the machine is running. By the time the mixture has fully thickened you will have made your own natural mayonnaise. Add the Sriracha sauce to the blender, and continue to blend until the mayo has taken on a light-orange color.

THE SANDWICH

Take the Cuban pork out of the oven once it is cooked, and pull the meat apart. It should fall apart when you attack it with tongs. Take a sandwich bun and layer it with sliced pickles, a slice of ham, a slice of Havarti cheese, some pulled pork, and some caramelized onions, and top with the chili aioli.

It's ready to serve, but technically it's not a true Cuban sandwich unless it's been grilled on a flat-top grill or grilling pan. Melt a little bit of butter in a nonstick pan and place the whole sandwich on the hot surface, pressing it down with a sandwich weight. Hold the sandwich down for approximately 3 minutes and then repeat on the other side. Now you have a Cuban pulled pork sandwich!

SAUCES ARE ALL SO EQUALLY IMPORTANT

PORK BELLY PO'BOY

SERVES 6 TO 8

I ALWAYS THOUGHT FRIED OYSTERS WERE WHAT MADE A PO'BOY A PO'BOY. AND THEN I WENT TO NEW ORLEANS AND LEARNED THAT ANYTHING CAN BE IN A PO'BOY — IT'S THE BREAD THAT MAKES IT PO'BOY-WORTHY. KNOWLEDGE IN THE FORM OF SANDWICH — WHERE WAS THIS IN HIGH SCHOOL?? (AND DON'T PANIC, IT'S FINE TO USE PLASTIC WRAP IN THE OVEN AT VERY LOW TEMPS.)

4 cups (1 L) canola oil

4 lb (2 kg) skinless pork belly

½ cup (125 mL) Dijon mustard

8 cups (2 L) Clamato juice

¼ cup (60 mL) dried thyme

2 tablespoons + 1 teaspoon (35 mL) kosher salt

1 cup (250 mL) apple cider vinegar

1 head Savoy cabbage

½ cup (125 mL) white vinegar

1 large carrot

2 eggs

3 cloves garlic

5 basil leaves

2 jalapeño peppers

Juice from 2 lemons

1 bottle (12 oz/355 mL) hoisin sauce

2 heirloom or beefsteak tomatoes

6–8 long, hoagie-style submarine buns

THE PORK BELLY

Make this belly the day before you're planning to eat it so that you can place it in the fridge and slice it properly. Just sayin'…

Pour 1 tablespoon (15 mL) of the canola oil into a skillet and bring it up to high heat. Place the pork belly in the skillet, and sear for approximately 4 minutes per side.

Preheat the oven to 300°F (150°C). In a large bowl, combine the mustard with the Clamato juice. Stir until mixed thoroughly. Add the dried thyme, 2 tablespoons (30 mL) of the salt, and the apple cider vinegar. Give it all a quick stir. Place the seared pork belly in a deep ovenproof pan and pour the mixture over it. Cover with a layer of plastic wrap and then a layer of aluminum foil. Cook for 3 to 4 hours, or until the meat is soft and almost falling apart. Remove the pork belly from the oven and let it cool to room temperature, then place it in the fridge.

THE SLAW

Peel the first few layers off the cabbage and then julienne the large piece until you reach the core. Discard the core. Place the shredded cabbage in a large bowl and lightly salt it. Pour in the white vinegar. Allow the cabbage to soak for approximately 1 hour. Remove it from the vinegar, dry it off with some paper towel, and place it in a clean, dry bowl. Shred the carrot into the cabbage slaw using a cheese grater. Crack the eggs into a blender or food processor. Blitz the eggs, and then add the garlic, basil, 1 teaspoon (5 mL) of salt, and the jalapeño peppers. Slowly pour in the canola oil while the machine is running and watch the egg mixture begin to thicken. Once the mixture is thick, gradually add the lemon juice, and then give one last blitz.

Add the aioli to the cabbage and carrot slaw. Toss until evenly coated and creamy.

OH BOY, HERE'S THE PO'BOY

Remove the pork belly from the fridge and slice it into ¼-inch (0.5 cm) strips. Grease a hot skillet or nonstick frying pan with a little bit of canola oil. Sear the pork belly over high heat for approximately 2 minutes on each side, allowing the fatty pieces of pork to crisp. Take the braising liquid from the pork belly pan and mix it with the hoisin sauce. You want the consistency of the hoisin mixture to be soft and a little on the loose side. Slice your tomatoes nice and thin, and layer some on the bottom portion of a bun. Add a layer of crispy pork belly pieces, and top with slaw. Drizzle with the braising liquid/hoisin sauce, close up the bun, and enjoy. Repeat with the remaining ingredients.

JOHN'S ROAST PORK, SOUTH PHILLY

WHEN YOU'RE IN PHILLY, MOST FOLKS AREN'T REALLY TALKING CHEESESTEAKS. IT MIGHT BE THE SO-CALLED SANDWICH OF TOURISTS, BUT THE LOCALS ONLY TALK ABOUT ROAST PORK.

KY DID SOME RESEARCH BEFORE WE HEADED TO THE CITY OF BROTHERLY LOVE, AND JOHN'S ROAST PORK IN SOUTH PHILLY CAME UP QUITE OFTEN. UPON FURTHER RESEARCH, WE LEARNED IT WAS A JAMES BEARD AWARD-WINNING SANDWICH SHOP. THE F*#@?!? JAMES BEARD AWARD-WINNING?? THIS I HAD TO TRY.

SO, FOR WHATEVER REASON, ON THE DAY WE DECIDED TO CHECK IT OUT THE SANDWICH GODS JUST WEREN'T ON OUR SIDE. A DETOUR TO GERMANTOWN AND SPENDING WHAT FELT LIKE ALMOST AN HOUR IN A BAKERY TALKING BREAD FOR AN EVENT ACTUALLY COST US OUR SANDWICH AS WE STOPPED LOOKING AT THE TIME AND ONLY FOCUSED ON GETTING FRESH BREAD. A FEW

WHEN YOU'RE IN PHILLY, MOST FOLKS AREN'T REALLY TALKING CHEESESTEAKS ... THE LOCALS ONLY TALK ABOUT ROAST PORK.

WRONG TURNS LATER BY OUR CAB DRIVER AND KY AND I WERE DROPPED OFF AT THIS LITTLE CAGED-UP SPOT ON THE SIDE OF THE ROAD IN SOUTH PHILLY. THE SIGN HAD NO ADVICE, NO WHIMSICAL ONE-LINER, AND DEFINITELY NO SANDWICH. ALL IT HAD WAS A CLOSED SIGN. DEFEATED AND SADDENED, WE WERE NONETHELESS DETERMINED TO RETURN A DAY LATER.

RETURN WE DID, AND THIS TIME AT 10:30 A.M. WE JOINED THE INCREDIBLY LONG LINEUP, HAPPY THAT WE WERE FAR MORE CAREFUL WITH OUR TIME THE SECOND TIME AROUND. IT WAS MY TURN TO ORDER, AND WHEN ASKED, "WHAT'LL YA HAVE?" I SAID VERY QUICKLY, "THE ROAST PORK." IN A SITUATION LIKE THIS, I ALWAYS TELL THE CRAFTSMAN TO SERVE IT THE WAY THEY WOULD EAT IT. IN THIS CASE, THAT MEANT STEWED HOT PEPPERS, OLD PROVOLONE, AND BROCCOLI RAAB (OTHERWISE KNOWN AS RAPINI). FOR WHATEVER REASON, I CHANGED MY ORDER IMMEDIATELY — I ORDERED THREE MORE WITH IT. THE DEDICATION PEOPLE HAVE FOR THESE SANDWICHES IS ASTONISHING. THEY WEAR THE QUALITY OF JOHN'S ROAST PORK LIKE A FATTY LITTLE BADGE OF HONOR.

PORK 'N' PEPPA DIP

SERVES 12

NOTHING BEATS A SUCCULENT, MOIST, MEATY ROAST PORK SANDWICH. THIS IS ONE OF THOSE SANDWICHES THAT WHEN DONE WELL, JUST MELTS IN YOUR MOUTH, BUT WHEN MESSED UP, IS JUST A CRIME AGAINST SWINE. LUCKY FOR YOU, I'VE GOT YOUR PIGGY BACK. GET IT? PIGGY BACK?

PLASTIC WRAP IN THE OVEN? YOU GOTTA BE KIDDING, RIGHT? NOPE. IT'S ALL GOOD AT VERY LOW TEMPS.

2 tablespoons (30 mL) fennel seeds

12 sprigs fresh thyme

3 tablespoons (45 mL) garlic powder

3 tablespoons (45 mL) kosher salt

1 tablespoon (15 mL) black pepper

1 tablespoon (15 mL) dried rosemary

¼ cup (60 mL) olive oil

8 lb (3.5 kg) boneless pork shoulder (ensure it is scored and tied)

2 red onions

1 cup (250 mL) white wine

2 bunches rapini

3 red bell peppers

4 cloves garlic

Juice from 1 lemon

4 rustic French baguettes

3 tablespoons (45 mL) grainy Dijon mustard (optional)

THE PORK

Pork shoulder, pork butt, Boston butt ... It has many names, but in the end, no matter what you call it, if you respect it, it will treat you right. Ask your butcher for a boneless (skin-on if possible) scored and tied pork butt. Not only will you score butcher points for sounding like you know a thing or two about pork, but you'll have snagged yourself the tastiest meat option possible.

Mix the fennel seeds with the fresh thyme in a food processor, and blend until it breaks it up. Transfer the blended spices to a bowl, and add the garlic powder, salt, pepper, and rosemary. Add the olive oil, and blend to make a spiced paste ready to be rubbed all over your butt ... pork butt ... cough, cough. When rubbing the pork with the spice mixture, make sure you get the paste into all the crevices of the pork. Then place the pork in a deep ovenproof pan. Cut the red onions into 1-inch (2.5 cm) cubes and add them to the pan. Pour the white wine and 3 cups (750 mL) of water (or chicken stock) into the pan, around the shoulder. Don't pour it over top as this will wash off the rub. At this point, the pork should be mostly submerged in the liquid. Cover the pan with a layer of plastic wrap and a layer of aluminum foil.

Preheat the oven to 275°F (135°C). Slowly cook the pork for approximately 6 hours, or until tender. While it cooks, enjoy a nice cold beverage and maybe even a cigar. Remove the pork from the oven, set it aside in the pan, and leave the oven on. ❯❯❯

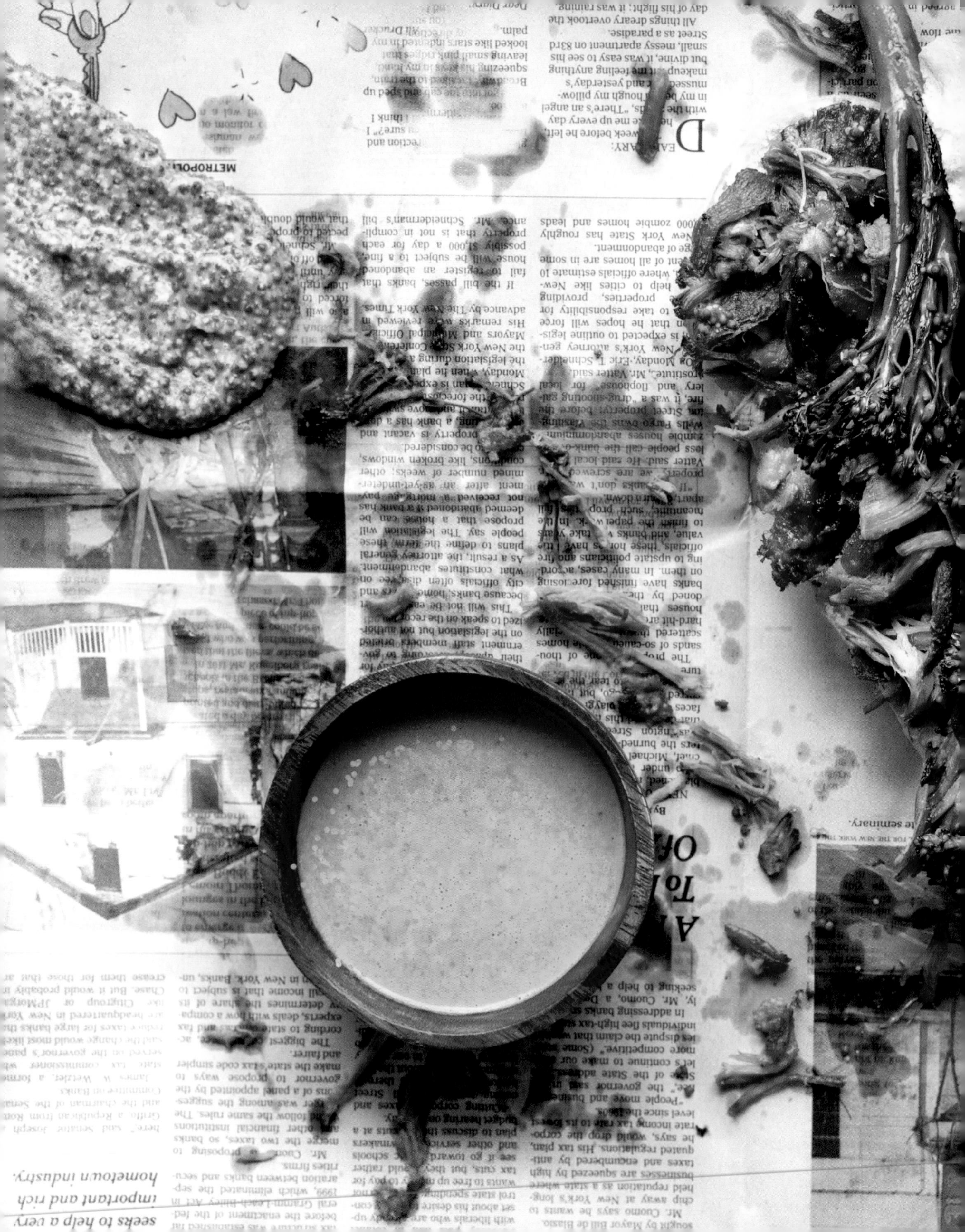

>>> THE SAUCE AND THE SANDWICH

Increase the temperature of the oven to 450°F (230°C). Remove the shoulder from the braising liquid and place it on a baking tray. Reserve the braising liquid for when you make your sauce. Place the braised meat in the hot oven, and cook, uncovered, for approximately 45 minutes, or until the skin becomes incredibly crispy but not burnt.

Prepare a bowl of ice water, and set it aside. Bring a pot of water to a boil over high heat. Add the rapini and cook for approximately 5 minutes, or until the greens darken. Remove the rapini from the pot and place it in the ice water until cooled. This shocks it and stops it from cooking any more. You can either use it as is or lightly sauté it in a pan over medium-high heat with garlic and olive oil until all the extra flavor has been soaked up by the bitter Italian vegetable. Actually, blanching the rapini before sautéing reduces its bitterness.

If you have a BBQ, I suggest roasting the peppers for approximately 10 minutes before you make the dipping sauce. If you don't have that option, broil the peppers in the oven for approximately 5 minutes on each side. Toss the peppers in a bowl and tightly cover it with plastic wrap. After about 10 minutes the peels will come off the peppers very easily. Pour the reserved braising liquid into a food processor. Add the roasted peppers, garlic, and lemon juice and blend until you have a velvety red sauce.

Pull the pork out of the oven and let it rest for approximately 10 minutes. Cut the pork into chunks. You'll notice at this point that the meat will just fall apart. If you're using the Dijon, spread some on both sides of each baguette — a little goes a long way with this sandwich. Put generous amounts of meat into the baguette and top with rapini. Now you can do three things with your red pepper sauce: pour the sauce over the pork and rapini in the sandwich, put it in a small dish and use it to dip your sandwich into, or do it the Fidel Gastro way, which is to do both. Cut each baguette into three pieces.

SUCCULENT, MOIST
MEATY ROAST PORK

LAMBAPEÑO BURGER

I LEARNED HOW TO MAKE THE JALAPEÑO MINT SAUCE IN THIS RECIPE AT A RODEO WITH ONE OF THE BEST DAMN BBQ PIT MASTERS I EVER MET. KEVIN FROM KB BBQ TOOK ME UNDER HIS WING AND LET ME IN ON HIS AMAZING JELLY. LADIES AND GENTLEMEN, THIS WAS MY FIRST RODEO. THERE'S NOTHING FANCY ABOUT IT, IT JUST GETS THE LAMB JOB DONE.

THE JALAPEÑO MINT SAUCE

Bring 1 ½ cups (375 mL) of water to a boil in a small pot over high heat. Toss in the jalapeños, and let them boil for approximately 5 minutes, or until soft. Remove the peppers from the water, but keep the water simmering over low heat. Remove the stems from the jalapeños. Place the jalapeños in a blender with the mint, thyme, basil, and garlic. Blend well, then transfer to the pot of simmering water. Add 1 tablespoon (15 mL) of salt, and then slowly add the sugar while stirring the mixture. Add the juice from one of the lemons and allow the jalapeño sauce to slowly reduce by half, approximately 30 minutes. Turn off the heat, and remove the pot from the burner. Stir the sauce lightly for approximately 30 seconds, and then let it stand until it comes down to room temperature. Transfer the sauce to an airtight container, and place it in the fridge to help the sugars congeal and give it a jelly-like consistency.

THE PATTY AND THE SLAW

Put the ground lamb in a bowl. Mix the remaining 1 tablespoon (15 mL) of salt, the black pepper, and the cumin into the meat. Make sure the seasoning is well distributed through the meat. Form the meat into four to six patties.

The slaw is incredibly simple to make. Very thinly slice the fennel, and place it in a bowl. Add the remaining lemon juice and lightly salt it. I sometimes like to give it a little splash of high-quality extra virgin olive oil because the flavor comes together very nicely with the lamb meat. Your choice.

THE BURGER

Place the lamb patties in a hot skillet or grill pan over high heat (no oil required). Sear the patties for approximately 2 minutes per side. Then turn down the temperature to medium-low, and cook the burgers for an additional 4 to 5 minutes per side. Set the burgers aside for approximately 1 minute to rest before you put them on the buns. Spread some goat cheese on the inside top and bottom of the burger buns. Add the lamb patty and top with fennel slaw and jalapeño mint sauce.

8 jalapeño peppers

1 bunch fresh mint

12 sprigs fresh thyme

10 basil leaves

5 cloves garlic

2 tablespoons (30 mL) kosher salt, divided

½ cup (125 mL) granulated sugar

Juice from 2 lemons, divided

2 lb (1 kg) ground lamb

1 teaspoon (5 mL) black pepper

1 tablespoon (15 mL) ground cumin

½ bulb fennel

4–6 classic burger buns

¼ cup (60 mL) creamy goat cheese

BUFFALO CHICKEN PATTY MELT

WHAT WE'RE TRYING TO DO WITH THIS DISH IS BRING ALL THE FUN AND FLAVOR OF A BUFFALO CHICKEN WING INTO A GRILLED CHEESE SANDWICH. THESE TWO SAUCES ARE WHAT MAKE THE DISH "BUFFALO CHICKEN-ESQUE." YOU ONLY USE ABOUT ¼ CUP (60 ML) OF THE SAUCES, BUT THE LEFTOVERS CAN BE REFRIGERATED SAFELY FOR A COUPLE OF WEEKS.

SERVES 4

THE SAUCES

To make the buffalo sauce, melt 1 ½ cups (375 mL) of the butter in a saucepan over medium heat. Add the Sriracha sauce and stir for 3 to 4 minutes, or until you have a creamy, velvety orange sauce. Add the vinegar and the juice from two of the lemons. Stir the sauce one last time. Remove from the heat and allow to cool to room temperature. Set aside in the fridge until needed.

The second sauce is the blue cheese dipping sauce. We dip the sandwich in this to make it extra badass. Crack the eggs into a food processor or blender with the garlic and give it a good blitz. Once everything is broken down, slowly pour in the canola oil while the machine is running. Continue to pour the oil in until the sauce begins to thicken up, then add the crumbled blue cheese and continue to blitz it until the cheese has been evenly distributed through the aioli. You will most likely need the entire 4 cups (1 L) of oil. Hit the dipping sauce with the remaining lemon juice right at the end. ❯ ❯ ❯

2 cups (500 mL) salted butter, divided

3 cups (750 mL) Sriracha sauce

¼ cup (60 mL) white vinegar

Juice from 3 lemons, divided

3 eggs

4 cloves garlic

4 cups (1 L) canola oil (approx)

3 ½ oz (100 g) blue cheese, crumbled

1 lb (500 g) ground chicken

Butter for frying

1 loaf bread (rye or white bread)

16 slices Havarti cheese

>>> THE PATTY AND ITS MELT

Place the ground chicken in a bowl, and mix it with about ¼ cup (60 mL) of the buffalo sauce. Combine well, and then form the ground meat into four evenly sized patties (the thinner the better). Melt a little butter in a nonstick skillet over medium heat. Place the chicken patties in the hot skillet and sear for approximately 2 minutes per side. Turn down the heat to medium, and cook for an additional 4 minutes per side. Take the patties off the heat, and let them rest for approximately 1 minute.

Take a clean nonstick pan and melt a little more butter over medium heat. On the countertop, lay out a piece of bread and place two slices of cheese on it, then place the chicken patty on top. Add about 2 teaspoons (10 mL) of buffalo sauce on top of the patty and top with two more slices of cheese. Finish by placing another slice of bread on top. Place the sandwich in the hot, buttery pan, and place a sandwich press or weight on top of it. Let this first side of the sandwich cook for 4 to 5 minutes. Flip the sandwich, and cook for another 4 to 5 minutes. When the sandwich is ready, remove from the heat and serve right away. Repeat with the remaining ingredients. Dip (and then double dip) in the blue cheese dipping sauce.

DIP (AND DOUBLE DIP)

DIP THE SANDWICH IN SAUCE TO MAKE IT EXTRA BADASS

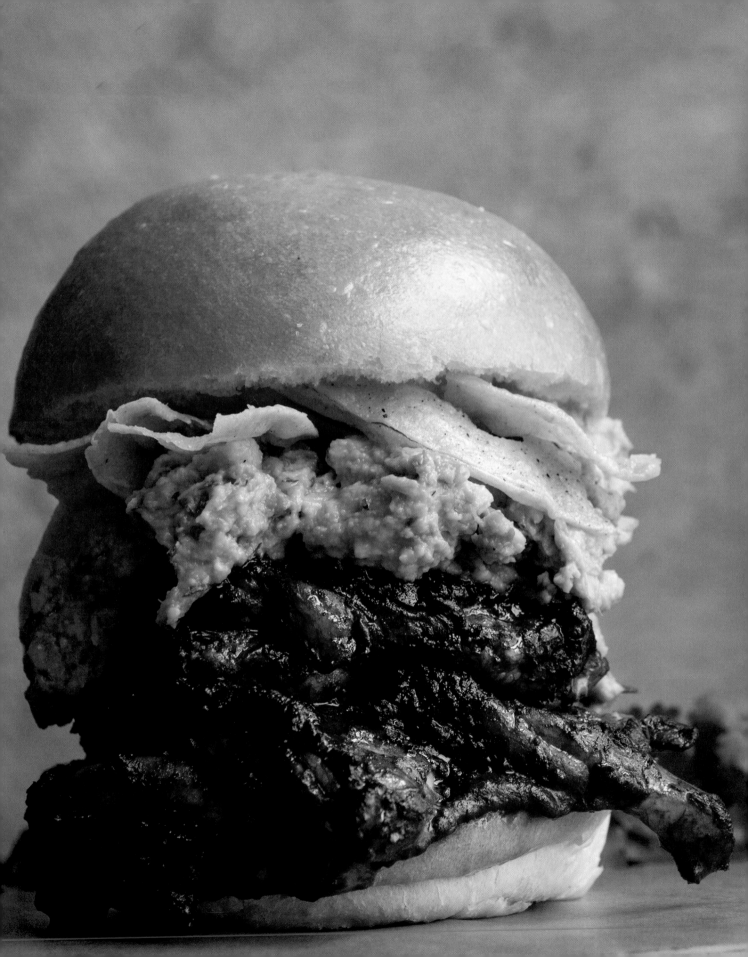

OLÉ MOLÉ GUACAMOLE CHICKEN SANDWICH

SERVES 4

THE MOLÉ SAUCE ACCOUNTS FOR THE MAJORITY OF THE WORK FOR THIS DISH. BUT IF DONE PROPERLY, IT'S TOTALLY WORTH IT. IT ALSO KEEPS VERY WELL, SO IF YOU MAKE EXTRA, BE SURE TO EXPERIMENT WITH THE ROBUST FLAVORS OF THE MOLÉ ON DIFFERENT PROTEINS: ANIMALS, FISH, AND OTHER STUFF. YOU CAN USE VERMOUTH IF YOU CAN'T FIND AMARO. › › ›

3 cans (7 oz/198 g each) chipotle
peppers in adobo sauce

8 cloves garlic

3 tomatoes

1 Spanish onion

2 tablespoons (30 mL)
unsweetened smooth
peanut butter

2 tablespoons (30 mL) ground
cinnamon

1 tablespoon (15 mL) dried
oregano

1 cup (250 mL) cold espresso

1 tablespoon (15 mL)
kosher salt, separated

1 cup (250 mL) salted butter

1 oz (30 mL) Amaro

21 oz (600 g) unsweetened dark
chocolate (baking chocolate
works well)

2 avocados

½ bunch cilantro, stems removed

3 limes

2 tablespoons (30 mL) olive oil

8 boneless, skinless chicken thighs

4 soft buns

5 oz (150 g) tortilla chips, crushed

THE MOLÉ SAUCE

Blitz the chipotles, garlic, tomatoes, onion, peanut butter, cinnamon, oregano, and then the espresso in a super-duty blender or food processor. Add 2 teaspoons (10 mL) of the salt.

Place the butter in a large saucepan and melt it over medium heat. Add the blended chipotle mixture to the melted butter and stir well. Once fully combined, add the Amaro and the unsweetened chocolate. Lastly, pour in 2 cups (500 mL) of water and continue to stir. Allow the sauce to simmer, uncovered, over low heat for approximately 1 hour. When the excess liquid has reduced and the sauce thickens up nicely, you've struck molé gold. If it looks like it's in danger of burning, turn down the heat even more. Once it's cooked, remove it from the heat and transfer to a container or bowl to let it cool at room temperature.

THE GUACAMOLE

Peel both avocados. Place them in a bowl and start to break the flesh down with a fork. Wash the cilantro and finely chop it. Add approximately 2 tablespoons (30 mL) of cilantro to the bowl with the avocado. Squeeze all the juice from the limes onto the mixture and keep working it down with the fork. I would leave it relatively chunky, because you can use a fork or spoon to add it to the sandwich. If you're planning to transfer it to a squeeze bottle, then make sure the guac is well blended. Add the olive oil and the remaining 1 teaspoon (5 mL) of salt for a little extra flavor. Normally I would suggest adding some finely chopped garlic, onions, and jalapeños to your guacamole, but the flavor from the molé sauce is so rich that these extra ingredients might get in the way. But hey, to each their own. Add some if you like.

THE SANDWICH

Preheat the oven to 325°F (160°C). Place the chicken thighs in a bowl and add just enough of the molé sauce to cover them. Toss the thighs around in the bowl until the meat is evenly coated. Drizzle a little vegetable oil in a large pan or skillet over high heat. Add the chicken and cook for approximately 2 minutes per side, or until the thighs have been browned on both sides. Remove the chicken from the pan, slather with more molé sauce, and place directly on a baking sheet in the oven for 15 to 20 minutes. The chicken is fully cooked when the juices run clear. If they run pink, it isn't fully cooked yet and will need a bit more time.

Put two pieces of chicken on each bun. Give it another blob of molé sauce, then top with a "healthy" portion of guacamole and crushed-up tortilla chips. Voilà, olé molé guacamole!

PEANUT BUTTER COOKIE FISH & CHIPS SANDWICH

SERVES 2

COOKIES AND FISH AND CHIPS ... I CAN'T BELIEVE THIS COMBO HAS NEVER BEEN DONE BEFORE. TRUTH BE TOLD, THE IDEA COMES FROM HOW MANY OTHER FISH AND CHIP PLACES USE POTATO CHIPS TO MAKE THEIR BATTER CRISPIER. THE COOKIES DO THE SAME THING, BUT WITH THE PEANUT BUTTER AWESOMENESS I'M ALWAYS LOOKING FOR. IF PB AIN'T YOUR THING, MAYBE JUST SETTLE FOR GOOD OL' POTATO CHIPS. BUT I WOULD LOOK TO THE COOKIE. ON THE DAY OF OUR PHOTO SHOOT, I DECIDED TO USE BLACK BASS FILLETS, BUT TILAPIA AND RED SNAPPER FRY JUST AS EVENLY. >>>

1 cup (250 mL) thinly sliced
  purple cabbage

½ cup (125 mL) rice wine vinegar

1 egg

2 cups (500 mL) canola oil

8 small gherkin pickles

2 cloves garlic

1 teaspoon (5 mL) kosher salt

Juice from 1 lemon

6 peanut butter cookies

1 teaspoon (5 mL) cayenne pepper

1 teaspoon (5 mL) kosher salt

1 teaspoon (5 mL) black pepper

1 ¼ cups (310 mL) rice flour,
  divided

1 pint (16 oz/470 mL) dark beer

1 fish fillet (1 lb/500 g) (tilapia,
  black cod, black bass, or red
  snapper)

1 sweet potato

1 teaspoon (5 mL) sea salt

¼ cup (60 mL) unsalted butter

2 brioche buns

THE COLESLAW

Soak the cabbage in the rice wine vinegar for approximately 1 hour. Crack the egg into a blender, and then gradually add the canola oil while the machine is running, until the consistency is thick. Add the pickles, garlic, kosher salt, and lemon juice to the mixture, and blend until all the pickles have combined with the egg mixture. Be careful not to overmix, otherwise the aioli could separate. Remove the cabbage from the rice wine vinegar. Dry with a paper towel, mix with the aioli, then transfer to a bowl. The more aioli you add, the creamier the slaw will be.

PICK YOUR FISH

Blitz the peanut butter cookies into fine crumbs and reserve about ¼ cup (60 mL) of them for later. Put the rest of the crumbs on a large plate, and add the cayenne pepper, salt, and black pepper. Use your fingers to gently combine the mixture. In a bowl, mix ¾ cup (180 mL) of the rice flour with beer until you have your preferred consistency. Add the beer gradually so that you can control the consistency. Place ¼ cup (60 mL) of rice flour in a separate bowl. Pour canola oil to a depth of 1 inch (2.5 cm) into a table-top deep-fryer or wok, and heat the oil to 340°F (170°C). Cut the fish fillet into two pieces, coat with rice flour, dip into the batter, and then coat evenly with the cookie crumbs. Carefully submerge the fish pieces in the hot oil, and cook for about 8 minutes total, or until golden brown, turning occasionally.

THE SWEET POTATO FRITES

Peel the sweet potato, then finely slice it into long shoestring pieces. Cover the shoestrings with the remaining rice flour and place them in the fryer at 340°F (170°C) for approximately 2 minutes, or until crispy. You don't need to change the oil for this. Remove the frites from the fryer and toss them in sea salt.

THE SANDWICH

Butter the inside of the brioche buns and briefly warm them, butter side down, in a clean pan or skillet over medium heat. Place half the frites in the warm bun first, followed by a piece of fish, then half the slaw. Sprinkle with the reserved cookie crumbs. Garnish with extra pickles, if you wish. Repeat with the remaining ingredients.

TEMPURA-FRIED CONEY ISLAND DAWG

DESPITE ITS NAME, THE CONEY ISLAND HOTDOG'S HOME IS DETROIT, NOT NEW YORK. THIS 90-YEAR-OLD HOTDOG IS TRADITIONALLY SERVED WITH CHILI, MUSTARD, AND ONIONS. I DECIDED TO PUT SOME NEW LIFE INTO IT VIA REAL HEARTY CHILI WITH BEANS AND A FRIED CHICKEN DOG. IT'S DIFFERENT, IT'S HUGE … AND IT'S A LOT OF FUN TO EAT. I USUALLY USE GROUND PORK FOR THE GROUND MEAT HERE, BECAUSE I THINK THE FAT FROM THE MEAT HELPS MAKE AN AMAZING CHILI SAUCE. BUT USE WHATEVER INGREDIENTS YOU LIKE!

6 pork, chicken,
  or turkey sausages

4 cloves garlic

1 Spanish onion

1 lb (500 g) ground beef,
  chicken, or pork

2 tablespoons (30 mL) olive oil

1 can (7 oz/198 g)
  chipotle peppers

½ cup (125 mL) salted butter

2 cans (28 oz/796 mL each)
  unseasoned chopped tomatoes

3 cups (750 mL) canned kidney or
  black beans, drained and rinsed

2 tablespoons (30 mL)
  kosher salt (approx)

2 tablespoons (30 mL)
  smoked paprika

2 tablespoons (30 mL)
  chili powder

1 tablespoon (15 mL) cumin

1 tablespoon (15 mL)
  cayenne pepper (approx)

2 red onions

¼ cup (60 mL) white vinegar

8 cups (2 L) canola oil

1 box (10 oz/283 g)
  tempura batter mix

6 standard white hotdog buns

Yellow mustard

PREPPING THE DAWG

Visit your local butcher and pick up six quality sausages — they can be pork, chicken, turkey, whatever you fancy. I tend to go with chicken for this recipe because the lightness of the meat works well with the heavy chili.

Bring a large pot of water to a boil over high heat. Add the sausages, and let them boil for 8 to 10 minutes. Remove the sausages from the water, and set aside until they reach room temperature. The meat is still cooking during this time. Once the sausages reach room temperature, place them in the fridge for approximately 1 hour, or until the fat begins to congeal and the meat begins to harden. ❯❯❯

>>> MAKING THE CHILI

Finely chop the garlic and the Spanish onion. Warm a large pot or skillet over medium heat and brown your meat. Add the garlic, onion, and olive oil. Stir the mixture as it cooks so you don't burn anything. Add the canned chipotles, and use a spoon to begin to break them down. Cook for approximately 5 minutes, or until the items in the pot begin to soak up all the oil. Add the butter and allow it to melt.

Turn down the heat to medium-low. Add the canned tomatoes, their juice, the beans, salt, paprika, chili powder, cumin, and cayenne. Allow the chili to simmer, uncovered, for approximately 1 hour, or until the liquid has been substantially reduced and the chili has become thicker and richer. At this point, feel free to add more salt if needed, or more cayenne if you want your chili a little spicier. The longer it cooks, the more mature the flavors get. Next-day chili isn't so bad ... Just sayin'.

Take the red onions and thinly slice them until you have nice little red onion rings. Place the onion slices in a bowl with the white vinegar. Allow the acid in the vinegar to cook the onion just enough so that it still has crunch but is definitely not raw anymore. Allow about 1 hour for this.

IT'S DIFFERENT, IT'S HUGE, AND IT'S A LOT OF FUN TO EAT

TEMPURA-FRYING THE EPIC DAWG!

This is the best part. I was working on someone else's food truck in Detroit the first time I did this, and they all looked at me like I was crazy. There's a fine line between crazy and creative, and I think this dish might just define that line.

Add canola oil to a depth of 1 inch (2.5 cm) to a deep saucepan, and heat it over medium-high heat. Using a cooking thermometer to monitor the temperature, bring it to and keep it at 350°F to 375°F (180°C to 190°C). If you have a table-top deep-fryer, set it to 350°F (180°C). Prepare the tempura batter mix as per the package instructions. Using cold water or cold soda water in the tempura batter mix creates a fluffier batter.

Bring the sausages out of the fridge and let them sit at room temperature for about 5 minutes before you start to prep them. Cover the sausages with the thick batter and gently place them in the hot oil, one at a time so you don't bring down the temperature of the oil. Cook the sausages for 4 to 5 minutes each, or until the batter is golden brown and crispy. Use tongs to remove the sausages from the oil. Place a crispy, golden sausage in a hotdog bun, top it with meaty, saucy chili, and add some slices of onion. Serve the bun whole or cut it in half. Drizzle with yellow mustard as a garnish, if you want to. If you are feeling a little frisky, you could also add shredded cheddar cheese to your chili. Repeat with the remaining ingredients.

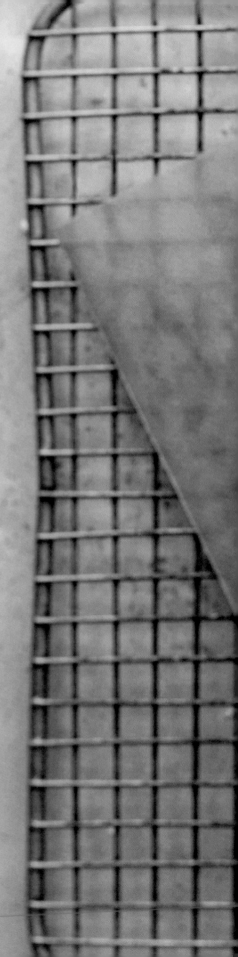

BANH MI SHRIMP

WHEN DONE PROPERLY, BANH MI SLAW IS INCREDIBLY REFRESHING. THIS IS ONE OF THE FEW RECIPES WHERE I'M COOL WITH A SANDWICH BEING 50/50 VEG AND PROTEIN. OKAY, MAYBE 50/50 IS A LITTLE OPTIMISTIC, BUT THE VEG CAN PLAY A MORE SIGNIFICANT ROLE THAN YOU MIGHT OTHERWISE EXPECT. THE FRESH HERBS AND CHUNKY PICKLED VEGETABLES BRING FRESHNESS AND CRUNCH TO EVERY BITE. ›››

SERVES 6 TO 8

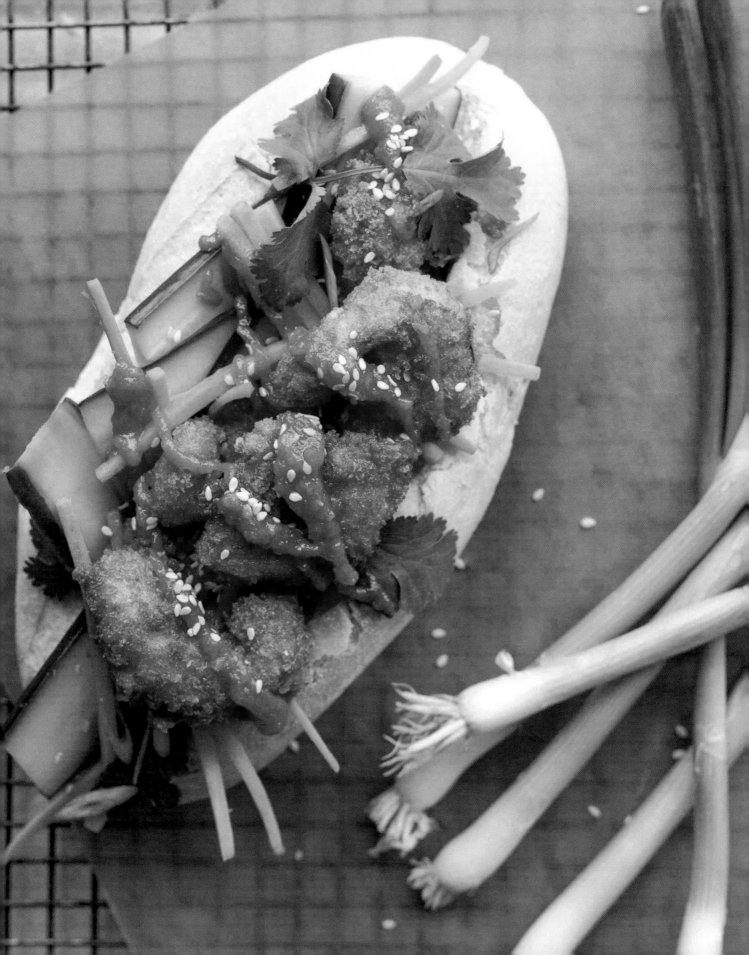

2 large English cucumbers,
  skin on

2 large carrots

4 Thai chili peppers

1 tablespoon (15 mL) kosher salt

2 cups (500 mL) rice wine vinegar

1 tablespoon (15 mL) sesame oil

1 can (17 oz/500 mL)
  pineapple chunks

4 cups (1 L) ketchup

3 cups (750 mL) Sriracha sauce

2 tablespoons (30 mL) prepared
  horseradish

1 cup (250 mL) all-purpose flour

6 eggs

1 cup (250 mL) Panko
  breadcrumbs

1 bag (1 lb/500 g) frozen 16-20
  shrimp (16-20 refers to how
  many shrimp are in 1 lb/500g),
  thawed

4 cups (1 L) canola oil, for frying

6–8 crusty French-style buns

1 bunch cilantro

1 tablespoon (15 mL) sesame seeds

THE SLAW

As in so many of my sandwich recipes, the slaw plays an important role. Quite often slaw is taken for granted, overshadowed by the protein. But what most people don't realize is that if you take the slaw away, the complexity of the sandwich changes. Flavor, freshness, texture ... The right slaw can really help define a sandwich, and the Vietnamese banh mi slaw is probably one of the most important.

Cut each cucumber into three equal parts, discarding the tips. Stand the pieces of the cucumber on one end and cut each piece into five or six thin strips. Do this with all the cucumber pieces. Peel the carrots, cut each one into three equal parts, and discard the tips. Lay the carrot on one side and cut each piece into five or six strips. Cut each carrot strip into really fine matchstick pieces. Finely chop the Thai chilies. Throw all the veg into a small bowl, lightly salt, and add the rice wine vinegar and sesame oil. Toss to coat the slaw, and set aside in the fridge until needed.

THE PINEAPPLE KETCHUP

Pour the can of pineapple with its juice into a blender or food processor, and blitz it until it is a chunky paste. Add the ketchup and Sriracha sauce, and blend until combined. Lastly, add the horseradish, and blitz again for approximately 30 seconds. Transfer the pineapple ketchup to a bowl, and set aside in the fridge until needed. This also acts as a great cocktail sauce, which is why it goes so well with our fried shrimp.

INCREDIBLY

REFRESHING

BUILDING THE BANH MI

Place the flour, eggs, and breadcrumbs into three separate bowls. Whisk the eggs thoroughly. Pull the shrimp shell and tails off the meat. There should be no shells or tails left on the meat of the shrimp. Cut each shrimp in half down the middle and toss the shrimps in the flour, then in the egg, and then in the breadcrumbs. I would do no more than ten at a time, as it gets a little messy.

Once your shrimps are breaded, use either a table-top deep-fryer to cook them or — my personal favorite — a wok. Pour the oil into the fryer or wok, and heat it to 345°F (175°C). Place the breaded shrimps in the hot oil, and let them fry for 4 to 5 minutes, or until golden brown. If you put too many shrimps in at one time, it will cool the oil down and then the shrimps won't fry properly. I recommend frying no more than ten at a time. Use either tongs or a metal strainer to remove them from the oil. Let the fried shrimps rest on some paper towel to remove the excess oil.

Remove the slaw from its vinegar bath and stuff some in a bun. Then add five or six fried shrimps and top with the pineapple ketchup, cilantro, and sesame seeds. Repeat with the remaining ingredients.

LA ROMANA

SERVES 6

ONCE IN A WHILE, A VEGGIE SANDWICH IS A GOOD THING. ESPECIALLY WHEN YOU USE A CHEESE AS DELICATE AND RICH AS BURRATA (A FRESH MOZZARELLA). REAL BURRATA IS ACTUALLY SEASONAL, SO IF YOU CAN'T GET YOUR HANDS ON IT, BUFFALO MOZZARELLA WILL DO JUST AS WELL. IT'S SOLD IN 2 OZ (50 G) PIECES.

THE VEG

Preheat the oven to 400°F (200°C). Slice the eggplant, red onions, and tomatoes into rounds of equal thickness. Place the sliced tomatoes in a bowl and drizzle with olive oil and balsamic vinegar. Set the bowl aside and allow the tomatoes to suck up the acid from the vinegar. Cut the bell peppers into quarters. Place the eggplant, red onion, and peppers on a baking sheet lined with parchment paper and drizzle with olive oil. Lightly season with salt and pepper, and cook for approximately 6 minutes, or until lightly browned.

Once cooked, remove the peppers from the pan and place them in a blender or food processor with the garlic and basil. Splash with a bit of olive oil and blitz the mixture until you have a chunky red pepper spread. Meanwhile, set the roasted onions aside on a plate, and place the pan of eggplant pieces back in the oven for an additional 5 minutes of cooking time. Remove the eggplant from the oven and set aside at room temperature.

- 1 Italian eggplant
- 2 red onions
- 4 Roma tomatoes
- Olive oil
- Balsamic vinegar
- 2 red bell peppers
- Kosher salt
- Black pepper
- 2 cloves garlic
- 10 basil leaves
- 1 loaf focaccia bread
- 2 Burrata cheese balls

GRILLING THE SANGWEECH

Take the loaf and cut it into 2 ½-inch (6 cm) wide strips. Cut each strip through the middle so it can be opened like a sandwich. Drizzle or brush olive oil on the outside of the top and bottom of the bread. Lightly grill the oiled pieces of focaccia on a grill pan or skillet over medium-high heat to get them nice and crispy. This only takes 2 to 3 minutes.

On each piece of warm focaccia, place some vinegar tomatoes as the first layer, followed by the roasted red onions, then roasted eggplant, and finally some red pepper spread.

Slice the Burrata cheese. It's incredibly soft and creamy, so it's the last thing to go on. As soon as you begin to cut the Burrata you will see its cream start to spill out of it. I wouldn't cut each ball into any more than three pieces or you'll lose the impact of the cheese. (You could also tear it with your hands for a more rustic look.) Place the Burrata pieces on top of the red pepper spread and then top with the final piece of focaccia. Repeat with the remaining ingredients.

If you wanted to make this a non-veggie sandwich, slices of prosciutto or Spanish ham would go very nicely with this combo.

STUFF
THAT'S
OPEN-
FACED

I'VE ALWAYS SAID THAT STREET FOOD HAS ABSOLUTELY NOTHING TO DO WITH DIRTY FOOD OR CHEAP FOOD. IN FACT, I THINK IT'S THE EXACT OPPOSITE.

TAKE ANYTHING SERVED OPEN: A TACO, A TOSTADA, SOMETHING ON A PITA, A LETTUCE WRAP … WHATEVER IT IS, ALL THE ELEMENTS HAVE TO COME TOGETHER VISUALLY FOR SOMEONE TO SAY, "I'D EAT THAT." NOTHING IS HIDDEN; EVERYTHING IS OUT IN THE OPEN. CONTRASTING COLORS AND TEXTURES. LAYERS OF SOMETHING FRIED, SPLODGES OF SOMETHING CREAMY, A HINT OF CITRUS, AND A VESSEL TO HOLD IT ALL TOGETHER. IT HAS TO BE BOTH ATTRACTIVE AND PRACTICAL. AND THE BEST PART IS, WE CAN BREAK AS MANY RULES AS WE WANT. A TACO DOESN'T HAVE TO BE JUST A TACO. A LETTUCE WRAP DOESN'T HAVE TO BE BORING. IT'S STREET FOOD. IT DOESN'T MATTER HOW YOU PACKAGE IT, IT JUST HAS TO BE FUN.

HOISIN BEEF WRAPS

SERVES 4 TO 6

THIS DISH IS FRESH AND LIGHT, AND BRINGS TOGETHER CRISP TEXTURES THAT MAKE FOR ONE CLEAN MEAL, IF I DO SAY SO MYSELF. AND BECAUSE IT'S BREADLESS, YOU CAN EAT LIKE FIVE OF THEM. REALISTICALLY, YOU COULD USE ANY THINLY SLICED MEAT FOR THIS DISH. PORK, LAMB, CHICKEN, BEEF … OH WAIT, WE DID DO BEEF. WELL THEN, BEEF ON, MY FRIENDS.

YOUR NON-MEAT PART OF THE LETTUCE WRAP

First, soak the rice noodles in salted water at room temperature. Allow them to soak for approximately 1 hour. You'll notice them soften and soak up a lot of the salt water. Drain them and reserve at room temperature. Cut the bell pepper in half, discard the seeds, slice the pepper into thin strips, and set it aside at room temperature. Peel the carrot and radish, and cut them into very thin matchsticks. You will only need about ½ cup (125 mL) of each. Use the leftovers for a Sweet 'n' Sour Beef Steak Sandwich (page 17). Mix the carrot, the radish, and the enoki mushrooms in a bowl, and pour the rice wine vinegar into the bowl to give them a light pickling. Set aside at room temperature until needed.

THE MEAT

Marinate the beef slices in a bowl with the hoisin sauce and half the lemon juice. Make sure you mix it thoroughly. The acid from the lemon will start cooking the beef. The hoisin sauce should be the predominant flavor and the lemon should just help bring out the flavors. Warm a nonstick pan over medium-high heat, add the marinated beef, and cook for 5 to 6 minutes, depending on how rare or lack thereof you want your meat. Remove the meat from the pan and return the pan of beautiful hoisin sauce to the warm burner.

THAT'S A WRAP

Add ¼ cup (60 mL) water to the hoisin sauce, and cook it for approximately 5 minutes to deglaze the hoisin from the bottom of the pan. Once the water has reduced a bit, give it a little stir, and add the finely chopped garlic and the red chili oil. Let it cook for approximately 1 minute, then add the bell pepper slices with a handful of the rice noodles. Squeeze in the remaining lemon juice and add salt to taste.

Grab the strongest-looking leaves of lettuce, lay them out on a plate, and add cooked noodles to each one. Top with cooked beef, layer with pickled veg, and throw in some cilantro and basil to add some extra freshness. Feel free to squeeze a little extra hoisin sauce over the whole wrap for some added flavor.

1 package (15 oz/450 g) rice noodles

1 yellow bell pepper

1 carrot

1 daikon radish

1 package (8 oz/225 g) enoki mushrooms

1 cup (250 mL) rice wine vinegar

1 lb (500 g) beef striploin, thinly sliced

1 cup (250 mL) hoisin sauce

Juice from 1 lemon, divided

4 cloves garlic, finely chopped

1 cup (250 mL) red chili oil

Kosher salt

1 head iceberg lettuce

¼ cup (60 mL) cilantro

¼ cup (60 mL) fresh basil

PHILLY CHEESESTEAK TOSTADAS

SERVES 6

TRADITIONALLY, THE CHEESESTEAK IS A SANDWICH, BUT BY DOING IT AS A TOSTADA YOU'RE MAKING THE SUPREME QUALITY AND FLAVOR OF THE BEEF THE STAR OF THE DISH RATHER THAN THE BREAD BEING THE MAIN ATTRACTION. A TYPICAL CHEESESTEAK HAS THREE INGREDIENTS: BEEF, CHEEZ WHIZ, AND WHITE ONIONS. SO, NOT ONLY HAVE I MESSED UP TRADITION BY PUTTING THIS ON A TOSTADA AND REPLACING THE CHEEZ WHIZ WITH CHEESE SLICES, I'VE ADDED INSULT TO INJURY BY THROWING IN A FEW MORE TOPPINGS.

THE TOPPINGS

Very thinly slice one of the jalapeño peppers. Place the sliced jalapeño with its seeds in a small bowl and add enough rice wine vinegar to cover them completely. Let the jalapeño slices soak for 10 to 15 minutes to lightly pickle them.

For the jalapeño aioli, chop the remaining two jalapeño peppers into large chunks. Blitz the eggs in a food processor or blender, and then add the jalapeño chunks with their seeds and the garlic. Blitz to blend well, then slowly blend in the oil while the machine is running. Once the aioli has thickened, squeeze in a little lemon juice and add a bit of salt to taste. Give it one last quick blitz to mix it all together.

BUILDING THE TOSTADA FROM THE BOTTOM UP

First you'll need a tostada shell. If you can't find any tostada shells, you can always deep-fry a soft-shell corn tortilla. Put about ½ inch (1 cm) of canola oil in a pot and bring it to 325°F (160°C). Place the tortilla in the hot oil, and cook for approximately 5 minutes, or until crispy, for the perfect tostada vessel. If you fry the tortilla in oil that's too hot, it will fry too quickly, burn, and break apart.

Slice the red onion into thin rings. Place the slices in a hot grill pan or skillet over high heat for 5 or 6 minutes, or until the onions have softened in texture and darkened in color. Remove from the pan and set aside at room temperature. Lightly salt and pepper the strips of beef striploin. Mix the onions with the raw beef, and stack them into a small clump. Place the beef and onion mixture in the hot pan. Leave the meat stacked while on the heat. Cook for approximately 5 minutes and then flip the beef. I suggest leaving it bunched up so that you can still have some parts undercooked while others parts are more cooked. Separate the meat into six piles while it's cooking. Place a slice of American cheese on top of each pile as it cooks, and cover with another pan or lid for just a few minutes to melt the cheese. (You can do this in two batches of three if it's easier.)

Remove your cheesy beef and place it on the tostada, giving it some height. Dress the top of the meat with a little bit of the jalapeño aioli, pickled jalapeño slices, and some washed and picked cilantro. Serve with a lime wedge. Repeat with remaining tostadas.

3 jalapeño peppers

1 cup (250 mL) rice wine vinegar

2 eggs

4 cloves garlic

4 cups (1 L) canola oil

Juice from 1 lemon

Kosher salt

6 tostada shells or crispy tortillas

1 red onion

1 lb (500 g) beef striploin, thinly sliced

Black pepper

6 thin slices American cheese

¼ cup (60 mL) cilantro

1 lime

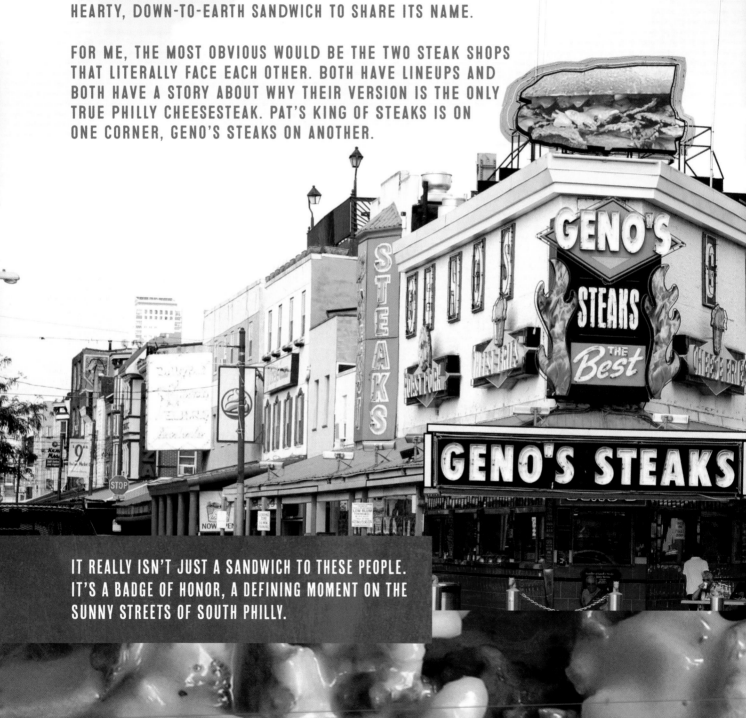

BREAD, MEAT, CHEEZ WHIZ, AND ONIONS. FOUR INGREDIENTS THAT ARE UP FOR CONSTANT DEBATE IN THE CITY OF PHILADELPHIA. LAYING CLAIM TO "BEST PHILLY CHEESESTEAK" IS KIND OF LIKE SAYING YOU'RE THE MOST "PHILLY," AND FROM WHAT I GATHERED FROM MY VERY SHORT TIME IN THE CITY, THAT'S CONSIDERED A BADGE OF HONOR. IT'S AN INCREDIBLY PROUD CITY WITH A HEARTY, DOWN-TO-EARTH SANDWICH TO SHARE ITS NAME.

FOR ME, THE MOST OBVIOUS WOULD BE THE TWO STEAK SHOPS THAT LITERALLY FACE EACH OTHER. BOTH HAVE LINEUPS AND BOTH HAVE A STORY ABOUT WHY THEIR VERSION IS THE ONLY TRUE PHILLY CHEESESTEAK. PAT'S KING OF STEAKS IS ON ONE CORNER, GENO'S STEAKS ON ANOTHER.

IT REALLY ISN'T JUST A SANDWICH TO THESE PEOPLE. IT'S A BADGE OF HONOR, A DEFINING MOMENT ON THE SUNNY STREETS OF SOUTH PHILLY.

PAT'S KING OF STEAKS AND GENO'S STEAKS, SOUTH PHILLY

I WAS LUCKY ENOUGH TO GET BEHIND ENEMY LINES AT BOTH SHOPS, AND TRUTH BE TOLD, THERE ACTUALLY ISN'T ANY RIVALRY. I MEAN, MAYBE AT ONE POINT THERE WAS, BUT IT SEEMS LIKE EACH PLACE HAS COME TO THE POINT OF NOT EVEN RECOGNIZING THE OTHER'S EXISTENCE. IT REALLY ISN'T JUST A SANDWICH TO THESE PEOPLE. IT'S A BADGE OF HONOR, A DEFINING MOMENT ON THE SUNNY STREETS OF SOUTH PHILLY. I ATE BOTH, I LIKED BOTH. THEY BOTH TASTE EXACTLY HOW YOU EXPECT THEM TO TASTE: AS UNIQUE AS BREAD, MEAT, CHEEZ WHIZ, AND ONIONS CAN TASTE. BUT WHEN YOU GET DOWN TO BRASS TACKS, IT'S THE WHOLE SANDWICH SHTICK OF PAT'S AND GENO'S THAT KEEPS THE TRADITION GOING AND THE PEOPLE COMING BACK FOR MORE CHEESESTEAKS.

NYC MEATBALL DEEP-FRIED PIZZA

SERVES 5 TO 6

NEW YORK CITY, HOME TO THE YANKEES, CONSTRUCTION WORKERS TEARING UP THE ROADS, AND BIG SAUCY MEATBALLS OVAH'HERE (VOICE À LA JOE PESCI). FOR THE PIZZA DOUGH PREP AND COOKING INSTRUCTIONS, SEE DUCK AND ASPARAGUS SLAW DEEP-FRIED PIZZA RECIPE (PAGE 76). FOR ALL MEATBALL-RELATED INQUIRIES, PLEASE READ ON. >>>

1 cup (250 mL) lukewarm water

1 package (2 ¼ tsp/12 mL)
   quick-rising dry yeast

2 cups (500 mL) all-purpose flour

Splash of olive oil

1 teaspoon (5 mL) kosher salt

1 tablespoon (15 mL)
   granulated sugar

½ lb (250 g) ground pork

½ lb (250 g) ground beef

½ cup (125 mL) dried
   breadcrumbs

3 tablespoons (45 mL)
   kosher salt, divided

1 tablespoon (15 mL)
   black pepper

1 tablespoon (15 mL)
   dried oregano

1 teaspoon (5 mL) chili flakes

1 teaspoon (5 mL) garlic powder

4 oz (100 g) piece
   Parmesan cheese

4 eggs

½ cup (125 mL) lukewarm
   water, divided

1 Spanish onion, diced

2 tablespoons (30 mL)
   finely diced garlic

¼ cup + 2 tablespoons (100 mL)
   olive oil

1 can (28 oz/796 mL)
   crushed tomatoes

2 cups (500 mL) arugula

½ cup (125 mL) fresh basil

Juice from 1 lemon

THE PIZZA DOUGH

Make the pizza dough according to the instructions on page 78.

THE SPICY MEATBALLS

Mix the ground pork and ground beef together in a bowl. Add the breadcrumbs, 2 tablespoons (30 mL) of the salt, the black pepper, oregano, chili flakes, garlic powder, and a little bit of grated Parm with the eggs and ½ cup (125 mL) of the water. Mix thoroughly with your mighty hands. Form the meatballs into roughly six imperfect balls. If you do the typical perfect ball thing, they just don't come out as tender. In a pan over high heat, sear each meatball for approximately 2 minutes on each side or until the exterior of the meatballs is brown. Set aside the seared meatballs until you are ready to add them to the sauce.

THE SUGO

Toss the onion and garlic into a food processor until still a little bit chunky. In a large pan over medium heat, warm the olive oil and add the garlic and onions. Cook for approximately 5 minutes, or until the onion becomes translucent. Be sure to stir them as they cook so the garlic doesn't burn. Add the can of tomatoes and one can of water (using the tomato can as your measure). Turn down the heat to medium-low, and cook the sauce, uncovered, for approximately 1 hour or until it has reduced a little. Throw the seared meatballs in at the 30-minute mark, and let them cook slowly in the sauce until the hour or so has been reached. Add additional Parmesan cheese to the sauce and meatballs.

BUILDING THE 'ZA

Place the arugula and basil in a bowl, and dress it with lemon juice and a little bit of salt for seasoning. Deep-fry the pizza dough. Dress the pizza crust with the arugula-basil salad. Top the pizza with the meatball sauce, and grate a little more cheese over it before serving.

BIG SAUCY MEATBALLS

OVAH'HERE

URBAN OVEN, LOS ANGELES, CALIFORNIA

I WAS TOTALLY AMAZED THAT THEY DIDN'T PLAY IT SAFE IN A NON-PIZZA TOWN. I HAD GRAPES, PROSCIUTTO, AND BRUSSELS SPROUTS ON MY 'ZA. WELL DONE, SIRS. WELL DONE.

PIZZA

I THOUGHT THAT LA HAD SOME AMAZING FOOD, BUT I WAS SHOCKED BY HOW FEW PIZZA JOINTS THERE WERE. PIZZA IS EVERYWHERE IN TORONTO — NEAPOLITAN, SICILIAN, ROMAN ... SO MANY TO CHOOSE FROM. LA HAD NOTHING. SO I HAVE TO TELL YOU, I WAS TOTALLY STOKED WHEN THE BEST PIECE OF PIZZA I HAD CAME FROM A FOOD TRUCK. ROBERT TREMONTI'S URBAN OVEN HAD A WOOD-BURNING OVEN ON THE TRUCK. THE SMELL OF FRESH-BAKED PIZZAS FILLED THE STREETS. I COULDN'T IMAGINE HOW HOT IT MUST HAVE GOTTEN IN THAT TRUCK.

BUT MOSTLY I WAS TOTALLY AMAZED THAT THEY DIDN'T PLAY IT SAFE IN A NON-PIZZA TOWN. I HAD GRAPES, PROSCIUTTO, AND BRUSSELS SPROUTS ON MY 'ZA. WELL DONE, SIRS. WELL DONE. AND GUESS WHAT? THE FOLKS ON THIS TRUCK WERE IN THE PROCESS OF OPENING UP A SHOP IN LA AS WELL.

BABY BACK BAO BUNS

. . . .
SERVES 8 TO 10
. . . .

I LOVE STEAM BUNS. MY MAIN THING WITH THEM IS THAT YOU NEED TO CONTRAST TEXTURES WHEN YOU STUFF THEM. THE BUNS THEMSELVES ARE INCREDIBLY SOFT, SO IF YOU STUFF THEM WITH MORE SOFT STUFF THEY GET INCREDIBLY MUSHY. BEAN SPROUTS, CARROTS, AND CABBAGE ALL ARE GREAT WAYS TO HELP BALANCE THE TEXTURES OF WHAT YOU STUFF IN YOUR BAO.

THE RIBS

Cut the rack of ribs into three equal parts. Season each piece with salt, pepper, and paprika. Sear the cap side (meat side) of the ribs in a grill pan over high heat for approximately 5 minutes, or until seared. Finely chop the onion. Rip three equal-sized pieces of aluminum foil to wrap the ribs. Preheat the oven to 275°F (135°C). Place the rib portions, meat side down, on each piece of foil. Fold the sides of the foil to make a bit of a pocket, and divide the beer evenly among the pouches. Then divide the onion between the pouches before sealing the ribs in the foil. You don't want the foil overly tight or too loose, just tight enough to keep the ribs snug. Place the ribs in the oven, meat side down, and cook for approximately 3 hours, or until they are fall-off-the-bone soft. Once cooked, remove the ribs from the foil and pour all the juice from the foil pouches into a bowl. Let the ribs cool for a few minutes before you start pulling the meat off the bones. This dish looks and tastes better if the meat is left chunkier and on the larger side. Set aside at room temperature until needed.

THE BAO BUNS

Pour the yeast into the lukewarm water and let it dissolve without touching it. Place 1 cup (250 mL) of the flour in a large bowl, and add the yeast-water mixture. Mix well until all the water has been completely absorbed. If you require a little more flour, add ¼ cup (60 mL) at a time to ensure you don't drown out the dough with water. Cover the bowl with a wet cloth and allow the dough to rest at room temperature for approximately 1 hour, or until it doubles in size. ❯❯❯

1 rack pork back ribs

1 tablespoon (15 mL) kosher salt

1 teaspoon (5 mL) black pepper

1 teaspoon (5 mL) smoked paprika

1 white onion

1 pint (16 oz/470 mL) dark beer

1 package (2 ¼ tsp/12 mL) quick-rising dry yeast

1 ½ cups (375 mL) lukewarm water

2 ½ cups (625 mL) all-purpose flour, divided

1 teaspoon (5 mL) granulated sugar

1 cup (250 mL) sesame oil, divided

6 cloves garlic

3 oz (75 g) piece fresh ginger

¼ cup (60 mL) rice wine vinegar

1 cup (250 mL) hoisin sauce

1 cup (250 mL) ketchup

1 cob of corn

1 large carrot

1 head iceberg lettuce

½ cup (125 mL) cilantro

½ cup (125 mL) fresh basil

››› In a pot, bring ½ cup (125 mL) of water to a boil over high heat, and add the sugar and a splash of the sesame oil. Stir well, and then remove the pot from the burner. Let the water cool to room temperature, and then add it to the bowl of risen dough. Knead the dough on a lightly floured board until smooth. Place it in an extra-large, greased bowl, cover with a damp cloth, and let it rise in a warm place until doubled in bulk, about 2 hours. Divide into two portions. Remove one portion. Using your hands again, mix the dough together and roll it out into portions that are roughly the size of your palm. Flatten each piece of dough with your hands, lightly brush some sesame oil on one side of each piece and then fold it in half so that the oil is on the inside and it looks like a half moon. Place in the fridge, covered, until needed. Repeat all of this with the other portion of dough.

THE SAUCE AND TOPPINGS

To make the BBQ sauce, blitz the garlic and ginger in a blender until you have a paste. Heat a pan over medium heat and warm a little bit of sesame oil. Toss the garlic-ginger mixture into the pan, and add the rice wine vinegar, hoisin sauce, and ketchup (in that order), and stir well to combine. Turn down the heat to low, and cook for 10 to 15 minutes, stirring a little for the first few minutes.

In a pot of salted water, boil the cob of corn for 6 to 8 minutes, or until tender. Slice all the corn kernels off the cob, throw them into a hot grill pan with some butter or olive oil, and cook over high heat for approximately 5 minutes, or until the kernels start to darken. Peel the carrot and cut it into three equal-sized chunks. Cut each chunk into thin, flat pieces (you don't want them to be matchsticks, though, so don't cut them too thin) and lightly salt to season.

BUILDING THE BAO

Cut a square of parchment or wax paper for each piece of dough.

Lightly brush the bottom of each half-moon of dough with sesame oil, and place each one on its own square of parchment. The easiest way to steam these buns is to purchase a bamboo steamer. They can be found at any restaurant store. Boil a pot of water or a wok filled with water over high heat, and place the bamboo steamer on top. If you don't have a bamboo steamer, you can use a metal rack that fits in the wok or on the pot, or use a pot that has a steamer compartment. Steam the buns for approximately 30 minutes or until they are nice and puffy.

Take the pulled rib meat and toss it in the BBQ sauce you made. Fill the buns with a layer of iceberg lettuce, seasoned carrots, and then the saucy pork. Finish them off with the corn, cilantro, and basil leaves. Tada, you just got bao'd!

ROASTED BONE MARROW

THIS DISH LOOKS INCREDIBLY INTENSE WHEN IT'S SERVED UP, DESPITE BEING RELATIVELY EASY TO PULL OFF. ANYTIME YOU COOK BONE LIKE A CHAMP PEOPLE WILL ASSUME YOU SPENT THE SUMMER IN PARIS LEARNING FROM A PRO. LITTLE DO THEY KNOW YOU JUST LEARNED THIS RECIPE IN ABOUT 5 MINUTES FROM A FOOD TRUCK GUY.

BUST OUT A BONE MARROW PLATTER AT A PARTY AND YOU WILL LEAVE PEOPLE IN SHOCK. IT MAY LOOK FIERCELY AVANT-GARDE, BUT IT'S ALSO A THROWBACK TO A MORE RUSTIC STYLE OF EATING. I GREW UP ON MARROW. IT WAS USED IN PASTA OR JUST SPREAD ON BREAD LIKE BUTTER. IT HAS SOME SERIOUS NATURAL FLAVOR AND ONLY NEEDS A FEW SELECT ELEMENTS TO HELP HEIGHTEN THOSE FLAVORS.

SERVES 4 TO 6

THE WHOLE DISH!

Preheat the oven to 450°F (230°C). Place the bones, marrow side up, on a baking sheet. Cut the lemon in half, and cut the top off the head of garlic. Dip the lemon and garlic into the olive oil and place on baking sheet. Place one sprig of rosemary on each bone marrow half and grate some fresh Parmesan cheese over everything. Drizzle some olive oil over the entire pan.

Place the marrow bones in the oven, and cook for 15 minutes, or until the fat starts to bubble. Remove from the oven, and enjoy the taste and smell. Grate some more fresh Parmesan cheese over top before you serve with roasted lemon and garlic.

3 marrow bones,
  cut in half lengthwise

1 lemon

1 head garlic

1 tablespoon (15 mL) olive oil

6 sprigs rosemary

1 piece (7 oz/200 g) fresh
  Parmesan cheese

DUCK AND ASPARAGUS SLAW DEEP-FRIED PIZZA

SERVES 8

4 skin-on duck legs

2 cups (500 mL) soy sauce

½ cup (125 mL) orange juice

1 cup (250 mL) duck fat

1 package (2 ¼ tsp/12 mL) quick-rising dry yeast

1 cup (250 mL) lukewarm water

2 tablespoons (30 mL) olive oil

1 tablespoon (15 mL) kosher salt

1 tablespoon (15 mL) granulated sugar

3 cups (750 mL) all-purpose flour, divided

1 Fuji apple, skin on

1 Bosc pear, skin on

1 bunch thick asparagus

1 package (8 oz/225 g) enoki mushrooms

1 cup (250 mL) sesame oil

Juice from 2 lemons

1 cup (250 mL) canola oil

Black pepper

1 tablespoon (15 mL) sesame seeds

4 green onions, finely chopped

THIS DISH IS PROBABLY THE ONLY TIME YOU'LL SEE THE WORDS DUCK, DEEP-FRYING, ASPARAGUS, AND PIZZA ALL IN ONE PLACE. GOOD THING THEY GO REALLY WELL TOGETHER. IT'S NOT A RECIPE FOR A PIZZA IN THE "PARTY SIZE" SENSE. THESE LITTLE GUYS ARE NOT MEANT TO BE SHARED. YOU'LL THANK ME LATER. YOU SHOULD HAVE ENOUGH DUCK FAT FOR THE RECIPE AFTER YOU'VE SEARED THE DUCK, BUT IF SOMETHING GOES WRONG YOU CAN BUY SOME TO MAKE UP THE DIFFERENCE. AND DON'T WORRY ABOUT USING PLASTIC WRAP IN THE OVEN. IT'S ALL GOOD AT LOW TEMPERATURES.

CONFIT THE QUACK

Score the skin of the duck legs. Pour the soy sauce and orange juice into a resealable plastic bag, and place the duck legs inside. Let the duck legs marinate in the bag in the fridge for a minimum of 1 hour and a maximum of 24 hours.

Take the duck legs out of the bag and reserve the marinade. Sear the duck legs, skin side down, in a hot skillet with a little bit of vegetable oil for approximately 3 minutes, or until the skin gets nicely browned. Preheat the oven to 200°F (95°C).

In a separate pot, warm the duck fat over medium-high heat, and melt it until it becomes a liquid. Put the duck legs in a deep oven-ready pan, skin side up, and pour the duck fat into the pan. Seal the pan tightly with a layer of plastic wrap and a layer of aluminum foil, then cook it in the oven for 2 to 3 hours, or until the meat is so tender that it just wants to jump off the bone. Woohoo! Now you're confitin' — a fancy French way of telling someone to cook something slowly in liquid fat. ❯❯❯

>>> THE PIZZA DOUGH

Add the yeast to the cup (250 mL) of lukewarm (make sure it's not hot) water. Let it stand for approximately 5 minutes at room temperature, or until it begins to bubble. Then add the olive oil, salt, and sugar to the cup. Stir it well.

Add a pinch of salt to 2 cups (500 mL) of the flour and place this and the yeast mixture in a large mixing bowl. Mix everything well with your hands until you have a bowl of dough. Add a splash more olive oil, and give one more mix before you cover the bowl with a damp cloth. Place it in a warm area for approximately 1 hour, or until the dough doubles in size. Pour the remaining 1 cup (250 mL) of flour onto a cutting board, dump the dough mixture onto it, and work it into the flour with your hands. Cut the dough into 3 oz (90 g) portions (about the size of your palm) and roll into individual balls. Place the dough balls on a baking sheet, cover it all with a plastic bag, and throw it in the fridge until you're ready to fry it.

THESE LITTLE GUYS

ARE NOT MEANT

TO BE SHARED

THE SLAW

Slice the apple and pear into matchsticks. Peel the asparagus with a vegetable peeler so you get long strands of asparagus. Mix the apple, pear, asparagus, and enoki mushrooms in a bowl with the sesame oil, lemon juice, and a pinch of salt. Giving it the occasional thorough stir, cook for approximately 30 minutes, so the lemon juice will start to cook the asparagus down.

YOUR UNCONVENTIONAL PIZZA PIE

Pull the duck skin off the legs and set it aside. Pull the moist duck meat off the bones. Warm the reserved duck marinade in a pan with 1 tablespoon (15 mL) of the duck fat over high heat. Bring the sauce to a boil, and add the duck meat with a little bit of salt to taste. Cook for approximately 1 minute, pulling apart the meat and coating it in the sauce.

Pour the canola oil into a wok or deep pot and heat it to 375°F (190°C). Flatten the dough balls with your hand. The dough shouldn't be much wider than the palm of your hand. Place a piece of dough very carefully in the hot oil and fry for 4 to 5 minutes, or until the dough is nice and puffy, and golden in color. Remove the dough from the oil, place on paper towel to absorb any excess oil, and lightly season with salt and pepper. Place the duck skin in the oil and cook for approximately 30 seconds, or until it becomes crispy. Lay out the cooked dough, layer each piece with slaw and duck meat, then drizzle some of the sauce over the meat. Top with sesame seeds and finely chopped green onions, and crumble the fried duck skin over it all for a delicious finish. Repeat with the remaining ingredients.

TACOZUNA

SERVES 4 TO 8

TRUE STORY. WHEN MY NONNO PASSED AWAY I WASN'T SURE IF I WANTED TO KEEP COOKING. BUT I DID. THE FIRST EVENT I DID AFTER HIS PASSING WAS A TACO COMPETITION WHERE KY AND I MADE THIS DISH. AND WE WON. THANKS, NONNO.

THE SLAW

First, shred the purple and green cabbage very thinly. Put the shredded purple cabbage in a bowl, lightly salt it, and then add ¼ cup (60 mL) of the rice wine vinegar. This will start to bleed out the purple in the cabbage so it doesn't stain the rest of the veg in the slaw. Place the green cabbage in a separate large bowl. Cut the cucumber and the carrot into matchsticks, and mix them into the bowl of green cabbage. Add the bean sprouts. Finely chop the Thai chilies, green onion, and cilantro, and toss them into the bowl of green cabbage. Remove the purple cabbage from the rice wine vinegar, and pat it dry with paper towel. Add the dried purple cabbage to the bowl of green cabbage. Lightly season the bowl of slaw with salt and pepper, and add the remaining ¼ cup (60 mL) of rice wine vinegar and the sesame oil.

THE CHICKEN

Preheat the oven to 325°F (160°C). Lightly season the chicken with salt and pepper. Place it in a skillet over high heat, and sear each side for approximately 2 minutes, or until the meat has a nice crust. Transfer the chicken to a roasting pan, and cook in the oven for approximately 10 minutes, or until the juices run clear. While the chicken cooks, prepare the tempura batter as per the package instructions. Add canola oil to a depth of 1 inch (2.5 cm) (about 2 cups/500 mL) to a table-top deep-fryer or a wok and heat it to 345°F (175°C). Take the chicken out of the oven and cut it in half. Dip the chicken in the tempura batter and deep-fry, in batches, for approximately 4 minutes, or until the batter is golden brown. ❯❯❯

¼ head purple cabbage

¼ head green cabbage

Kosher salt

½ cup (125 mL) rice wine vinegar, divided

1 English cucumber

1 large carrot

1 cup (250 mL) bean sprouts

6 Thai chili peppers

1 green onion

1 bunch cilantro, stems removed

Black pepper

1 teaspoon (5 mL) sesame oil

4 boneless, skinless chicken thighs

1 box (10 oz/283 g) tempura batter mix

6 cups (1.5 L) canola oil

2 tablespoons (30 mL) wasabi powder

2 eggs

4 cloves garlic

Juice from 1 lemon

8 soft corn tortillas

1 tablespoon (15 mL) hoisin sauce

¼ cup (60 mL) pea shoots

1 tablespoon (15 mL) sesame seeds

>>> BUILDING THE TACO

In a bowl, gradually add up to ½ cup (125 mL) of water to the wasabi powder and mix until it turns into a paste. Crack the eggs into a food processor with the garlic and 4 cups (1 L) canola oil. Blend until the aioli starts to thicken, gradually add the wasabi paste, and hit it with the lemon juce. Blend until smooth.

In a pan, warm the tortillas over medium-low heat for approximately 2 minutes per side. Place some seasoned slaw on each warm tortilla and top with a piece of chicken. Zig-zag hoisin sauce and wasabi aioli over it all. Garnish the taco with pea shoots and sesame seeds. Serve immediately.

THANKS, NONNO

IT'S AMAZING WHEN YOU CAN CARVE OUT THE LIFE YOU WANT FOR YOURSELF, ESPECIALLY IF IT'S DOING SOMETHING STEEPED IN FAMILY TRADITION. WHEN FATIMA CAME TO NEW YORK IN 1987, SHE BROUGHT WITH HER THE RECIPES AND TRADITIONS TAUGHT TO HER BY HER FAMILY. STREET FOOD WAS IN ITS INFANCY IN NEW YORK AT THAT TIME, AND IT CERTAINLY DIDN'T REFLECT THE CULTURAL DIVERSITY OF THE CITY. FATIMA USED HER FAMILY RECIPES TO CREATE A LIFE FOR HERSELF AND FILL A GAP IN THE FOOD WORLD.

TRINI PAKI BOYS CART – HALAL FOOD, NYC, NEW YORK

FATIMA USED HER FAMILY RECIPES TO CREATE A LIFE FOR HERSELF AND FILL A GAP IN THE FOOD WORLD.

TRINI PAKI BOYS · HALAL FOOD

FATIMA AND HER SON, MOHAMMED, WORK THE INCREDIBLY POPULAR TRINI PAKI BOYS CART IN NYC. TWENTY-FIVE YEARS AGO, IT WAS THE CITY'S FIRST HALAL CART. SHE MAKES TRADITIONAL TRINIDADIAN FOOD, ALL HALAL, SUCH AS DOUBLES AND GOAT MEAT ROTI. IMAGINE BEING THAT INCREDIBLY FORWARD-THINKING IN A CITY AS LARGE AND DYNAMIC AS NYC! LINEUPS SNAKED AROUND THE BLOCK WHEN THE CART FIRST OPENED, DOUSING THE STREET FOOD SCENE WITH THE SCENT OF TURMERIC AND TAMARIND CHILI SAUCES.

NO WONDER THEY WERE ALL SOLD OUT BY THE TIME KY GOT TO THE WINDOW.

TILAPIA DOUBLES

I NEVER UNDERSTOOD WHERE THE WORD "DOUBLES" CAME FROM IN THE FOOD SENSE. I LEARNED FROM THE TRINI PAKI CART THAT TRADITIONALLY THEY ARE STUFFED WITH A CURRIED CHICKPEA (GARBANZO BEAN) CONCOCTION, AND GOOGLE TELLS ME THAT ALTHOUGH IT CAME AS ONE SINGLE FLATBREAD, PEOPLE WOULD ASK FOR DOUBLES OF THEM.

SERVES 6

SEEING DOUBLES

Pour the yeast into the lukewarm water and allow it to dissolve for approximately 5 minutes, or until it begins to bubble. In a large bowl, combine the flour, the baking powder, 1 teaspoon (5 mL) of the salt, the black pepper, and the turmeric. Pour 1 cup (250 mL) of water into the bowl and add the yeast water. Mix well to work the dough. If the mixture looks dry, add some more water. Once fully worked, cover the dough with a damp cloth and set it aside in a warm place. Let the dough sit for approximately 1 hour, or until it has doubled in size. Cover a cutting board with some flour and roll the dough, working in the excess flour to reduce some of the dough moisture. Roll the dough out with your hands and portion it into six evenly sized balls using the palm of your hand. Put the dough on a flat surface (like a baking sheet), cover it with a plastic bag, and place it in the fridge until needed.

Fill a deep saucepan or wok with the canola oil, and heat the oil to 345°F (175°C). Flatten each ball of dough with the palm of your hand and fry it in the hot oil for approximately 2 minutes per side. Fry the dough one ball at a time, as too many at once will cool the oil. Remove the double from the oil and lightly salt. ❯ ❯ ❯

1 teaspoon (5 mL) quick-rising dry yeast

1 cup (250 mL) lukewarm water

2 cups (500 mL) all-purpose flour

1 tablespoon (15 mL) baking powder

2 teaspoons (10 mL) kosher salt, divided

1 teaspoon (5 mL) black pepper

1 teaspoon (5 mL) turmeric

1 cup (250 mL) canola oil

1 Spanish onion

4 cloves garlic, chopped

1 can (14 oz/398 g) chickpeas, drained and rinsed

2 tablespoons (30 mL) salted butter

½ cup (125 mL) finely chopped cilantro

½ cup (125 mL) curly parsley

1 cup (250 mL) plain Greek yogurt, divided

2 tilapia fillets

1 teaspoon (5 mL) smoked paprika

1 teaspoon (5 mL) ground cumin

Juice from 2 lemons

>>> THE FISH AND THE FILLING

Cut the onion into thin rings. Warm a small amount of canola oil in a skillet over medium-high heat and toss in the onion and the garlic. Allow them to cook, stirring well, for approximately 5 minutes, or until the onion starts to brown. Add the chickpeas, butter, cilantro, parsley, a pinch of turmeric, and the remaining 1 teaspoon (5 mL) of salt. Turn down the heat to medium-low, and cook for 6 or 7 minutes. Remove the pan from the heat, and add 2 tablespoons (30 mL) of yogurt. Allow the yogurt to slowly melt over the chickpeas before you stir it in.

Cut each tilapia fillet into three strips, and season them with salt, paprika, and cumin. Cook the fish in a hot grill pan over medium-high heat for approximately 4 minutes per side, or until crispy and flaky. Once the fish is cooked, squeeze the lemon juice into the pan for added flavor.

Spoon the chickpea and onion filling onto one side of the double, and place the fish next to it. Top the double with a little more yogurt for good measure.

ASK FOR DOUBLES

HOLLYWOOD CEVICHE

HONESTLY, IT'S CEVICHE WITH A CITRUS MARINADE IN AN AVOCADO CUP. THE HOLLYWOOD PART IS BECAUSE IT'S RIDING AROUND IN A CONVERTIBLE. GET IT?!? AND DON'T USE FROZEN CORN FOR THIS.

PESCA!

Take the albacore tuna and cut it into ¼-inch (0.5 cm) cubes. Toss the tuna cubes in a bowl with the salt, sugar, juice from both limes, juice from one lemon, the apple cider vinegar, shallots, cilantro, and chives. Add a splash of cold water as well to bring down the intensity of the acid and then give it all a little mix. The fish is now "cooking" in the citrus bath you just made for it. Set aside in the fridge until needed.

THE JALAPEÑO AIOLI

Blitz the eggs in a food processor or blender with the garlic and the jalapeño peppers. Slowly add the canola oil while the machine is running, and mix until the aioli starts to thicken. Once it's thickened, season it with salt and the juice from half the remaining lemon.

WELCOME TO HOLLYWOOD

Halve the avocados and remove the pits. Keep the meat in the avocado skin, spray it with some lemon juice, and season with salt. Cut the cucumber, leaving the skin on, into quarters, and then cut the seeds right out. Dice the cucumber quarters into small pieces, and add them to the bowl of tuna. In a pot, boil the cobs of corn over high heat for approximately 8 minutes, or until tender. Cut the corn kernels off the cobs, and add them to the bowl of tuna. Toss the ceviche around, and add a little more salt, the remaining lemon juice, cilantro leaves, and the olive oil. Fill the avocados with the ceviche, and drizzle with jalapeño aioli for extra flavor.

8 oz (225 g) albacore tuna

1 tablespoon (15 mL) kosher salt

½ teaspoon (2.5 mL) granulated sugar

Juice from 2 limes

Juice from 2 lemons, divided

1 tablespoon (15 mL) apple cider vinegar

2 shallots, finely chopped

¼ cup (60 mL) cilantro

1 tablespoon (15 mL) finely chopped chives

2 eggs

4 cloves garlic

2 jalapeño peppers

4 cups (1 L) canola oil

2 ripe avocados

1 English cucumber

2 cobs of corn or 1 can (12 oz/341 g) of corn

Handful of cilantro leaves

1 tablespoon (15 mL) olive oil

OPEN-FACED BOSTON CRAB

SERVES 4 TO 6

I'VE BEEN EATING A LOT OF CRAB THIS YEAR. BEING IN BOSTON AND CAPE BRETON HAS GIVEN ME EASY ACCESS TO CRABMEAT. BUT YOU CAN ALSO USE LOBSTER OR SHRIMP MEAT.

3 lb (1.5 kg) cooked snow crab

1 russet potato, skin on

¼ red onion, finely diced

1 stalk celery, finely chopped

1 green onion, finely chopped

¼ teaspoon (1 mL) black pepper

1 lemon

2 tablespoons (30 mL) grainy Dijon mustard

1 ½ tablespoons (22 mL) mayonnaise

3 radishes

1 loaf rustic bread

1–2 tablespoons (15–30 mL) salted butter

GET CRABBY

Shuck all the beautiful shell from the snow crab. The best way to crack the long pieces is to snap them in half from the bottom side (non-orange side). It cracks easiest from there, and you should be able to pull most of that meat cleanly out of its shell. Crack the claw by snapping the loose single claw off first. If you look at where the orange and off-white color meet on the claw you should be able to see a hairline crack. If you can't see it, that's the easiest place to apply some pressure and make your own hairline crack. Use the first piece of claw you broke off to pick away at the rest of the crab. Once all your crab is shucked, squeeze the excess water from the meat and place it in a bowl.

DRESS IT UP

Prepare an ice water bath large enough to hold the potatoes. Dice the potato into ¼-inch (0.5 cm) cubes. Bring a pot of salted water to a boil over high heat, add the potato cubes, and cook for approximately 6 minutes, or until tender but still with some texture and bite. Drain them and toss them into the ice water bath to shock them and stop the cooking process.

Add one-quarter of the red onion and the celery, green onion, and black pepper to the bowl of crabmeat. Add juice from about half the lemon. Add the grainy mustard and mayo, and mix gently, ensuring you don't break up the crabmeat. That would be a sin! I suggest you add the mayo and mustard gradually to gauge just how creamy you want the crab mixture to be. You don't want to disguise your good crab behind the mayo. That said, the mayo and the mustard help bind all the flavors together and make the crab salad more cohesive. Once the potato has cooled down, add it to the bowl as well.

BUTTER UP!

Slice the radishes into thin rounds, and toss them in a bowl with the juice from the other half of the lemon. Cut the loaf of bread into ¼-inch-thick (0.5 cm) pieces and butter both sides of each slice. Grill the bread in a skillet for 2 minutes on each side, or until golden brown or darker. Slap on a healthy portion of the crab salad and garnish with radish slices.

ROASTED BEET TOSTADA

THE TOSTADA IS A GREAT VESSEL FOR FOOD. IT HOLDS TOGETHER QUITE FIRMLY AND BASICALLY ACTS AS AN EDIBLE PLATE. NOT REALLY WHAT IT WAS INTENDED FOR, BUT HEY, WHEN IN ROME ... THIS DISH BRINGS TOGETHER MY LOVE OF WHITE BEANS AND ROASTED BEETS IN A UNIQUE WAY THAT LOOKS FANTASTIC, THANKS TO THE VIBRANT COLORS OF THE INGREDIENTS AND THE ALMIGHTY TOSTADA VESSEL. AND IT'S VEGGIE!

SERVES 10

THE BEETS

First things first, get those beets in the oven. I used red beets, but they all cook the same, and if you mix and match the kind of beets you use, it makes for a visually more interesting plate. Preheat the oven to 350°F (180°C). Place the beets on a baking sheet, and cook for approximately 1 hour, or until soft. Let them cool for approximately 10 minutes before you start peeling them. Once peeled, slice them into very thin rounds, and set aside at room temperature until needed.

THE WHITE BEAN MASH

White beans are scientifically proven to be a magical fruit. They actually bring all the flavors in this dish together atop the crispy tostada. Throw the beans in a blender. Add the leaves from the sprigs of thyme, the olives, and the sundried tomatoes. Blitz it all together until mostly creamy with just a little bit of chunkiness.

Melt the butter in a pan over medium-high heat. Lightly salt the mushrooms and allow them to cook for approximately 5 minutes, or until they have browned. Remove them from the pan and place them in a bowl until you're ready to use them. Place the white wine and white bean purée in the pan, and cook over medium heat. Stir well. Season to taste with salt, and then cook until all the wine has been soaked up into the bean purée, 5 to 10 minutes. Once the wine has soaked up, squeeze the juice from half a lemon into the beans. I suggest stirring the white beans semi-frequently so that they don't stick to the bottom of the pan.

THE CILANTRO PESTO

Preheat the oven to 400°F (200°C). Put the pine nuts on a baking sheet, and place them in the oven for 5 to 10 minutes, or until roasted. Remove from the oven and set aside at room temperature. Wash the cilantro and the fresh basil, and toss them into a blender with the garlic, roasted pine nuts, olive oil, and juice from the remaining lemons. Blend until the mixture is smooth like a sauce.

BUILDING THE TOSTADA

Layer about five slices of beets on each tostada. Spread a generous helping of white bean purée on the beets, add some mushrooms, and finish with a drizzle of the pesto.

4 red, candy cane, or golden beets

1 can (14 oz/398 g) white beans, rinsed and drained

10 sprigs fresh thyme

10 pitted green olives

2 tablespoons (30 mL) sundried tomatoes in oil

2 tablespoons (30 mL) salted butter

10 shitake mushrooms

Kosher salt

¼ cup (60 mL) white wine

Juice from 2 lemons, divided

¼ cup (60 mL) pine nuts

Handful of fresh cilantro

Handful of fresh basil

6 cloves garlic

½ cup (125 mL) olive oil

10 tostada or flat and crispy tortilla shells

TACO SEOUL

2 eggs

4 cups (1 L) canola oil

1 ¾ cups (430 mL)
  Sriracha sauce

1 tablespoon (15 mL) kosher salt

1 tablespoon (15 mL)
  smoked paprika

3 tablespoons (45 mL)
  brown sugar

4 lb (2 kg) skinless pork belly

1 pint (16 oz/470 mL) dark beer

½ cup (125 mL) soy sauce

8 oz (225 g) Hallumi cheese

1 tablespoon (15 mL) canola oil

10 soft-shell corn tortillas

½ cup (125 mL) Kimchi
  (see page 118)

½ cup (125 mL) cilantro

1 cup (250 mL) bean sprouts

THE KOREAN TACO CREATED BY HIS STREET FOOD MAJESTY ROY CHOI HAS BECOME INCREDIBLY POPULAR ON THE STREET FOOD SCENE. NOW, HALLUMI CHEESE MIGHT NOT REALLY REFLECT KOREAN CUISINE, BUT MAN IT'S GOOD AND IT'S FUN TO MAKE.

THE SRIRACHA AIOLI

Blitz the eggs in a food processor, and slowly add the canola oil while the machine is running. Once the mixture has thickened, pour in the Sriracha sauce. If you want it spicier, you can add more. The Sriracha alone provides a lot of flavor, so you shouldn't have to add too much more than just those three ingredients.

MA BELLY

Combine the salt and smoked paprika in a bowl. Add the brown sugar. Rub the pork belly with the dry mixture. Heat a skillet or griddle pan over high heat, and sear the pork belly for approximately 3 minutes per side, or until crispy.

Preheat the oven to 300°F (150°C). In a deep roasting pan, pour in the beer and soy sauce. Give it a good mix until it becomes one cohesive liquid, and place the seared pork belly into it. Cover the pan very tightly with a layer of plastic wrap and a layer of aluminum foil. Cook the pork belly in the oven for approximately 4 hours, or until soft.

IT'S KOREAN TACO TIME

Take the pork belly out of the oven and allow it to cool. If you can let it cool overnight in the fridge, that's even better. The fat will have time to harden so when you slice and grill it, you have nice meaty pieces of pork belly. If you slice it and then try to grill it from warm, it will most likely fall apart. Wah wahhh! So, resist the urge to dive in and just let it cool overnight.

Slice the pork belly into perfect taco-sized portions, about ¼ inch (0.5 cm) thick. Slice your Hallumi cheese into generous rectangular portions, about ¼ inch (0.5 cm) thick and a little wider than the pork belly pieces. Warm a nonstick skillet over high heat, then add the 1 tablespoon (15 mL) oil and get the pan hot. Add the cheese slices to the pan. You should only need to flip the cheese once, so place it on one side of the pan and cook for 3 to 4 minutes, and then flip to cook the other side. You're basically going to do the exact same thing with the belly. Place the cut pieces in a separate hot nonstick skillet, and cook for 3 or 4 minutes per side.

In a dry pan over medium-low heat, lightly warm the tortillas. Layer the taco with Hallumi cheese, grilled pork belly, and kimchi. Drizzle with some Sriracha aioli, and top with cilantro, or another green sprout for color and freshness, and the bean sprouts.

STUFF THAT MAKES YOU SWEAT

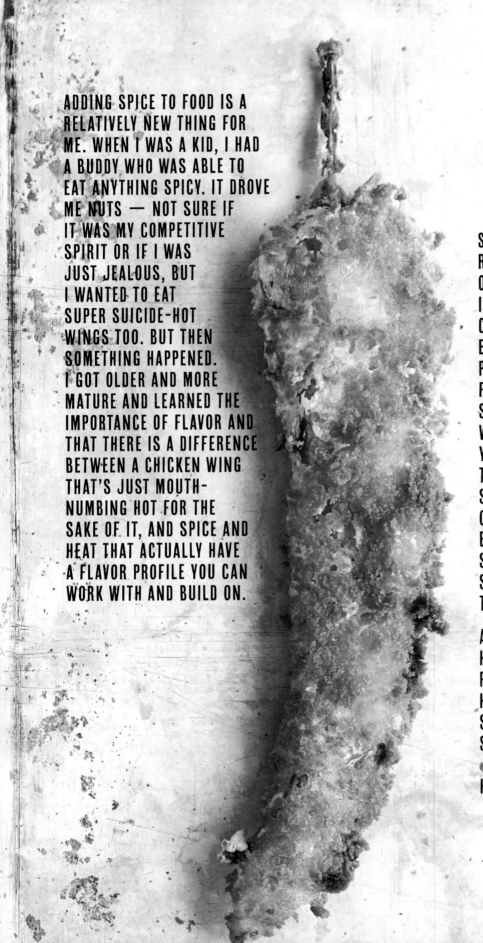

ADDING SPICE TO FOOD IS A RELATIVELY NEW THING FOR ME. WHEN I WAS A KID, I HAD A BUDDY WHO WAS ABLE TO EAT ANYTHING SPICY. IT DROVE ME NUTS — NOT SURE IF IT WAS MY COMPETITIVE SPIRIT OR IF I WAS JUST JEALOUS, BUT I WANTED TO EAT SUPER SUICIDE-HOT WINGS TOO. BUT THEN SOMETHING HAPPENED. I GOT OLDER AND MORE MATURE AND LEARNED THE IMPORTANCE OF FLAVOR AND THAT THERE IS A DIFFERENCE BETWEEN A CHICKEN WING THAT'S JUST MOUTH-NUMBING HOT FOR THE SAKE OF IT, AND SPICE AND HEAT THAT ACTUALLY HAVE A FLAVOR PROFILE YOU CAN WORK WITH AND BUILD ON.

STREET FOOD AND SPICES REALLY DO GO HAND-IN-HAND. OFTENTIMES THE CULTURAL INSPIRATIONS OF STREET FOOD COME FROM CUISINES THAT EMBRACE A VARIETY OF HOT PEPPERS AND SPICES. AND FROM THAT, I LEARNED HOW SPICE IS USED IN DIFFERENT WAYS — SOMETIMES IT'S ALL YOU TASTE, OTHER TIMES IT'S THE LINGERING AFTERTASTE; SOMETIMES IT CREEPS UP ON YOU, OTHER TIMES IT'S BALANCED WITH ACID OR SWEETNESS. SO, THIS IS A SECTION DEVOTED TO STUFF THAT MAKES YOU SWEAT.

AND BECAUSE I'M A NICE GUY, HOW ABOUT WE HAVE A LITTLE POINT RATING SYSTEM FOR HOW MUCH SWEAT CERTAIN STUFF WILL MAKE YOU HAVE? SO 🔥 IS ON THE LOW END AND 🔥🔥🔥🔥 IS BORDERLINE HEAT WAVE. ENJOY!

MOROCCAN
BEEF SHORT RIBS

SERVES 8 TO 10

I FIRST MADE THIS DISH WHILE COOKING UP GRUB FOR
FOLKS AT A RODEO IN TEXAS. MY CHALLENGE THEN AND
NOW WAS MAKING THE MOROCCAN SPICES TRANSLATE TO
SOMETHING THAT WAS INCREDIBLY LARGE AND BEEFY. WHEN
I FIRST MADE THE DISH, THE MEAT WAS SMOKED, SO THERE
WAS THAT FAMILIARITY THAT THE TEXAS FOLK COULD RELATE
TO, DESPITE THERE BEING CRUSHED NUTS ON THEIR BBQ.
WHEN I DECIDED TO BRING THE RECIPE BACK HOME I LEARNED
THAT AS LONG AS THE MEAT IS FALL-OFF-THE-BONE TENDER,
THE SPICES WILL WORK NO MATTER WHAT. >>>

RUBBIN' IS LOVIN'

First you need to make your Moroccan rub to completely cover your ribs. Combine the salt, pepper, cinnamon, ground ginger, cumin, and turmeric in a bowl. Mix it all together so it makes one very robust-smelling spice.

Preheat the oven to 250°F (120°C). Cover each and every part of the ribs with the rub until it's layered on thick. Place the ribs, meat side up, in a baking pan with approximately ½ cup (125 mL) of liquid (water is fine, but dark beer is better). Slow-roast the ribs, uncovered, for approximately 6 hours. Every hour or so, try to baste them with the liquid from the pan.

For the Moroccan dark sauce, you will need to blitz one onion, the garlic, cilantro, peeled ginger, and lime juice in a blender or food processor. There should be no lumps. Pour the contents into a large saucepan and add the beer, Worcestershire sauce, ketchup, molasses, and honey. Stir it all really well, then toss in the butter and the remaining Spanish onion (keep it whole but peel it first!). Cook the sauce, uncovered, over medium heat for approximately 1 hour.

SUCCULENT RIBS

Take the ribs you've been slow-roasting and place them in the sauce. Cook them in the sauce for about another hour, or until the meat just looks incredibly soft and tender. Take the ribs out of the sauce and top them with crushed pistachios before serving.

2 tablespoons (30 mL) kosher salt

2 tablespoons (30 mL) black pepper

2 tablespoons (30 mL) ground cinnamon

2 tablespoons (30 mL) ground ginger

2 tablespoons (30 mL) ground cumin

2 tablespoons (30 mL) ground turmeric

4 whole long-bone beef short ribs

2 Spanish onions

10 cloves garlic

1 bunch cilantro

4 oz (100 g) piece fresh ginger, peeled

Juice from 6 limes

2 pints (16 oz/470 mL each) dark beer

2 cups (500 mL) Worcestershire sauce

2 cups (500 mL) ketchup

½ cup (125 mL) molasses

2 tablespoons (30 mL) honey

1 cup (250 mL) salted butter

¼ cup (60 mL) crushed pistachio nuts

FLYING CARPET, AUSTIN, TEXAS

The Flying Carpet
Moroccan Souk Food

Flying Carpet
n Souk Food

MOROCCAN FOOD REALLY IS QUITE DIFFERENT IN ALL THE RIGHT WAYS.

AUSTIN, TEXAS, REALLY IS A MECCA FOR STREET FOOD. CARTS AND FOOD TRUCKS LINE THE STREETS OF THE CITY, CREATING A VIBRANT, COLORFUL BACKDROP TO AN ALREADY COOL CITY.

TACOS AND BBQ DOMINATE THE SCENE. SOME ARE INCREDIBLE, SOME NOT SO MUCH; THE ONES THAT STOOD OUT HAD A PASSIONATE AND DEVOUT FOLLOWING. BUT THEN THERE'S A DIFFERENT KIND OF STANDOUT. TUCKED BEHIND A MOROCCAN TEASHOP WAS A LITTLE FOOD CART CALLED THE FLYING CARPET. MOROCCAN STREET FOOD IS PRETTY DIFFERENT, BUT BECAUSE I WAS TACO'D AND BBQ'D OUT, I THOUGHT THIS WOULD BE AWESOME, NOT YOUR TYPICAL STREET FARE.

I MET THIS MASSIVE MAN, ABDUSOUKTOURI, NICKNAMED THE BIG ABDU. COINCIDENTALLY ENOUGH HE HAS AN ITEM ON HIS MENU ALSO NAMED THE BIG ABDU. I KIND OF FELT LIKE I WAS MEETING A WRESTLER FROM THE EARLY '90S. IN THIS CORNER, BIG ABDU! SO I ORDERED THE BIG ABDU AND IT TURNED OUT TO BE A MASSIVE MOROCCAN BURRITO STUFFED WITH AN EGG AND BEEF KEFTA. THE FLAVOR WAS RIDICULOUSLY INTENSE IN ALL THE RIGHT WAYS. HE BROUGHT ME IN HIS CART, WHERE HE HAD ALL THE SPICES LINED UP AND DOUBLE-BAGGED. YOU COULD SMELL THEM PERFECTLY THROUGH THE BAG. I MEAN, I'VE HAD SPICED FOOD BEFORE BUT THIS WAS A WHOLE DIFFERENT BAG (LITERALLY) OF SPICE. I'M SURE THIS WASN'T MY FIRST TIME EATING MOROCCAN BUT FOR WHATEVER REASON, I KNEW I WOULD BE ABLE TO REMEMBER THIS ONE. THE FLAVORS WERE JUST TOO INTENSE NOT TO REMEMBER, AND PLUS, HOW CAN YOU FORGET EATING SOMETHING CALLED THE BIG ABDU, PREPARED BY A GUY NAMED BIG ABDU? AFTER WE ATE AND TALKED ABOUT FOOD, HE AND HIS WIFE JOINED ME OUTSIDE THE CART AND WE HAD SOME MOROCCAN TEA TOGETHER BECAUSE AS IT TURNED OUT THEY HAD THE TEA PLACE IN FRONT AND RENTED THE BACK LOT OUT TO NUMEROUS CARTS AND TRUCKS.

I'VE ALWAYS BEEN A BELIEVER THAT YOU NEED TO BE DIFFERENT IN ORDER TO SURVIVE IN THIS INDUSTRY, AND IN A WORLD OF BBQ AND TACOS, MOROCCAN FOOD REALLY IS QUITE DIFFERENT IN ALL THE RIGHT WAYS.

CHIPOTLE BUTTER OXTAIL AND POTATOES

BUTTER AND SPICE HAVE A VERY INTERESTING RELATIONSHIP. IT'S KIND OF LIKE A WOLF IN SHEEP'S CLOTHING. YOU TASTE THE SAUCE AND THE BUTTER DOES A GREAT JOB OF LETTING YOU THINK IT'S JUST A RICH, VELVETY-SOFT SAUCE … AND THEN IT HITS YOU. KAPOW! THE SPICE. IN THIS DISH WE COMBINE SOME CHIPOTLES WITH BUTTER — THE BATMAN AND ROBIN OF THE SPICY, SMOOTH SAUCES. TOGETHER THEY BRING OUT THE RICHNESS AND FATTINESS IN THE OXTAIL.

SERVES 2 TO 4

1 Spanish onion

6 cloves garlic

1 cup (250 mL) unsalted butter, divided

3 cans (7 oz/198 g each) chipotle peppers in adobo sauce

2 cups (500 mL) Clamato juice, divided

4 large pieces (10 oz/300 g each) oxtail

20 fingerling or small roasting potatoes

2 cups (500 mL) basmati rice

1 teaspoon (5 mL) kosher salt

MEAT AND POTATOES

Finely chop the onion and crush the garlic. Lightly cook them in a medium-sized saucepan with 1 teaspoon (5 mL) of the butter over high heat for 4 to 5 minutes, or until their aroma fills your nose with garlic butter bliss. Then add the rest of the butter and allow it to melt.

Blitz the chipotles in a blender, and add a splash of the Clamato juice so that no chipotle flavor gets left behind. Add the chipotles to the butter pot, and then add the rest of the Clamato juice. Give everything a nice stir, and add the oxtail. Cook the oxtail, covered, over low heat for approximately 3 hours. At the 3-hour mark, cut all your potatoes in half lengthwise and sear them in a separate pan over high heat for approximately 2 minutes, or until brown. Once seared, add them to the pot of oxtail, and cook, covered, for another hour.

GIVE THAT TAIL SOME LOVE

Into a large saucepan, pour 4 cups (1 L) of water and the rice. Add about 1 teaspoon (5 mL) of salt and let the water come to a boil over high heat. Give it one good stir, and then turn down the heat to low, cover the pot, and cook for approximately 8 minutes, or until the rice has absorbed the water.

Place the rice on a plate, and put the potatoes and oxtail on top. Don't you dare discard that braising sauce! Pour it over the whole dish for some extra heat and flavor.

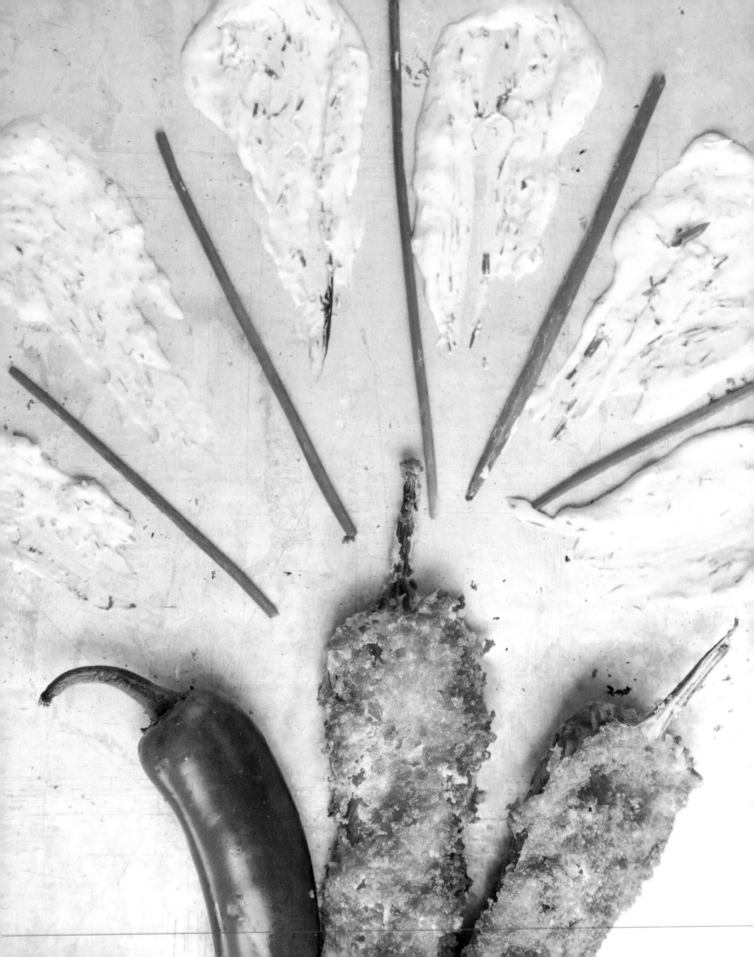

GOAT CHEESE AND PORK BELLY POPPERS

IF I HAD TO CHOOSE BETWEEN LIVING IN A STUFFED PEPPER KIND OF WORLD OR A NON-STUFFED PEPPER KIND OF WORLD, I'D SAY, "STUFF ME UP, BUTTERCUP." PEPPERS WERE MEANT TO BE STUFFED, AND IN THIS CASE WE HAVE THE MOTHER OF ALL STUFFINGS — GOAT CHEESE AND PORK BELLY ... SAY WHAAAA?

PEPPER FOR THE POPPERS

Preheat the oven to 425°F (220°C). Cut the jalapeño peppers and banana peppers in half lengthwise and discard the seeds, but try to keep the stems on the peppers. Place the peppers on a baking sheet, skin side up, and roast them for approximately 10 minutes, or until the skin darkens and the peppers soften. Take them out of the oven and let them cool at room temperature.

NOW FOR THE FILLING

Blitz two cloves of the garlic with the chives in a food processor. Add the juice from two of the lemons, the ricotta cheese, and goat cheese. Blitz again until the mixture is very smooth. Take the cheese mix and scoop it all into a plastic bag. Squeeze the bag tightly so that all the cheese is in one corner. Cut one corner off the bag, and pipe the cheese evenly into each pepper half. Cut the pork belly into thin 1-inch-wide (2.5 cm) strips, and stuff two pieces into the cheese in each pepper. It actually looks better if the pork belly strips are longer than the pepper. Set aside until needed.

NEED MORE THYME!

Blitz two of the eggs in a food processor or blender, and add the thyme and the remaining two cloves of garlic. Slowly add the canola oil while the machine is running, and then the juice from three of the remaining lemons. Season to taste with salt.

POPPER TIME

Break the remaining four eggs in a bowl, and whisk. Toss the stuffed peppers in the flour, then dip them in the whisked eggs, and lastly dunk them in the Panko breadcrumbs. Fill a table-top deep-fryer to the line with canola oil, or add oil to a depth of 1 inch (2.5 cm) to a deep saucepan, and heat it to 350°F (180°C). Place the poppers in the oil, and fry for approximately 1 to 2 minutes on each side, or until golden brown.

Dress the poppers with the lemon thyme aioli, and serve with wedges of the final lemon.

4 jalapeño peppers

3 hot banana peppers

4 cloves garlic

1 bunch chives

Juice from 6 lemons, divided

1 lb (500 g) ricotta cheese

1 cup (250 mL) goat cheese

2 lb (1 kg) pork belly
(see page 94, divided in half)

6 eggs

½ cup (125 mL) fresh thyme,
stems removed

4 cups (1 L) canola oil

Kosher salt

1 cup (250 mL) all-purpose flour

1 cup (250 mL)
Panko breadcrumbs

HOT AND SOUR HENS

THE CORNISH HEN IS OTHERWISE KNOWN AS THE MUCH SMALLER CHICKEN. I ACTUALLY REALLY ENJOY COOKING HENS — FOR ONE THING, THEY'RE LESS LIKELY TO DRY OUT WHEN YOU COOK THEM. UNLIKE THE CHICKEN, MOST OF THE COMPONENTS OF THE HEN ARE EVENLY SIZED AND THEREFORE FINISH COOKING AT APPROXIMATELY THE SAME TIME. AND IF YOU DECIDE TO EAT A WHOLE HEN IN ONE GO, YOU FEEL LESS GUILTY BECAUSE THEY'RE SMALLER. #STREETFOODPROBLEMS.

2 Cornish hens cut into 4 pieces each (cut down the middle and then drum and thigh separated from breast and wing)

1 cup (250 mL) salted butter, at room temperature

1 teaspoon (5 mL) kosher salt

1 teaspoon (5 mL) black pepper

1 teaspoon (5 mL) dried rosemary

1 teaspoon (5 mL) cayenne pepper

1 cup (250 mL) sambal oelek

¾ cup (180 mL) plum sauce

¼ cup + 2 tablespoons (100 mL) rice wine vinegar

Juice from 1 lemon

1 cup (250 mL) sour cream

1 lime

FEELING HOT, SOUR HOT (LIKE THE SONG)

Sear the Cornish hen pieces in a lightly oiled grill pan over high heat for approximately 3 minutes, or until the skin is a nice golden brown. Remove the pan from the heat.

Preheat the oven to 325°F (160°C). Rub the butter over the pieces of hen to cover them lightly but evenly. Sprinkle with salt, black pepper, rosemary, and cayenne pepper. Place the hens in a roasting pan and bake for approximately 25 minutes, or until the juices run clear.

Combine the sambal, plum sauce, and rice wine vinegar in a bowl, and give it a stir so that it has one cohesive spicy, sweet flavor with an acidy kick.

Take the hens out of the oven and hit them with the fresh lemon juice and a little more salt.

Place the hen pieces on a serving platter. Using two squeeze bottles, zig-zag the sour cream and the hot and sour sauce over the hens, and serve with a wedge of lime.

MAPLE HABANERO TURKEY WINGS

SERVES 4 TO 6

ONE OF MY FAVORITE WAYS TO BALANCE FLAVOR IS BY TAKING SOMETHING SWEET AND SOMETHING HOT AND BRINGING THEM TOGETHER IN A DISH. THIS DISH IS KIND OF THE EPITOME OF THAT BECAUSE WE ARE TAKING THE HOTTEST AND THE SWEETEST ENDS OF THE SPECTRUM AND FORCING THEM TO DANCE ALL OVER A TURKEY WING. I WAS INSPIRED TO MAKE THIS SAUCE WHILE IN NEW ORLEANS — THE UNBELIEVABLE AMOUNT OF FRENCH CANADIAN INFLUENCE PROMPTED THE FRESH MAPLE SYRUP, AND ACCESS TO SOME OF THE FRESHEST PEPPERS I HAD EVER COME ACROSS IN AN URBAN GARDEN PROMPTED ME TO ADD THE HEAT.

¼ cup + 2 tablespoons (100 mL) canola oil

6 turkey wings, 3 drums and 3 flats separated

4 large carrots

2 Spanish onions

1 teaspoon (5 mL) fresh thyme

6 cups (1.5 L) chicken stock (optional)

2 tablespoons + 1 ½ teaspoons (37.5 mL) kosher salt

5 habanero peppers

6 cloves garlic

2 lemons

½ cup (125 mL) white vinegar

1 ½ cups (375 mL) maple syrup

Black pepper

BUT WHAT REALLY CAME FIRST, THE CHICKEN OR THE TURKEY?

Put 2 tablespoons (30 mL) of the canola oil in a pan over high heat and get it super hot. Sear the turkey wings for approximately 3 to 4 minutes per side, or until all the sides have a crust on the skin. The skin should be a nice dark brown. This will take a few minutes per side. The skin is very fatty, so be careful — it might pop some hot oil onto your forearm.

When you're done searing the wings, roughly chop the carrots and onions and throw them into a deep roasting pan with the thyme and about 6 cups (1.5 L) of water (or chicken stock, if using).

Preheat the oven to 275°F (135°C). Place the wings in the liquid, and add the 2 tablespoons (30 mL) of salt. Tightly wrap the pan with a layer of plastic wrap and a layer of aluminum foil. Place the wings in the oven and braise for approximately 3 hours, or until fall-off-the-bone tender.

GET SAUCY

While the wings are braising, blitz the habanero peppers with the garlic, the flesh of one lemon, and the white vinegar in a blender or food processor. Thicken the sauce with the remaining ¼ cup (60 mL) of canola oil while the machine is running, and then add the maple syrup into the mixture while the machine is still running. Add the remaining 1 ½ teaspoons (7.5 mL) of salt. Give it one last blitz to combine. Give it a taste. You will taste the sweet maple, followed immediately by furious heat.

After the wings are braised, place them back in the pan, and sear them for 3 to 4 minutes per side. Season them with an extra sprinkle of salt and a dash of pepper. The braising makes the meat fall off the bone, but you need this last searing to make the wings super crispy on the outside. You could also dust them with some flour first, but you don't have to.

Take the wings out of the pan, place them on a plate, and paint them with the maple habanero sauce. Serve with a lemon wedge.

POLLO, POLENTA, AND PICO

THREE P'S — POLLO IS YOUR CHICKEN, POLENTA IS YOUR CHARRED CORNMEAL CAKE, AND PICO IS YOUR TOMATO AND ONION-BASED SALSA.

SERVES 6 TO 8

POLLO

Sear the chicken thighs in a saucepan or large cast iron pan over high heat for approximately 2 minutes, or until nicely browned. Once the chicken is seared on both sides, toss in the Roma tomatoes with their seeds and one of the jalapeño peppers, finely diced, the butter, the salt, and ½ cup (125 mL) of water. Give it a good stir, and let the sauce cook, uncovered, over medium-low heat for approximately 45 minutes, or until the tomatoes have cooked down. As the sauce cooks, pull the chicken apart to let it soak up more sauce.

POLENTA

On to the polenta cake! Boil 4 cups (1 L) of lightly salted water over high heat. Toss in the polenta. Stir it up and then turn down the heat to medium. Add the milk and Parmesan cheese. Cook the polenta, stirring, for approximately 2 minutes, or until the liquid is fully absorbed. Spread the polenta about ¼ inch (5 mm) thick onto a baking sheet lined with parchment paper, and cool in the fridge for approximately 20 minutes. Once cooled, cut the polenta into 2-inch (5 cm) squares.

AND PICO!

Now for the last "P" of the dish — the pico. Finely chop the three remaining jalapeño peppers and the onions, garlic, and heirloom tomatoes. Throw them all together in a bowl with the olive oil, cilantro, and lemon juice. Season to taste with salt and pepper.

Warm some olive oil in a nonstick skillet and cook the polenta pieces over high heat for 1 to 2 minutes on each side, or until they have a nice char on them. Portion the polenta out onto individual plates, top with the chicken tomato sauce, and then dollop with spicy pico. Serve it with a lime wedge and some extra cilantro to help ease the spice of the pico.

- 8 boneless, skinless chicken thighs
- 12 Roma tomatoes, chopped into small chunks
- 4 jalapeño peppers
- 2 tablespoons (30 mL) unsalted butter
- 1 tablespoon (15 mL) kosher salt
- 1 cup (250 mL) polenta
- 2 cups (500 mL) 2% milk
- ¼ cup (60 mL) freshly grated Parmesan cheese
- 2 Spanish onions
- 4 cloves garlic
- 6 heirloom tomatoes
- 2 tablespoons (30 mL) olive oil
- ¼ cup (60 mL) chopped cilantro
- Juice from 1 lemon
- Black pepper
- 1 lime

EL REY
DEL SABOR,
NYC, NEW YORK

THE OWNERS OF EL REY DEL SABOR,
OFELIA "ROSA" CARDOSO AND VILIO
VILIULFO, OPERATE THREE MEXICAN
FOOD CARTS IN MIDTOWN, NEW YORK.
THEY WERE NOMINATED FOR ROOKIE OF
THE YEAR AT THE 2006 VENDY AWARDS,
AND THEN FOR THE VENDY CUP IN 2010.
FYI, THE VENDYS ARE KIND OF A BIG DEAL.
THIS BROTHER AND SISTER DUO FROM
PUEBLA, MEXICO, RUN THEIR THREE-CART
BUSINESS TOGETHER. HIS BACKGROUND
WAS COOKING AUTHENTIC MEXICAN STREET
CUISINE, AND HERS WAS WORKING IN OTHER
CARTS IN NEW YORK'S STREET FOOD SCENE.
NOW, I COULDN'T MAKE THIS UP IF I TRIED,
BUT AT CERTAIN TIMES OF YEAR THEY OFFER
GRASSHOPPER TACOS, WHICH APPARENTLY
SELL OUT VERY QUICKLY. I'VE GOT TO SAY,
THAT WAS A NEW ONE FOR ME.

I COULDN'T MAKE THIS UP IF I TRIED, BUT AT CERTAIN
TIMES OF YEAR THEY OFFER GRASSHOPPER TACOS ...

KIMCHI

SERVES 10+

LIKE EVERY OTHER GOOD OL' ITALIAN-CANADIAN BOY, I LOVE MAKING KIMCHI. OKAY, OKAY, THAT MAKES NO SENSE, BUT I DO LOVE MAKING KIMCHI. IT'S ONE OF THOSE ITEMS THAT YOU CAN MAKE AND KEEP, AND THE BEST PART IS THAT IT GETS BETTER OVER TIME. IN FACT, AGED KIMCHI JUST TASTES BETTER. IT HAS A MATURE, FERMENTED FLAVOR — AND I MEAN THAT IN A GOOD WAY. IF YOU DON'T BELIEVE ME, TRY MAKING IT IN BATCHES OVER A FEW WEEKS. MAKE ONE BATCH AND LET IT REST IN THE FRIDGE FOR THREE WEEKS, THEN MAKE ANOTHER BATCH AND LET IT REST FOR A WEEK, AND THEN A THIRD BATCH AND LET IT REST FOR A DAY. EAT THEM ALL AND SEE WHICH YOU LIKE BEST. NOW, DESPITE THIS BEING MY RECIPE FOR KIMCHI, IT IS NOT HARDCORE, TRADITIONAL, AGED KIMCHI. FOR THAT YOU NEED TO BURY IT AND HAVE A KIMCHI FRIDGE, AND I'M SURE I'M STILL MISSING SOME TRADITIONAL STEPS. THINK OF THIS AS A QUICK AND TO-THE-POINT KIMCHI RECIPE THAT DOES THE TRICK.

½ cup (125 mL) kosher salt

1 napa cabbage

2 Fuji apples, skin on

2 Bosc pears, skin on

6 cloves garlic

4 oz (100 g) piece fresh ginger

1 bunch green onions

2 lemons

2 cans (7 oz/198 g each) chipotle peppers in adobo sauce

2 cups (500 mL) rice wine vinegar

1 cup (250 mL) Sriracha sauce

¼ cup + 2 tablespoons (100 mL) sesame oil

1 tablespoon (15 mL) fish sauce

1 bunch cilantro, stems removed

1 tablespoon (15 mL) cayenne pepper

KIMCHI BATH

Boil a large pot of water over high heat, add the salt, and turn off the heat. Let cool for approximately 10 minutes.

Cut the cabbage into 1-inch (2.5 cm) squares, or leave them as long full leaves and cut them into squares after fermenting. Soak the cabbage in the cooled water for 30 minutes to 1 hour, and then drain it for at least 1 hour to get as much of the salt water out of the cabbage as you possibly can.

KIMCHI DANCE

While the cabbage drains, make your kimchi marinade. First, throw the apples, pears, garlic, ginger, and green onions in a blender or food processor. Remove the flesh from the lemons and throw that in as well. Blitz it all. Transfer the resulting paste to a bowl, and set aside at room temperature. In the same blender or food processor (you don't need to wash it out), toss in the chipotles, rice wine vinegar, Sriracha sauce, sesame oil, fish sauce, cilantro, and cayenne pepper. Blitz these until they become a paste as well. Combine the two pastes, and add the new paste to the drained napa cabbage in a large bowl. Mix well to cover the cabbage. Add a little more sesame oil, and some salt to taste. Allow to rest for at least 24 hours in the fridge before using. This allows the spices and flavors to fully mature. The longer you let the kimchi stand, the better it tastes.

MAC 'N' CHEESE ARRABIATA

I HAVE A WEIRD RELATIONSHIP WITH ANY SORT OF PASTA ARRABIATA. YOU SEE, *ARRABIATA* LITERALLY TRANSLATES TO "ANGRY" IN ITALIAN. OR AT LEAST IN MY FAMILY'S DIALECT. ALL THROUGH MY CHILDHOOD THE WORDS *FATTO ARRABIATA* WERE FOLLOWED BY THE APPROACH OF MY NONNA'S WOODEN SPOON. SO YOU CAN IMAGINE MY CONFUSION WHEN I SAW IT ON MENUS SOME 15 YEARS LATER. SPICY … ANGRY … SAME DIFFERENCE, SO LONG AS THERE'S NO FLYING WOODEN SPOON.

SERVES 4 TO 6

- 8 oz (225 g) elbow or orecchiette pasta
- ½ cup (125 mL) salted butter
- ½ cup (125 mL) all-purpose flour
- 1 jar (10 oz/298 mL) Italian chilies in oil
- 4 cups (1 L) whipping cream
- 1 cup (250 mL) shredded mozzarella cheese
- 1 cup (250 mL) shredded jalapeño Monterey Jack cheese
- 2 cups (500 mL) ricotta cheese
- ½ cup (125 mL) freshly grated Parmesan cheese
- 6 slices Velveeta or American cheddar
- ½ cup (125 mL) dried breadcrumbs
- 2 tablespoons (30 mL) dried chilies
- 1 lemon

YOU'RE SO ROUX

Boil some water in a saucepan over high heat and cook the pasta for approximately 6 minutes, or until it's very, very al dente. But don't overcook it, or it will come out like mush after you bake it. Keep in mind that elbow and orecchiette pastas cook differently, so just make sure you are happy with it before it comes out. Drain it and toss it in olive oil before you let it fully cool on a baking sheet.

In a separate saucepan, start a roux by melting the butter over medium-low heat and slowly stirring in the flour until a paste-like mixture begins to form. Add three-quarters of the jar of chilies in oil and the whipping cream, all while stirring constantly. If you find the sauce too thick, gradually add more cream (but don't add any more than another 4 cups/1 L). The key to making a good cheese sauce is constant stirring over medium-low heat, so just assume you have to keep stirring until I say to stop.

Start to add the cheeses. First, the grated mozzarella, then the Monterey Jack, followed by the ricotta. Cook the cheeses, still stirring, for approximately 5 minutes, or until they've mostly melted. Add the Parmesan cheese with the Velveeta slices. Stir the cheese sauce until the cheeses have fully melted.

MACARONI (OR ORECCHIETTE) AND CHEESE TIME

Preheat the oven to 400°F (200°C). Transfer the cooled pasta to a deep baking pan — cast iron ovenproof skillets or deep porcelain dishes work best. Pour the cheese sauce over the pasta so it is well covered. In a small bowl, combine the breadcrumbs with the dried chilies and then sprinkle the mixture over the surface of the mac 'n' cheese. Bake for approximately 6 minutes, or until the breadcrumbs start to brown. Remove from the oven, drizzle chili oil from the jar over the top of the pasta, and serve with a lemon wedge.

MAC SHACK, DETROIT, MICHIGAN

WHEN KY AND I WERE IN DETROIT WE WENT TO THE EASTERN MARKET. A THREE-DAY-A-WEEK FARMERS' MARKET, IT TRUMPS THE SIZE OF ANY OTHER MARKET THAT I HAD VISITED BEFORE. AND IT WAS ONE OF THE MOST IMPRESSIVE AS WELL.

I'M A BIT OF A SPICE AND HERB NERD. I GET EXCITED WHEN I FIND PLACES THAT SPECIALIZE IN THE MOST ELUSIVE SPICES AND HERBS, SO WHEN I FOUND SUCH A PLACE AT THIS MARKET, I DECIDED TO PARK AT IT FOR A BIT. I WAS PLANNING TO MAKE A PIG'S CHEEK CHILI, AND I WANTED SPICES AND HERBS THAT STOOD OUT JUST AS MUCH AS THE PIG'S CHEEK. KY VENTURED OFF AND CAME BACK WITH A PAD THAI VERSION OF MAC 'N' CHEESE. IT WAS FANTASTIC — JUST ENOUGH SPICE, CRUNCH, AND FRESHNESS ON TOP OF THE MUCH-NEEDED GOOEYNESS OF THE MAC 'N' CHEESE. I THOUGHT IT WAS A GREAT STREET FOOD DISH. KY EVEN THOUGHT IT TASTED FAMILIAR, LIKE SOMETHING I WOULD MAKE.

IT WAS AMAZING TO HEAR SOMEONE NOT SHIT ON THEIR CITY OF DETROIT. DAN AND LINDSAY MADE EVERY OPPORTUNITY POSSIBLE, AND I HAD SOME SERIOUS, SERIOUS RESPECT FOR THEM ... AND THEIR MAC 'N' CHEESE.

The Mac Shack

Mac 'N' Cheeses:
- Our shack-made, untopped: 6 75

7 50 • The Bacon Made Me Do It : bacon, tomato, green onion

7 50 • Cheech's Trip : chorizo, pico, jalapeno, cilantro

7 50 • Cluck Like a Buffalo : spicy chicken, blue cheese, green onion, buffalo sauce

7 50 • Papa Smurf : sautéed mushrooms + onions, fresh parmesan

7 50 • Koh San Road : sprouts, green onion, cilantro, sriracha, peanuts, limes

7 50 • Dune Climber : artichokes, capers, tomato, green onion

7 50 • I-80 : sautéed mushrooms + onions, beef gravy + a fried egg

4 50 • Garlic Parmesan Fries

4 50 • Amaze Balls : 3 deep fried mac n cheese balls topped w/ ranch, marinara or buffalo sauce

THE NEXT DAY, WE GOT TO MEET THE OWNER OF THE TRUCK, DAN, AND HIS WIFE, LINDSAY, AT THE DO IT YOURSELF FESTIVAL WHERE WE WERE FILMING FOR *REBEL WITHOUT A KITCHEN*. WE WERE TALKING, AND I WAS LIKE, "CRAZY-GOOD MAC 'N' CHEESE, MAN," AND HE WAS ALL LIKE, "OH, DID YOU EAT OFF OUR CART OR TRUCK?" FROM THERE WE FOUND OUT THAT THEY OWNED THREE FOOD TRUCKS AND ONE CART, AND RAN A COMMISSARY KITCHEN IN DETROIT. WE HIT IT OFF INSTANTLY. WE EVEN HAD DINNER TOGETHER AT THEIR CONDO IN DETROIT. IT WAS GREAT TO SIT DOWN WITH SOMEONE WHO GETS EVERYTHING YOU'RE GOING THROUGH AS A BUSINESS OWNER ... SOMEONE WHO JUST PLAIN GETS IT. THE SIMILARITIES WERE UNBELIEVABLE. IT WAS AMAZING TO HEAR SOMEONE NOT SHIT ON THEIR CITY OF DETROIT. DAN AND LINDSAY MADE EVERY OPPORTUNITY POSSIBLE, AND I HAD SOME SERIOUS, SERIOUS RESPECT FOR THEM ... AND THEIR MAC 'N' CHEESE.

SPICY ROASTED CAULIFLOWER WITH CUCUMBER MINT DIPPING SAUCE

SERVES 6 TO 10

THIS DISH IS THE PERFECT EXAMPLE OF MY BEING A GLUTTON FOR PUNISHMENT. IT'S INCREDIBLY HOT YET INCREDIBLY ADDICTIVE. I WENT BACK FOR MORE ABOUT FOUR OR FIVE TIMES, DESPITE BEING IN PAIN.

IT BURNS

Break off pieces from both of the cauliflower heads. Use the florets plus a little bit of stalk. They can be different sizes. In fact, the dish comes out better when all the pieces are a different size. Using a BBQ brush, paint Sriracha sauce all over every piece of cauliflower. I'm not talking a little drizzle of sauce, I'm talking a heavy-duty layering of sauce all over every piece.

Preheat the oven to 450°F (230°C). Place the pieces of cauliflower on a rimmed baking sheet, and drizzle with the olive oil. Throw in the Thai chilies, and bake the cauliflower for approximately 25 minutes, or until well roasted. Remove the baking sheet from the oven, and sprinkle the cauliflower with the cayenne pepper and dried chilies. Turn the oven to broil and broil for approximately 5 minutes, or until the cauliflower gets nice and crispy.

TRUST ME, YOU WANT THIS. CORRECTION ... YOU NEED THIS.

For the dipping sauce, peel and roughly chop the cucumber. Blitz it with the garlic, mint, and yogurt in a blender. Transfer this sauce to a dish and serve with the spicy cauliflower. This is a perfect cooling agent to help temper the spiciness.

1 head white cauliflower

1 head orange cauliflower

3 cups (750 mL) Sriracha sauce

1 tablespoon (15 mL) olive oil

12 red Thai chilies

1 teaspoon (5 mL) cayenne pepper

1 tablespoon (15 mL) dried chilies

1 English cucumber

2 cloves garlic

¼ cup (60 mL) finely chopped fresh mint

¾ cup (180 mL) plain Greek yogurt

TOMATO BRAISED GREEN BEANS

SERVES 4 TO 6

I STOLE THIS RECIPE FROM MY MOTHER. ACTUALLY, I STOLE IT AND MADE IT BETTER. THANKS, MOM. YOU MIGHT WANT TO SERVE THIS DISH WITH SOME MASSIVE CHUNKS OF BREAD TO SOAK UP ALL THAT SAUCE AND TO HELP STOP YOUR MOUTH FROM BURNING. IF YOU THINK I LIED AND PUT A TWO-STAR WHEN REALLY IT WAS A THREE-PLUS, MY APOLOGIES.

2 cloves garlic

10 whole fresh red chili peppers

1 tablespoon (15 mL) olive oil

1 can (28 oz/796 mL) chopped tomatoes

12 white pearl onions or cipollini onions

1 lb (500 g) green beans, topped and tailed

2 tablespoons (30 mL) unsalted butter

7 oz (200 g) freshly grated Parmesan cheese

YOU'VE HEARD OF THE JUMPING BEAN? WELL, THIS ONE KICKS.

Finely chop the garlic and chilies. Warm the olive oil in a saucepan over high heat, and toss in the garlic and chilies. Cook for approximately 2 minutes, and then add the can of tomatoes with their juice. Cook the tomatoes, stirring occasionally, for 30 minutes. Add 2 cups (500 mL) of water to the sauce, stir to combine, and continue cooking for another 30 minutes.

In a separate saucepan, boil some water over high heat, and add the onions. All you want to do here is blanch the onions briefly so that you can peel the skins off properly and so that they get really soft when you cook them with the beans and sauce. Cook the onions for 5 or 6 minutes, and then remove them from the water and peel them immediately.

LOW, SLOW, AND SUGO

After the sauce has been cooking for 1 hour, throw in the green beans and the peeled onions. You can either blanch the beans in boiling water first for a few minutes or toss them in raw. Raw beans will have a darker, more rustic color and blanched beans will stay brighter. I lean toward the rustic approach. Give the ingredients a good stir so that they're completely covered with the sauce. Add the butter, an additional ½ cup (125 mL) of water, and the Parmesan. Turn down the heat to low and allow the beans to slowly cook in the sauce for at least another 30 to 45 minutes, or until the beans and onions are melt-in-your-mouth soft. Transfer the saucy beans to a large dish and grate Parmesan cheese all over them.

PRETTY FLY FOR A FRY GUY

FRYING FOOD JUST MAKES SENSE. CONTRARY TO POPULAR BELIEF, IT'S NOT THE EASY WAY OUT OF COOKING. I MEAN, YES, IF YOUR UNDERSTANDING OF FRYING MEANS GOING TO THE BAR, ORDERING A TEAM PLATTER, AND EATING 5 LB OF DEEP-FRIED GOD-KNOWS-WHAT THAT HAS GONE FROM FREEZER, TO BOX, TO FRYER, TO PLATE, THEN YES, IT'S THE EASY WAY OUT. BUT FOR ME IT'S SO MUCH MORE.

BY PUSHING THE BOUNDARIES OF FRIED FOOD, YOU CAN ACTUALLY SEE A MATURE TECHNIQUE THAT HAS THE CAPABILITY TO HEIGHTEN SOMETHING'S FLAVOR AND GIVE IT A COMPLETELY NEW IDENTITY. THERE'S THAT PIECE OF FISH, THEN THERE'S THAT PIECE OF FISH WHEN IT'S DEEP-FRIED. PIECE OF CHEESE, PIECE OF CHEESE DEEP-FRIED. YOU GET THE IDEA. STREET FOOD FOR THE MOST PART GETS THIS ASPECT OF DEEP-FRYING. IT ADDS NEW FLAVORS, PROVIDES A WOW FACTOR WHEN YOU TALK ABOUT IT, AND CAN BE QUITE EASY TO PULL OFF IF YOU HAVE THE FRYING TECHNIQUE DOWN PAT. THIS SECTION WILL ULTIMATELY TEACH YOU THAT IF YOU CAN EAT IT, THEN YOU CAN FRY IT.

THE RECIPES IN THIS SECTION WILL ALWAYS BE EASIER IF YOU USE A TABLE-TOP DEEP-FRYER, OR AT THE VERY LEAST A WOK. CANOLA OIL FOR ALL OF THE DEEP-FRYING IS YOUR BEST OPTION. HOW MUCH OIL TO USE? FOR A TABLE-TOP DEEP-FRYER, FILL THE OIL TO THE LINE (EASY, EH?). IF YOU'RE USING A WOK OR A DEEP SAUCEPAN, ADD ENOUGH OIL SO THAT IT'S AT LEAST 1 ½ INCHES (4 CM) DEEP. IF YOU'RE DEEP-FRYING SOMETHING CHUNKY, USE YOUR JUDGMENT AND MAYBE GO TO 2 INCHES (5 CM).

DEEP-FRIED JUICY LUCY

TRADITIONALLY, A JUICY LUCY BURGER IS ONE THAT IS STUFFED WITH CHEESE VERSUS BEING TOPPED WITH IT. THE CHEESE MIXED WITH THE JUICY MEAT MAKES FOR A VERY MEMORABLE CALIFORNIA-INSPIRED BURGER. I OBVIOUSLY COULDN'T LET THE STATE OF CALIFORNIA BEAT ME, SO I DECIDED TO DEEP-FRY MY VERSION. NOTICE THAT YOU NEED TWO TYPES OF EGGS FOR THIS RECIPE — CHICKEN EGGS AND QUAIL EGGS.

SERVES 6

WHERE'S THE DEEP-FRIED BEEF? OH, WAIT ...

Put the ground beef in a bowl, and add the salt, pepper, and paprika. Using your hands, mix it well. Make six beef balls, and then shove a cube of cheese into the middle of each ball. Mold the beef around the cheese and then form little hockey pucks.

Put the flour in one bowl, beat the chicken eggs in another bowl, and place the breadcrumbs in a third bowl. Dip the stuffed beef patties in the flour, then the eggs, then the breadcrumbs. Bring the fryer or wok with the oil (see page 129) to 310°F (155°C). The oil needs to be at a lower temperature for this dish to work properly, otherwise the meat will still be raw in the middle, the cheese won't melt, and the outside will burn. This temperature cooks the meat through at a slower rate and gradually darkens it. Fry the patties for approximately 10 minutes, or until the meat has fully cooked. Do not fry more than three patties at a time or you'll crowd the basket and bring the temperature of the meat right down.

LIL' EGGY

Fry the quail eggs in a little bit of olive oil in the smallest pan possible over medium heat. The smaller the pan the better, and only do one egg at a time. Although this process is incredibly annoying, it is the best way to cook them. These lil' eggys don't take very long. Cook them for approximately 2 minutes, or until the egg white is fully cooked and the yolk is still runny. When all your frying is done, top each deep-fried cheeseburger with a pickle and a quail egg.

1 lb (500 g) ground beef

1 tablespoon (15 mL) kosher salt

1 tablespoon (15 mL) black pepper

1 tablespoon (15 mL) smoked paprika

½ cup (125 mL) cubed aged cheddar

1 cup (250 mL) all-purpose flour

3 chicken eggs

1 cup (250 mL) dried breadcrumbs

6 quail eggs

6 coin-sliced dill pickles

POPCORN CHICKEN LIVERS WITH PUTTANESCA DIPPING SAUCE

SERVES 6 TO 8

I WAS IN PHILLY (SURPRISE, SURPRISE) AT THIS SANDWICH SHOP IN SOUTH PHILLY CALLED PAISANOS WHEN I WAS TOTALLY BLOWN AWAY BY THEIR USE OF CHICKEN LIVERS. THEY WERE FRIED AND COVERED WITH PROVOLONE CHEESE AND BOLOGNESE SAUCE. INCREDIBLY DECADENT AND ONE OF THE BEST SANDWICHES I HAVE EVER EATEN. THE TOMATO AND FRIED CRISPY CHICKEN LIVER COMBO REALLY STUCK IN MY MIND. I FELT LIKE THIS WAS A MORE ACCESSIBLE WAY OF EATING CHICKEN LIVERS.

1 lb (500 g) chicken livers

4 cups (1 L) buttermilk

10 pitted black olives

4 cloves garlic

12 anchovies

1 small can (5 ½ oz/156 mL) tomato paste

½ cup (125 mL) white wine vinegar

Juice from 1 lemon

1 tablespoon (15 mL) olive oil

1 cup (250 mL) basil leaves

1 cup (250 mL) all-purpose flour

2 tablespoons (30 mL) garlic powder

1 teaspoon (5 mL) kosher salt

1 tablespoon (15 mL) black pepper

1 teaspoon (5 mL) mustard powder

1 lemon

WINNER, WINNER, CHICKEN LIVER DINNER

The first thing is to soak the livers in buttermilk. Make sure all the tendons and sinew have been removed off the livers first. Soak them for at least 1 hour in the fridge. The longer they soak, the more tender they will be.

SOAK IT UP

While the livers soak up all that buttermilk goodness, you can make the cold, raw puttanesca dipping sauce. Throw the olives, garlic, anchovies, and tomato paste into a blender, and blitz until you have a thick paste. Add the white wine vinegar, lemon juice, olive oil, and basil. Give it another quick blitz. The acid from the vinegar and lemon juice cuts the thickness of the tomato paste.

In a bowl, place the flour and season it with the garlic powder, salt, pepper, and mustard powder. Dredge the chicken livers in the seasoned flour, and place them in the table-top deep-fryer with the oil (see page 129) at 350°F (180°C). Fry them in batches for 5 to 6 minutes, or until golden brown. Serve with lemon wedges and the puttanesca dipping sauce.

MOZZARELLA AND MARROW SANGWEECH

THIS DISH TASTES LIKE A GRILLED CHEESE SANDWICH THAT CHUGGED AN ENERGY DRINK. AS LONG AS THE BREADING AROUND THE SANDWICH IS FIRM, NONE OF YOUR AMAZING FILLINGS WILL FALL OUT WHILE YOU DEEP-FRY. YOU WANT THE BREAD WRAPPED TIGHTLY AROUND THE CHEESE AND BONE MARROW TO HUG IT IN TIGHT. AND THEN — OBVIOUSLY — DEEP-FRIED.

4 veal marrow bones, halved lengthwise

1 loaf focaccia bread

4 large buffalo mozzarella cheese balls

1 tablespoon (15 mL) coarse ground salt

2 cups (500 mL) all-purpose flour

6 eggs

1 cup (250 mL) dried breadcrumbs

1 teaspoon (5 mL) black pepper

1 lemon

SANGWEECH — ITALIAN-ESE FOR SANDWICH

The first thing you have to do for this dish is roast your marrow. The marrow gets used as a spread, so before you even think of frying your little mozzarella sangweech, you need that marrow roasted. Preheat the oven to 450°F (230°C), put the marrow bones cut side up on a baking pan, and roast for 15 to 20 minutes, or until the fat starts to bubble.

Slice the focaccia into pieces no thicker than your index finger, then cut each piece in half. Slice each mozzarella cheese ball into three or four, depending on how many sangweeches you're making, and lightly salt. Slather some hot marrow on each side of the bread, and place one or two pieces of salted mozzarella on half the slices of bread. Top with the remaining slices of bread to finish off the sangweeches.

Place the flour in a bowl, whisk the eggs in another bowl, and place the breadcrumbs in another bowl.

FRY THE SANGWEECH TIME

Heat the oil (see page 129) in your table-top deep-fryer to 360°F (185°C). Dredge the sangweeches in the flour, then the egg, and finally the breadcrumbs. Place one sangweech at a time in the deep-fryer, and fry for 4 to 5 minutes, or until golden brown. Try to use some sort of weight to keep the whole sangweech submerged so that it fries evenly. Tongs can help, and so can the top of the basket. Lightly season with salt and pepper, and serve with a slice of lemon. The acid really cuts through the oil and the cheese, so you have a cleaner deep-fried taste.

RED SNAPPER FISH TACOS

SERVES 12

FISH TACOS ARE ALL THE CRAZE ON THE STREETS THESE DAYS. TO ME, WHAT MAKES THE DIFFERENCE BETWEEN A MEDIOCRE FISH TACO AND A GREAT FISH TACO IS THE QUALITY OF THE FISH. YES, ALL THE OTHER INGREDIENTS ARE WHAT BRING IT ALL HOME, BUT HAVING A NICE LIGHT, FLAKY FISH THAT FRIES EVENLY AND QUICKLY IS SUPER IMPORTANT. SNAPPER IS ONE OF MY FAVORITES AND MAKES A GREAT FISH TACO. TILAPIA AND HALIBUT AIN'T SO BAD EITHER.

THE SLAW

Preheat the oven to 400°F (200°C). Put the garlic cloves on a square of aluminum foil, and drizzle with the olive oil. Wrap the foil around the garlic to create a pouch and roast in the oven for approximately 10 minutes, or until golden brown.

Crush the roasted garlic with a spoon in a large bowl. Add the mayo and lemon juice, and mix well to combine. Shred both cabbages (you should have 2 cups/500 mL of each color). Toss the shredded cabbage into the mayo mixture, lightly season with salt, and then place this slaw in the fridge until needed.

Slice the red onion thinly, and lightly pickle in a bowl with the rice wine vinegar until the acid starts to cook the onions and bleed out some of the color of the red onion.

Remove the root and the green tops of the green onions. Starting on an angle, very thinly slice the meaty part in the middle.

TACO TACO TACO

Cut each fish fillet into three long pieces. Season each piece with salt and tandoori spice. Set aside ¼ cup (60 mL) of the flour in a bowl. Place the remaining flour in a separate bowl and mix in the beer. Cover the seasoned fish with the ¼ cup (60 mL) of flour and then submerge it in the beer batter. Bring the canola oil (see page 129) to 350°F (180°C) in the table-top deep-fryer. Slowly drop the coated fish pieces, two or three at a time, into the fryer, and fry for approximately 5 minutes, or until the batter is a nice golden brown color.

Top each corn tortilla with slaw and then fried fish. Add some pickled onion, sesame seeds, and green onion as garnish. Taco, taco, taco time!

6 cloves garlic

1 tablespoon (15 mL) olive oil

1 cup (250 mL) mayonnaise

Juice from 2 lemons

¼ head purple cabbage

¼ head Savoy cabbage

1 tablespoon (15 mL) kosher salt

1 red onion

2 cups (500 mL) rice wine vinegar

1 bunch green onions

4 boneless red snapper fillets

1 tablespoon (15 mL) tandoori spice

1 cup (250 mL) all-purpose flour, divided

1 pint (16 oz/470 mL) light beer

12 corn tortillas

2 tablespoons (30 mL) sesame seeds

SNOW CRAB POGOS

SERVES 4 TO 8

SNOW CRAB POGOS ARE ESSENTIALLY CRAB CAKES ON A STICK. I REALLY
HAVE A STRONG OPINION WHEN IT COMES TO CRAB CAKES. SOMETIMES YOU
BITE INTO THEM AND YOU MIGHT AS WELL CALL THEM POTATO CAKES THAT
COME WITH A WARNING: MAY CONTAIN TRACES OF CRAB. CALL IT WHAT IT
IS, USE FRESH CRABMEAT, AND COMPARE THE DIFFERENCE BETWEEN WHAT
YOU HAVE AND WHAT SOME RESTAURANTS HAVE. SURE, CRAB IS EXPENSIVE,
BUT THE DIFFERENCE IS WORTH THE EXTRA COIN.

NOTHING WRONG WITH BEING CRABBY

Let the crab thaw in cold water before you start shucking it. I know, pretty obvious, but you never know. Each piece of crab leg has two sides: the top, which is orange and much harder, and the bottom, which is a creamish color and much softer. The best way to crack the long pieces is to snap it in half using the bottom side (non-orange side). It cracks easiest from that side and you should be able to pull most of that meat cleanly out of its shell. The best way to crack the claw is by snapping the loose single claw off first. If you look at where the orange and off-white colors meet on the claw, you should be able to see a hairline crack. If not, that is the easiest place to apply some pressure and make your own hairline crack. Then you can use the first piece of claw you broke off to pick away at the rest of the crab. Once all the crab has been shucked, squeeze the excess water from the meat, and place the meat in a bowl.

Finely dice the green onions and mix them with the crabmeat. Add ½ cup (125 mL) of Panko breadcrumbs and four of the eggs. Mix it all together, and start to form the crabmeat into little 3-oz portions (90 g) in the shape of tubes; kind of like a crab dog. Most people will argue that you need potato in the crab to stretch out the meat, but those are the people who enjoy eating mediocre crab cakes. Potato doesn't stretch the crab, it masks it completely.

Once all the crab cakes have been formed, make my Triple X scotch bonnet dipping sauce. Blitz the scotch bonnets with their seeds in the blender, and add the flesh from the lemons while the machine is running. Peel the ginger, then toss it into the blender with the garlic, salt, canola oil, and vinegar. Once fully blitzed, put the sauce in the fridge for approximately 30 minutes to allow it to congeal a little bit.

IT'S POGO TIME

Place the flour in a bowl and whisk the remaining five eggs in another bowl. Dredge the crab cakes in the flour, then the eggs, and then the remaining breadcrumbs. Bring the oil (see page 129) in a table-top deep-fryer to 340°F (170°C), and fry the crab cakes, two or three at a time, for 5 or 6 minutes, or until they are a nice golden brown color. Jam a stick in the bottom of each, and serve with the Triple X dipping sauce. The crabmeat should have quite a bit of natural salt, but if you want a little more, lightly salt the fried pogo crust.

4 lb (2 kg) cooked snow crab or king crab

1 bunch green onions

2 cups (500 mL) Panko breadcrumbs, divided

9 eggs

4 yellow scotch bonnets

3 lemons

4 oz (100 g) piece fresh ginger

2 cloves garlic

1 tablespoon (15 mL) kosher salt

1 cup (250 mL) canola oil

½ cup (125 mL) rice wine vinegar

1 cup (250 mL) all-purpose flour

BEER-BATTERED CLAMS

SERVES 2 TO 4

THE PROCESSES OF SHUCKING AND FRYING OYSTERS AND CLAMS ARE IDENTICAL. WHAT MAKES EACH FRIED SHELLFISH DISH DISTINGUISHABLE IS THE ACTUAL FLAVOR. CLAMS, DESPITE BEING MUCH SMALLER, PACK A SWEETER FLAVOR THAN OYSTERS. OYSTERS TEND TO HOLD THE SEA WATER FLAVOR WHEREAS CLAMS HAVE A LESS INTENSE FLAVOR BUT PACK AN OVERALL SWEETNESS. IF YOU'RE LIKE ME, YOU LIKE BOTH AND JUST TAILOR HOW YOU USE EACH. OYSTERS I LOVE IN PO'BOY SANDWICHES, CLAMS I PREFER AS BITE-SIZED SNACKS. >>>

1 bulb fennel

¼ purple cabbage

Juice from 2 lemons, divided

Kosher salt

Black pepper

4 large kosher pickles

4 cloves garlic

1 cup (250 mL) mayonnaise

1 tablespoon (15 mL)
  Dijon mustard

2 lb (1 kg) little neck clams

1 cup (250 mL) all-purpose flour

2 pints (16 oz/470 mL each)
  lager beer, divided

I LOVE FENNEL. JUST THOUGHT I'D SHARE.

Thinly slice the bulb of fennel. Pick off the fennel tips and keep them in cold water to use as garnish. Thinly slice the purple cabbage and place it in a large bowl with the juice from half of one of the lemons. Place the thinly sliced fennel in a separate bowl with the juice from the other half. Lightly salt and pepper both bowls, and let them sit at room temperature until needed.

BIG DIPPIN' SAUCE

Toss the pickles, garlic, mayo, and mustard with juice from the remaining lemon into a blender. Blitz these for approximately 30 seconds. You want this sauce chunky but you don't want massive pickle pieces. Transfer the sauce to a bowl, cover, and place in the fridge until you are ready to serve with the clams.

SHUCKER FOR PUNISHMENT

Shuck all the clams. To do this, you will need a proper oyster/shellfish shucking tool and a clean rag. Put the rag in one hand and firmly place it on top of the clam. Using your shucking tool, find the point on the backside of the clam where it hinges together. If you were steaming these clams, they would open in the front but stay connected at the back. The back end is what you are trying to pry open. Use the point of your tool to find the divot and push and wiggle until you feel like you have cracked through the seal. Once you have, it becomes very easy to pop off the entire top shell. Use the tool to break the membrane connecting the clam to the shell. Once it's free, toss the clam into a bowl containing ½ cup (125 mL) of flour. Repeat until all the clams are shucked. In a separate bowl, combine the remaining ½ cup (125 mL) of flour with half of the beer. Whisk the two ingredients together really well. Because the clams aren't the meatiest, you want this to be a thinner batter. Use some of the second pint if you need to thin it out … If not, well … Cheers!

Add oil to a deep saucepan (see page 129), and bring it to 350°F (180°C). Take the clams from the flour, dip them in the beer batter, and then carefully place them in the hot oil. Cook about 10 clams at a time, and use a spider/perforated tool to get them out of the oil. Fry the clams for approximately 2 minutes, or until golden brown.

Remove the cabbage and fennel from the lemon juice and toss them together in a bowl with about 1 tablespoon (15 mL) of the dipping sauce you made. Mix the slaw all around and top with the reserved fennel tips. Lightly salt your fried clams, and serve with the slaw and dipping sauce.

DEEP-FRY SOMETHING TODAY

CREOLE "POUTINE"

NOT YOUR TRADITIONAL POUTINE BY ANY MEANS. NO GRAVY, NO FRENCH FRIES, BUT ALL THE SAME FUN. WE SUBSTITUTE TEMPURA-FRIED SWEET POTATO COINS FOR THE FRIES, NEW ORLEANS–STYLE TRINITY SAUCE FOR GRAVY, AND GRATED PARMESAN CHEESE FOR CURDS. AND JUST FOR THE FUN OF IT, WE TOSS IN HEAD-ON PRAWNS.

TRINITY FTW

The most important element of this entire dish is the trinity sauce. I learned very quickly that it's not a tomato sauce that contains peppers, onions, and celery, but a pepper, onion, and celery sauce held together by tomato.

Finely chop the onions, peppers, and celery. In a large saucepan with a little bit of olive oil over medium-high heat, lightly cook them for approximately 5 minutes, or until soft and brown. Toss in the paprika, salt, and pepper, and stir until the veg absorbs all the seasoning. Hit the pan with ¼ cup (60 mL) of water and 1 cup (250 mL) of the butter. Continue to stir the veg until all the butter is melted, leaving a thick buttery sauce that covers the vegetables. Add in the dried chilies, and give it all one last stir. Dump in the can of tomato sauce and the other 1 cup (250 mL) of butter, and let it reduce for 20 to 30 minutes, or until thick.

Prepare an ice bath. Peel your yams, and slice them into fairly thin coins. Boil a saucepan of salt water over high heat, and blanch the sweet potato coins in the hot water for approximately 6 minutes, or until soft. Once cooked, throw the sweet potatoes into the ice bath to shock them. This will soften the sweet potato but will also halt the cooking process so the sweet potatoes don't get mushy when you attempt to batter and fry them. Set aside at room temperature until needed. ❯ ❯ ❯

2 Spanish onions

2 red bell peppers

1 stalk celery

2 tablespoons (30 mL) smoked paprika

1 tablespoon (15 mL) kosher salt

1 tablespoon (15 mL) black pepper

2 cups + 1 tablespoon (515 mL) salted butter, divided

1 tablespoon (15 mL) dried chilies

1 can (14 oz/398 mL) unseasoned tomato sauce

2 yams

16 head-on prawns

4 cloves garlic, thinly shaved

1 package (10 oz/283 g) tempura batter mix

1 piece (7 oz/200 g) fresh Parmesan cheese

›› ON WITH THEIR HEADS

Take your head-on prawns and carefully remove the shell from around the body, but leave the tails and heads intact. Run a knife down the back side of the prawns and use your finger to scrape down the back of the prawns to clean the ... well ... the poop.

Melt the remaining 1 tablespoon (15 mL) of butter in a skillet over high heat for approximately 2 minutes, or until it starts to brown. Add the thinly shaved garlic with the head-on prawns. Cook the prawns in the brown butter and garlic for approximately 4 minutes per side.

Following the directions on the package, make the tempura batter and dip the blanched sweet potato coins in it. Using a table-top deep-fryer, fry the sweet potato in small batches in the oil (see page 129) at 360°F (185°C) until the coins are nice and crispy. Place them on paper towel to absorb any excess oil, then lightly salt them. Place about six coins together on a plate, and pour the trinity sauce all over them. Top with the head-on prawns and brown butter garlic sauce. Finish with some grated Parmesan cheese.

NOT YOUR TRADITIONAL POUTINE, BUT STILL FUN!

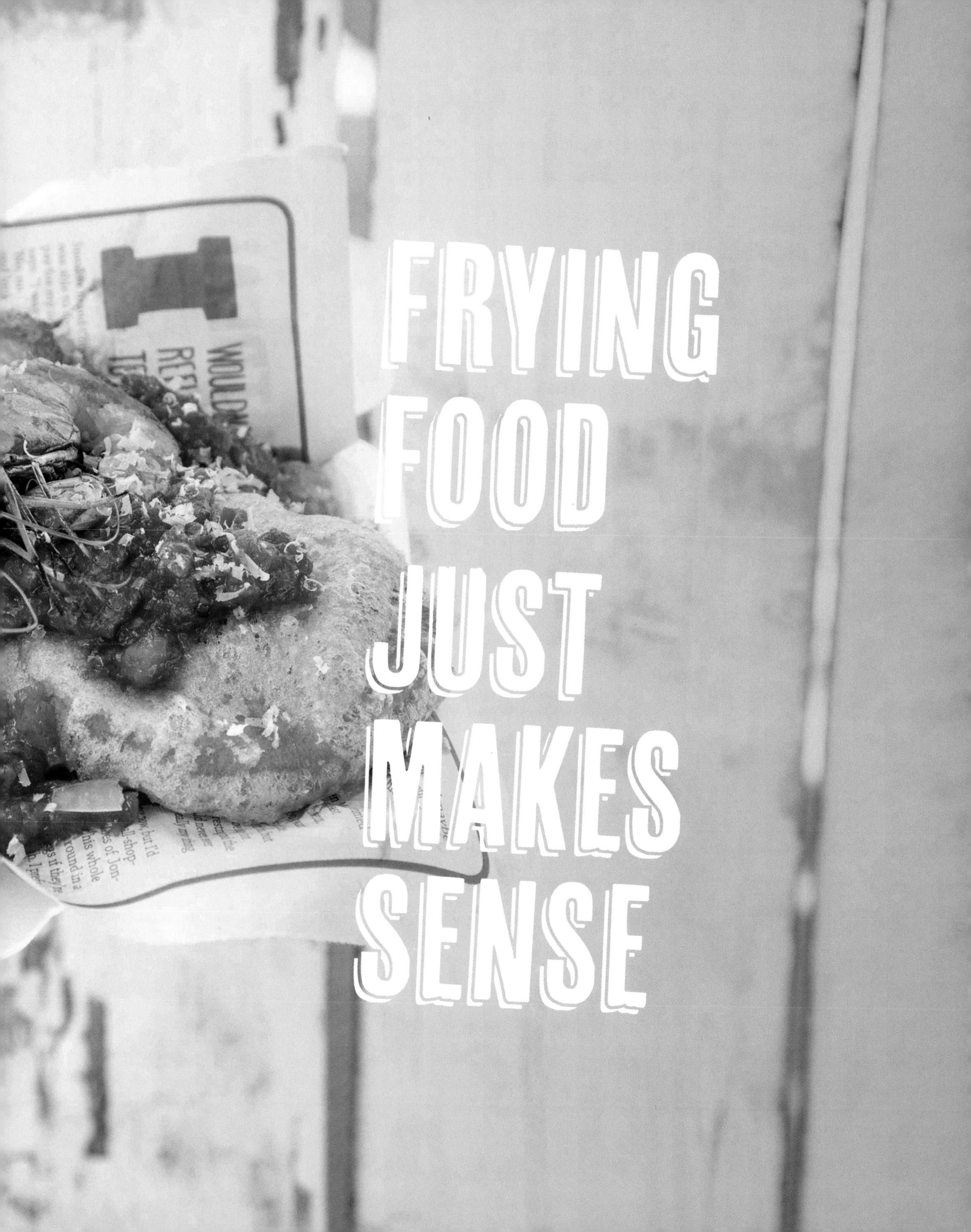

FRYING FOOD JUST MAKES SENSE

I MET NIGEL THE MORNING AFTER HE HAD DONE AN INCREDIBLY LATE SERVICE. DESPITE HAVING ONLY SLEPT FOR A FEW HOURS, HE WAS MORE THAN HAPPY TO INVITE ME INTO HIS NOLA TRUCK AND SHOW ME SOME OF HIS CLASSIC DISHES.

I WANTED LEGITIMATE NEW ORLEANS STREET GRUB, SO HE GOT CLASSIC ON ME — PO'BOYS AND TRINITY SHRIMPS. I LEARNED VERY QUICKLY THAT NEW ORLEANS IS A CITY OF LINGO. FOR EXAMPLE, NOLA STANDS FOR NEW ORLEANS, LOUISIANA. PO'BOY STANDS FOR POOR BOY, AND TRINITY ... WELL, THAT'S JUST THE NOLA WAY OF SAYING, MAKE SAUCE WITH THESE THREE ESSENTIAL INGREDIENTS AND YOU CAN'T GO WRONG. AS GOOD AS HIS PO'BOY WAS, I WAS MORE INTRIGUED TO HEAR HIM TALK ABOUT HOW IF IT'S NOT ON A FRENCH STICK IT'S NOT A PO'BOY. I HAD NO IDEA. I JUST THOUGHT IT WAS A FRIED SANDWICH. NOPE, IT MUST HAVE LETTUCE AND TOMATO, AND MUST BE ON A FRENCH STICK. IT'S A NOLA LAW APPARENTLY. THAT'S HOW YOU MAKE A PO'BOY IN LOUISIANA.

TRINITY ... WELL, THAT'S JUST THE NOLA WAY OF SAYING, MAKE SAUCE WITH THESE THREE ESSENTIAL INGREDIENTS AND YOU CAN'T GO WRONG.

THE NOLA TRUCK, NEW ORLEANS, LOUISIANA

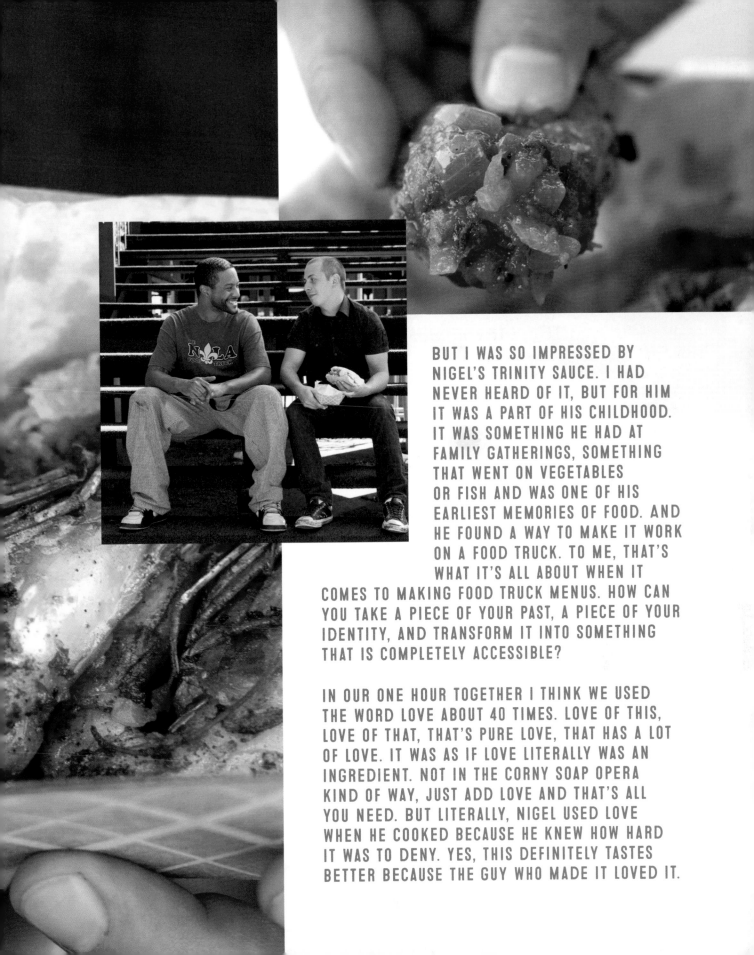

BUT I WAS SO IMPRESSED BY NIGEL'S TRINITY SAUCE. I HAD NEVER HEARD OF IT, BUT FOR HIM IT WAS A PART OF HIS CHILDHOOD. IT WAS SOMETHING HE HAD AT FAMILY GATHERINGS, SOMETHING THAT WENT ON VEGETABLES OR FISH AND WAS ONE OF HIS EARLIEST MEMORIES OF FOOD. AND HE FOUND A WAY TO MAKE IT WORK ON A FOOD TRUCK. TO ME, THAT'S WHAT IT'S ALL ABOUT WHEN IT COMES TO MAKING FOOD TRUCK MENUS. HOW CAN YOU TAKE A PIECE OF YOUR PAST, A PIECE OF YOUR IDENTITY, AND TRANSFORM IT INTO SOMETHING THAT IS COMPLETELY ACCESSIBLE?

IN OUR ONE HOUR TOGETHER I THINK WE USED THE WORD LOVE ABOUT 40 TIMES. LOVE OF THIS, LOVE OF THAT, THAT'S PURE LOVE, THAT HAS A LOT OF LOVE. IT WAS AS IF LOVE LITERALLY WAS AN INGREDIENT. NOT IN THE CORNY SOAP OPERA KIND OF WAY, JUST ADD LOVE AND THAT'S ALL YOU NEED. BUT LITERALLY, NIGEL USED LOVE WHEN HE COOKED BECAUSE HE KNEW HOW HARD IT WAS TO DENY. YES, THIS DEFINITELY TASTES BETTER BECAUSE THE GUY WHO MADE IT LOVED IT.

BEER-BATTERED CAPRESE SALAD

I THINK I'VE HAD ABOUT A THOUSAND CAPRESE SALADS. ONE DAY I WAS PLAYING AROUND WITH SOME RECIPES AND THOUGHT IT WOULD BE FUN TO DEEP-FRY ONE. I'M NOT SURE WHY ... BUT MY GOODNESS, AM I EVER HAPPY THAT I FOLLOWED MY GUT ON THAT ONE. BEER-BATTERING AND FRYING THE TOMATO AND CHEESE INTENSIFY THE FLAVORS AND MAKE THEM POP IN YOUR MOUTH.

SERVES 6 TO 8

6 cloves garlic

1 tablespoon (15 mL) olive oil

½ cup (125 mL) mayonnaise

½ cup (125 mL) Worcestershire sauce

1 tablespoon (15 mL) Dijon mustard

½ cup (125 mL) freshly grated Parmesan cheese

1 cup (250 mL) cherry tomatoes

1 lb (500 g) bocconcini

2 cups (500 mL) all-purpose flour

2 pints (16 oz/470 mL each) light beer (pilsner or lager), divided

½ cup (125 mL) fresh basil

STRATEGICALLY DIPPING

Because the actual act of frying food really doesn't take that long, you're better off getting your dipping sauce ready first. Preheat the oven to 425°F (220°C). Toss the garlic in the olive oil and then place it on a piece of aluminum foil. Fold the foil into a pouch to hold the garlic in place and place in the oven for approximately 10 minutes, or until the garlic is brown.

When the garlic is done, transfer it to a bowl and smash it up into a paste. Add the mayo, Worcestershire sauce, mustard, and last but not least, the Parm. Throw the sauce in the fridge to keep it cold until needed.

Wash the tomatoes and place them in a large bowl. Place the bocconcini balls in a separate bowl. Add ½ cup (125 mL) of the flour to each bowl and toss the tomatoes and the cheese separately, making sure they are fully covered. In a separate bowl, add the remaining 1 cup (250 mL) of flour and slowly pour in 1 pint of the beer. The less beer you use, the thicker the batter will be. The more beer you use, the thinner the batter ends up. I usually go for a medium batter, which means 1 pint of beer for the balls, and 1 pint of beer for you! But don't get started on your beer too soon. If you find the batter is too thick, you'll need to add some beer to thin it out. Add it gradually to avoid making it too thin.

CRAZY CAPRESE TIME

Now that you have a consistency of batter you like, get your deep-fryer or wok with oil (see page 129) to 350°F (180°C). Dip the flour-covered tomatoes in beer batter, and immediately place them in the fryer, three at a time. Cook for 2 to 3 minutes, or until they are golden brown. Do the same for the cheese (three at a time again). Wash and pick the fresh basil, and place a leaf underneath every ball of tomato and/or cheese as you place them on a plate. Wrap the basil leaves around the balls when you dip them in your sauce. Give the balls a light salting and a light drizzle of olive oil before dipping.

KB'S BBQ, VICTORIA, TEXAS

I MET KEVIN, THE OWNER OF KB BBQ, WHILE SHOOTING MY TV SHOW, *REBEL WITHOUT A KITCHEN*, IN TEXAS. AFTER BEING IN AUSTIN FOR A FEW DAYS AND EATING BBQ MORE TIMES THAN I HAD FINGERS, CLEARLY IT WAS ONLY RIGHT TO VENTURE AN HOUR OR SO OUT OF AUSTIN TO VICTORIA, TEXAS, WHERE I WAS ABOUT TO HOOK UP WITH KEV AND COLLABORATE ON SOME BBQ BEEF SHORT RIBS FOR A RODEO. YES, FOLKS, IT'S TRUE — THIS WAS MY FIRST RODEO. I CAN'T TELL YOU HOW MANY TIMES I USED THIS LINE WHILE AT THE RODEO. IT NEVER GOT OLD.

KEV AND I REALLY BONDED. I MEAN, WE HAD NO CHOICE REALLY — BBQ SHORT RIBS TAKE AT LEAST 8 HOURS TO MAKE, AND I WAS AT A RODEO IN TEXAS. IT WAS FUNNY TOO BECAUSE THE DAY WAS REALLY INTENSE FOR THE FIRST HOUR — SPICING UP THE MEAT, GETTING THE SMOKER HOT, JUST GENERALLY MAKING SURE EVERYTHING WAS PERFECT. THEN THE MEAT WENT ON — AAAAAAAND, THAT WAS PRETTY MUCH IT. I MEAN, OBVIOUSLY I HAD TO SPRAY THE MEAT ONCE IN A WHILE TO KEEP IT MOIST, AND THEN PLAY WITH THE CHAMBER TO CONTROL THE HEAT, BUT OVERALL, WE JUST HAD A FEW BEERS AND TALKED LIKE OLD BUDS.

TEXAS

KEV AND I REALLY BONDED. I MEAN, WE HAD NO CHOICE REALLY — BBQ SHORT RIBS TAKE AT LEAST 8 HOURS TO MAKE, AND I WAS AT A RODEO IN TEXAS.

I THINK IT WAS AT THE 4- OR 5-HOUR MARK WHEN WE BOTH GOT A LITTLE PECKISH. KEV WENT INTO HIS BBQ TRAILER AND GRABBED SOME BRISKET STRIPS AND THIS GREEN SAUCE. I DIPPED THE MEAT IN IT AND TOOK A BITE — AND WAS BLOWN AWAY. JALAPEÑO MINT JELLY: REFRESHING, SPICY, AND WORKED PERFECTLY WITH THE MEAT. KEV EXPLAINED HIS PROCESS TO ME, AND I WAS TOTALLY IMPRESSED. HERE WAS THIS BBQ GUY FROM VICTORIA, TEXAS, GETTING VERY TECHNICAL AND REFINED WHEN IT CAME TO MAKING THIS SAUCE. I ALMOST FEEL BAD SAYING THIS, BUT — KEV'S BBQ WAS REALLY, REALLY GOOD, BUT I JUST COVERED EVERYTHING WE ATE IN THAT SAUCE BECAUSE IT WAS JUST THAT AMAZING. NOT A BAD FIRST RODEO, I HAVE TO SAY.

EGGPLANT "MEATBALLS" WITH JALAPEÑO MINT DIPPING SAUCE

THE MEATLESS MEATBALL … I KNOW, I KNOW … IT SOUNDS LIKE SACRILEGE. BUT TO BE FAIR, THE EGGPLANT TEXTURE WORKS VERY WELL IN PLACE OF MEAT AND CAN BE SEASONED AND TREATED JUST LIKE GROUND MEAT. KB'S INFAMOUS JALAPEÑO MINT SAUCE GIVES THESE VEGGIE BALLS THE OOMPH THEY DESERVE. ›››

2 large eggplants

1 tablespoon (15 mL) olive oil

2 tablespoons (30 mL) kosher salt, divided

1 tablespoon (15 mL) black pepper

8 oz (225 g) goat cheese

10 basil leaves

1 tablespoon (15 mL) onion powder

1 tablespoon (15 mL) dried chilies

7 eggs

2 cups (500 mL) Panko breadcrumbs, divided

8 jalapeño peppers

1 bunch fresh mint

12 sprigs thyme, stems removed

1 cup (250 mL) finely chopped fresh basil

10 cloves garlic

½ cup (125 mL) granulated sugar

Juice from 1 lemon

2 cups (500 mL) all-purpose flour

THE MEATLESS MEATBALL

Preheat the oven to 400°F (200°C). Cut each eggplant in half lengthwise, and score the flesh with X's. Drizzle the olive oil over the scored flesh of the eggplant and lightly season with salt and pepper. Roast in the oven for approximately 20 minutes, or until the eggplant meat is very soft.

Scoop the softened meat out of the eggplant, place it in a bowl, and season to taste with some salt and pepper. Add the goat cheese, basil, onion powder, and dried chilies to the bowl, and mix it all around just like you would with a meat meatball. Crack two eggs into the mix and add ¼ cup (60 mL) of the breadcrumbs to bind everything. Mix well, and form into 24 evenly sized balls. Place the balls on a baking sheet and then put them in the fridge for 2 to 3 hours to harden a little bit.

THE JALAPEÑO MINT DIPPING SAUCE

Bring 1 ½ cups (375 mL) of water to a boil in a small pot over high heat. Discard the stems from the jalapeño peppers, and cook the jalapeños for approximately 5 minutes, or until soft. Remove the peppers from the water, but keep the water. Blend the jalapeños with the mint, thyme, basil, and garlic. Bring the reserved pot of cooking water back to a simmer over low heat. Pour in the jalapeño mixture, add 1 tablespoon (15 mL) of salt, and then slowly add the sugar. Be sure to stir the mixture as you do so. Add the lemon juice and allow the jalapeño sauce to reduce slowly for approximately 30 minutes, or until thick. Remove from the heat and let stand until the sauce cools down to room temperature. Once cooled, place the sauce in the fridge for 2 to 3 hours, or until the sugars congeal and give the sauce a jellyish consistency.

Whisk the remaining five eggs and put them in a bowl. Place the flour in another bowl, and the remaining 1 ¾ cups (425 mL) of breadcrumbs in another. Take your eggplant balls out of the fridge, and dredge them in the flour, then the eggs, and then the breadcrumbs. Deep-fry the eggplant meatballs in the deep-fryer or a wok with oil (see page 129) at 340°F (170°C) for approximately 2 minutes, or until golden brown. Lightly salt the fried balls, and serve with the jalapeño mint dipping sauce.

IF YOU CAN EAT IT, THEN YOU CAN FRY IT

PAD THAI FRIES

SERVES 4
(BUT MOST LIKELY
1 PERSON BECAUSE
THIS RECIPE ROCKS)

OF ALL THE DISHES THAT ARE IN THIS COOKBOOK THAT I SERVE EITHER ON THE FIDEL GASTRO FOOD TRUCK OR IN MY RESTAURANT, LISA MARIE, NOTHING MAKES PEOPLE GO CRAZIER THAN PAD THAI FRIES. PEOPLE JUST GET WEIRD FOR THEM. THE RECIPE IS SO, SO, SO, SO EASY, BUT IT'S THE PERFECT EXAMPLE OF HOW A FUN STREET FOOD CONCEPT CAN ACTUALLY BE INCREDIBLY MEMORABLE IF YOU USE THE BEST INGREDIENTS. AND IN THIS CASE, BEST MEANS CAVENDISH DOUBLE-COATED FRIES. NO OTHER FRY KEEPS ITS INTEGRITY AND ABSORBS SAUCE QUITE LIKE THESE DO. I AM GIVING AWAY ALL MY SECRETS WITH THIS ONE.

2 cups (500 mL) salted butter

3 cups (750 mL) Sriracha sauce

1 cup (250 mL) lemon juice (about 4 large lemons)

1 large bag (1 lb/500 g) oven fries

1 cup (250 mL) bean sprouts

1 cup (250 mL) cilantro

4 limes

¼ cup (60 mL) crushed peanuts (optional)

AND NOW YOU KNOW ...

Melt the butter in a pan over high heat. Stir in the Sriracha sauce and lemon juice. Turn down the heat to low, and cook for approximately 5 minutes, or until the sauce is a nice velvety, orange color. Let the sauce cool and congeal so when you apply it to your fries it's more of a paste than a sauce.

I STILL CAN'T BELIEVE I'M GIVING THIS RECIPE AWAY

Fry the fries in the deep-fryer with the oil (see page 129) at 360°F (185°C) for 5 or 6 minutes, or until they're crispy and golden brown. If you are gung-ho about making your own, check out Carbonara Fries (see page 197) for how to do this.

In a large bowl, toss the cooked fries in the sauce. This lets you coat the fries without making them soggy. Transfer the coated fries to a serving dish, and top with bean sprouts, cilantro, and lime wedges. If you want to make it even more pad Thai-y, you can always top it with crushed peanuts.

MEAT-ER

I SPENT MY FORMATIVE YEARS WORKING IN A BUTCHER SHOP IN TORONTO, ONTARIO, CANADA. AT 14 YEARS OLD, I SAW MEAT, REAL BUTCHERED MEAT, AND IT TAUGHT ME A LOT ABOUT FOOD AND MORE SPECIFICALLY HOW TO SELL IT TO PEOPLE. PEOPLE LOOKED AT THESE RAW SLABS AND I HAD TO TRANSFORM IT RIGHT BEFORE THEIR EYES, TELL THEM ALL THE THINGS THEY COULD DO WITH IT, AND DESCRIBE HOW IT WOULD TASTE WHEN COOKED PERFECTLY. NOT AN EASY TASK. ONCE IN A WHILE YOU GET PEOPLE WHO KNOW WHAT THEY WANT, BUT MOST PEOPLE NEED A BIT OF HELP — SOME MEAT EDUCATION, AS IT WERE — SO THAT THEY FEEL LIKE THEY ARE GETTING THE ABSOLUTE BEST CUT, TENDER, TOP-GRADE, WELL-MARBLED PIECE OF MEAT.

AS WE TRAVELED ACROSS THE U.S. AND CANADA WE ENCOUNTERED A LOT OF LOCAL MEAT PURVEYORS. WHEN WE WERE IN TEXAS, I GOT TO GO TO BASTROP CATTLE COMPANY RANCH. I MET WITH PATTI, WHO OWNS THE RANCH. SHE LOVES WHAT SHE DOES, KNOWS ALL HER CATTLE BY NAME, AND IS AN INDEPENDENT FEMALE SMACK DAB IN THE MIDDLE OF THE MALE-DOMINATED CATTLE INDUSTRY. HER RANCH IS SMALL-SCALE, BUT PRODUCES

MISSION

100% GRASS-FED BEEF. I'VE ALWAYS BEEN A BIG SUPPORTER OF GRASS-FED BEEF. IT DEFINITELY DOES NOT GET THE SAME MARBLING THAT CORN-FED BEEF GETS, BUT IT DOES HAVE AN INCREDIBLY CLEAN TASTE. GRASS ON GRASS FINISH IS A VERY LEAN CUT — ABSOLUTELY NO FAT. I'VE HAD GRASS WITH A BARLEY FINISH BEFORE AND IT MAKES A HUGE DIFFERENCE. CORN-FED BEEF CAN ALSO BE RAISED LOCALLY, DEPENDING ON WHERE IN THE WORLD YOU ARE. CORN-FED BEEF HAS A HIGHER FAT CONTENT. FAT — BETTER KNOWN AS MARBLING IN THE STEAK WORLD — ADDS MORE FLAVOR, BUT IT ISN'T CONSIDERED HEALTHY, FOR EITHER THE CATTLE OR THE PERSON EATING IT.

YAY MEA

Quality MEATS & SAUSAGE

PORK HAS BECOME MY FAVORITE MEAT TO COOK WITH IN RECENT YEARS. IT HAS SUCH A RANGE OF FLAVORS AND CUTS FROM NOSE TO TAIL. WHEN WE WERE IN LA, I GOT TO HANG OUT (NO PUN INTENDED) AT LINDY & GRUNDY, A WHOLE-ANIMAL BUTCHER SHOP THAT SPECIALIZES IN LOCALLY AND ETHICALLY RAISED PRODUCTS. THE CONCEPT OF NOSE-TO-TAIL BUTCHERY ALLOWS PEOPLE LIKE ME TO MAKE THINGS LIKE BIG CHEEK CHILI OR PIG TAIL NACHOS. YOU FIND UNIQUE AND CREATIVE WAYS TO USE ALL THE PARTS OF THE ANIMAL.

YOU FIND UNIQUE AND CREATIVE WAYS TO USE ALL THE PARTS OF THE ANIMAL.

QUITE OFTEN I'M VERY SPECIFIC IN THIS BOOK ABOUT WHAT TO ASK FOR WHEN IT COMES TO BUYING MEAT. IT'S SO IMPORTANT TO HAVE A LOCAL BUTCHER SHOP THAT YOU CAN TRUST, ONE THAT YOU CAN WALK INTO AND HAVE A CONVERSATION WITH THE PERSON WHO IS FEEDING YOU. YOU WANT TO KNOW THAT YOU ARE GETTING THE ABSOLUTE BEST PRODUCT TO ENSURE YOU ARE MAKING THE BEST RECIPE. ACTUALLY SEEING THE MEAT THAT GOES INTO YOUR BURGERS VERSUS PICKING UP A FROZEN BOX OF GOD-KNOWS-WHAT MAKES ALL THE DIFFERENCE. WHETHER IT'S FOR MY TRUCK, MY RESTAURANT, OR MY FRIENDS, I ALWAYS MAKE SURE THE MEAT IS THE MEAT OF THE MEAL. YAY MEAT!

I LOVE BACON

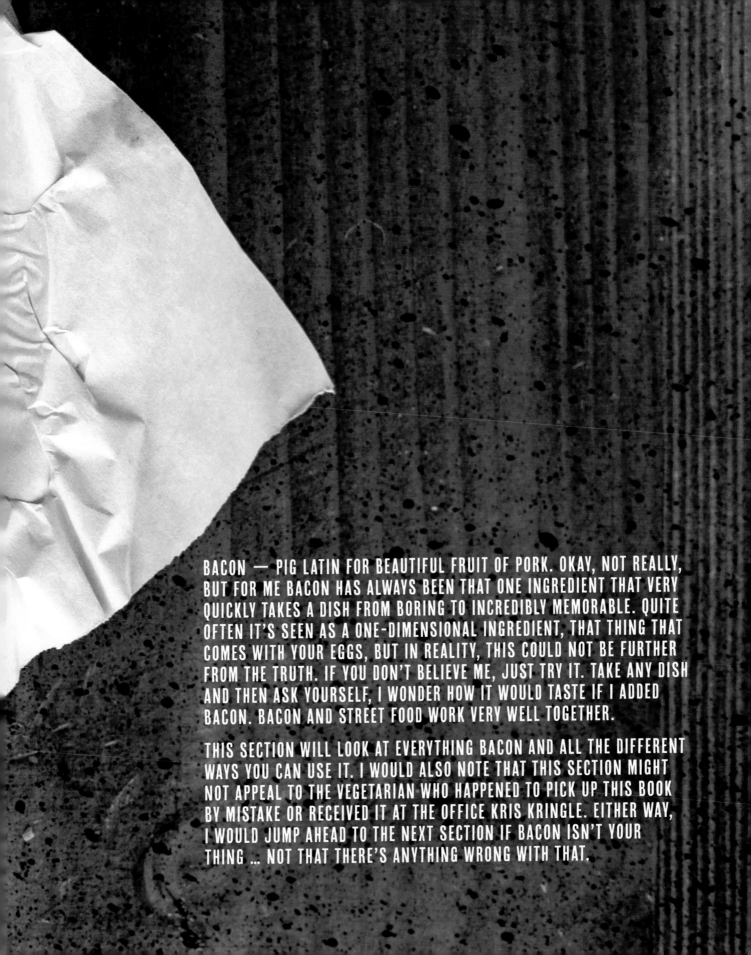

BACON — PIG LATIN FOR BEAUTIFUL FRUIT OF PORK. OKAY, NOT REALLY, BUT FOR ME BACON HAS ALWAYS BEEN THAT ONE INGREDIENT THAT VERY QUICKLY TAKES A DISH FROM BORING TO INCREDIBLY MEMORABLE. QUITE OFTEN IT'S SEEN AS A ONE-DIMENSIONAL INGREDIENT, THAT THING THAT COMES WITH YOUR EGGS, BUT IN REALITY, THIS COULD NOT BE FURTHER FROM THE TRUTH. IF YOU DON'T BELIEVE ME, JUST TRY IT. TAKE ANY DISH AND THEN ASK YOURSELF, I WONDER HOW IT WOULD TASTE IF I ADDED BACON. BACON AND STREET FOOD WORK VERY WELL TOGETHER.

THIS SECTION WILL LOOK AT EVERYTHING BACON AND ALL THE DIFFERENT WAYS YOU CAN USE IT. I WOULD ALSO NOTE THAT THIS SECTION MIGHT NOT APPEAL TO THE VEGETARIAN WHO HAPPENED TO PICK UP THIS BOOK BY MISTAKE OR RECEIVED IT AT THE OFFICE KRIS KRINGLE. EITHER WAY, I WOULD JUMP AHEAD TO THE NEXT SECTION IF BACON ISN'T YOUR THING ... NOT THAT THERE'S ANYTHING WRONG WITH THAT.

BACON AND CORN CHOWDAH

I DID THE UNTHINKABLE WHEN I COMPETED IN A CLAM CHOWDAH COMPETITION IN BOSTON — I TOTALLY MESSED WITH THE RECIPE. I ADDED CURRY AND COCONUT MILK, WHICH GAVE IT MORE OF A TRINIDADIAN TWIST. FROM WHAT THE LOCALS TOLD ME, THIS WAS ABSOLUTE SACRILEGE. CHOWDAHS COME IN ALL SHAPES AND SIZES, BUT THE BASE NEEDS CONSISTENCY SO THOSE FLAVORS CAN BE A PROPAH CHOWDAH FOUNDATION NO MATTER WHICH DIRECTION YOU DECIDE TO TAKE IT.

SERVES 4 TO 6

1 stalk celery

1 leek

1 large carrot

2 lb (1 kg) slab double-smoked bacon

6 cobs of corn

2 cups (500 mL) salted butter

2 tablespoons (30 mL) ground turmeric

1 tablespoon (15 mL) curry powder

2 tablespoons (30 mL) kosher salt

2 cans (14 oz/390 mL each) chickpeas, drained and rinsed

1 cup (250 mL) coconut milk

4 cups (1 L) whipping cream

IT'S PRONOUNCED *CHOWDAHHHH*

Before you do anything, finely chop the celery, leek, and carrot. Also, cut the bacon into small cubes. In a large pot, boil water over high heat and cook the corn for approximately 6 minutes, or until tender. Remove the corn from the water, reserving the water for the chowdah stock. Cut all the kernels off the cobs and place them in a bowl.

In a large soup pot, cook the bacon over high heat for approximately 4 minutes (no oil required). As the bacon begins to get a little crispy, add the celery, leek, and carrot. Stir well, and continue to cook. When the contents in the bottom of the pot start to brown a little, add about a ladle's worth of the reserved corn cooking water and add the butter. Stir everything thoroughly so that all the flavors get picked up by the veg.

BUILDING ON THE BASE

At this point, toss in all the turmeric, curry powder, salt, corn kernels, and chickpeas. Give everything yet another good, solid stir so that all these flavors are picked up by the bigger ingredients. Add the coconut milk and reserved corn cooking water (you'll need 16 to 20 cups/4 to 5 L or so) to your chowdah. Turn down the heat to low, add your cream slowly, stirring it in, and allow the soup to simmer, uncovered, for 3 to 4 hours, or until the curry flavors have matured. Every hour, add another 2 cups (500 mL) of corn water ONLY if the soup is looking dry.

I highly suggest blending the soup just enough that it's still chunky but the chickpeas can help thicken it. You can either let the soup cool a bit and blend it all or just take a portion of it, blend it, and then stir it back into the pot. Always taste the soup and add salt if you feel you need it. Soup is one of those things where everyone has their own salt tolerance.

And just like any other soup, it always tastes better the next day.

BACON ALMIGHTY GRILLED CHEESE SANDWICHES

SERVES 2

THIS IS THE SUPER BOWL SUNDAY OF BLTS AND GRILLED CHEESE SANDWICHES ALL IN ONE GO. IT'S LIKE THE TWO HAD A BABY ON KRYPTON AND THEY BIRTHED THE SUPERHERO BACON VERSIONS OF THEMSELVES. IMAGINE A THICK-CUT-BACON BLT WITH A FRIED GREEN TOMATO, HELD TOGETHER BY TWO GRILLED CHEESE SANDWICHES. CRAZY TALK? I THINK NOT. BACON.

1 head romaine lettuce

2 large green tomatoes

Unsalted butter

8 slices white bread

8 slices cheddar cheese

8 thick slices side bacon

1 cup (250 mL) all-purpose flour

6 eggs

1 cup (250 mL) cornmeal

¼ cup (60 mL) mayonnaise

8 baby gherkin pickles

GET IT ALL READY

Let's get all your prep done first. Shred the lettuce and slice the tomatoes. Don't slice the tomatoes too thin, though, or they'll just dissolve when you place them in the deep-fryer. Prep done! Now it's matter of managing three pans at one time. In one pan, you'll grill the bacon, in another you'll make the grilled cheese sandwiches, and in the last you'll fry the green tomatoes.

GRILL THAT MONSTER

First, the grilled cheese. Spread butter on both sides of each slice of bread. Lay two slices of cheese on four of the bread slices and top them with the remaining four buttered bread slices to complete the prep on the sandwiches.

Butter a skillet, and grill two sandwiches over medium heat for approximately 5 minutes per side, or until the bread is golden brown. Press the sandwiches down, just a little bit, using a spatula or a weight as you cook them. I'm a firm believer in doing the grilled cheese on a lower heat once you get some color on the bread so you don't burn it without melting any of the cheese. Repeat this process with the remaining two sandwiches. ❯ ❯ ❯

BLT AND GRILLED CHEESE
ALL IN ONE GO

››› Take another pan for your thick-cut bacon. If you can, go to a deli and have the butcher slice the bacon — that makes for the best sandwich texture. Grill the thick pieces of bacon over medium-high heat for 3 to 4 minutes per side. You have to keep an eye on bacon, otherwise it will burn. You don't want that!

Your third pan will need slightly higher sides so that you can pour in about ½ inch (1 cm) of canola oil to fry the green tomato slices. Bring the oil to 340°F (170°C). Before you fry the tomato slices, place the flour in one bowl, beat the eggs in another bowl, and place the cornmeal in a third bowl. Cover the tomato slices in flour, then egg, and then cornmeal. Gently place them in the oil and fry for approximately 5 minutes, or until golden brown. Remove the tomato from the oil, place it on paper towel to absorb any excess oil, and salt it.

BUILD THE MONSTER

First you take one grilled cheese sandwich and spread a little bit of mayo on the top of it. Then layer the lettuce, fried tomatoes, and bacon on top of it. Top with the second grilled cheese sandwich, and stick a massive skewer through it with some pickles just chilling at the very top. Repeat to create one more sandwich.

BEAUTIFUL
FRUIT OF
PORK

BACON JAM GRILLED CHEESE SANDWICHES

. . . .
SERVES 8 TO 10
. . . .

THESE BAD BOYS COULD RUN FOR MAYOR. WHO WOULDN'T VOTE FOR BACON JAM AND MELTED CHEESE? THIS GRILLED CHEESE IS VERY DIFFERENT FROM THE BACON ALMIGHTY GRILLED CHEESE (PAGE 172). THIS IS A MUCH SMALLER PORTION, IT USES BUFFALO MOZZARELLA, WHICH IS A MUCH FRESHER AND CREAMIER CHEESE, AND IT'S CUT WITH THE BACON JAM, WHICH IS SHARPER AND MUCH SMOKIER THAN REGULAR BACON.

1 loaf sourdough bread

½ cup (125 mL) Bacon Jam
(see page 192)

5 large balls (1 oz/25 g each)
buffalo mozzarella cheese

8 leaves basil

6 cloves garlic

2 shallots

1 tablespoon (15 mL) olive oil

Kosher salt

1 tablespoon (15 mL)
unsalted butter

GETTING CHEESY IN HERE

Cut the loaf of bread in half, and then into slices ¼ inch (0.5 cm) thick and 3 inches (7.5 cm) long. Spread bacon jam on one side of each bread slice — not too thick, though, as you don't want it to overwhelm the cheese. Then cut the buffalo mozzarella cheese balls into four or five slices, depending on how large the balls are. My inner child wants to ask you if you have big balls or little balls, but I'll refrain.

Finely chop the basil, the garlic, and the shallots. Combine these in a bowl. Add the olive oil and a little bit of salt, and stir to combine. Dip the mozzarella slices into the mixture. Be sure to get both sides! The garlic, basil, and shallots should just stick to the cheese. Put about three pieces of cheese, depending on the size, onto half the slices of bread — you want to cover one side of the bread.

GRILL IT REAL GOOD

Add the top half of the sandwiches, press each one together, and lightly grill in a pan with a little bit of butter over medium-low heat for 4 to 5 minutes per side, or until the mozzarella cheese starts oozing out of the side of the sandwich. If you have an appropriate weight or are able to apply some pressure to the sandwich while it's grilling, I highly recommend you do so. Serve immediately for some gooey-goodness.

BACON EXPLOSION

THE BACON EXPLOSION IS ONE EPIC BACON-INFUSED PORK LOAF THAT WILL BLOW EVERYONE WHO TRIES IT OUT OF THE PARK! THE MOST IMPORTANT PART OF THIS WHOLE DISH IS YOUR BACON WEAVE.

. . . .
SERVES 4 TO 8
. . . .

BACON WEAVE

Take a slice of bacon and twist it into an L-shape on a large piece of aluminum foil (you need the foil to help you roll the explosion). Then alternate placing bacon strips above and below the piece of bacon on the left hand side. Once you have made it all the way to the top, you repeat the same thing but from the bottom going left to right. When you're all done you should have a perfect blanket of lattice-weaved bacon. It makes more sense when you're actually doing it (see page 181).

MIX THE MEAT

Slice the onion, and add it to a skillet with about 1 tablespoon (15 mL) vegetable oil. Cook, stirring, over medium heat for approximately 8 minutes, or until soft. Remove from the heat and allow to cool to room temperature. In a bowl, combine the ground pork, eggs, barbecue sauce Sriracha sauce, bacon jam, salt, and cooled cooked onion. Using your hands, mix everything together. Place the meat along the bottom of the bacon blanket, making sure it goes from one side to the other but leaving a margin of about 1 inch (2.5 cm) on both sides. Pack it in tightly. Now use the aluminum foil to tightly roll the explosion. After every time you roll it, use your hands to continue to tighten it up and adjust the foil to keep it tight. You should end up with an incredibly tight roll that's a perfect cylinder. ❯ ❯ ❯

1 package (16 oz/450 g) thin-cut bacon

1 large Spanish onion

1 tablespoon (15 mL) vegetable oil

2 lb (1 kg) ground pork

4 eggs

2 cups (500 mL) barbecue sauce

1 cup (250 mL) Sriracha sauce

1 cup (250 mL) Bacon Jam (see page 192)

2 tablespoons (30 mL) kosher salt

Jalapeño peppers (optional)

¼ cup (60 mL) rice wine vinegar (optional)

8 American cheese slices (optional)

8 burger buns (optional)

1 head iceberg lettuce

¼ cup (60 mL) Sriracha aioli (see page 94) (optional)

> > > Preheat the oven to 325°F (160°C). Place the bacon explosion on a baking sheet, and bake in the oven for between 1 hour and 1 ¼ hours, or until the juices run clear. Once the juices run clear, increase the oven temperature to 425°F (220°C), and continue to cook until the bacon is brown and crispy on the outside, 5 minutes at most. Remove it from the oven and behold, the bacon explosion.

BACON EXPLOSION BURGER

Now you can eat your bacon explosion any way you want. Some folks like to eat it as is, almost like a meatloaf with some side dishes. Truth be told, you could save all the bacon drippings and make one kickass mashed potato to go alongside the sliced explosion. But if I had to choose one way to serve up the explosion it would be this ...

Let the explosion cool down to room temperature. Slice some jalapeños really thin and lightly pickle them in the vinegar for 15 minutes. Take two 1-inch-thick (2.5 cm) pieces of explosion and grill them in a pan over high heat for 3 minutes, until there's a nice crust on both sides of the bacon. Flip the pieces of explosion and place a slice of cheese on top of them. Cover the skillet so the cheese melts over both pieces quickly. Place the cheesy explosion meat on a bun and top with pickled jalapeños, lettuce, and Sriracha aioli.

PERFECT BLANKET OF LATTICE-WEAVED BACON

KALE BACON CAESAR SALAD

KALE HAS BECOME A MASSIVE FIXTURE IN THE WORLD OF SALAD LATELY. I LOVE IT BECAUSE IT REALLY DOES SOAK UP FLAVOR LIKE A SPONGE. THE MORE ACID IN YOUR DRESSING, THE MORE "COOKED" THE KALE BECOMES. I LOVE USING IT TO MAKE CAESAR SALADS BECAUSE THERE IS SO MUCH FLAVOR — THE BACON, THE CHEESE, THE LEMON … NOW THAT'S A SPONGE WHERE #YOUCANMAKEFRIENDSWITHSALAD.

SERVES 4 TO 6

DRESS IT UP AHEAD OF TIME

Try to make the dressing the day before you want to make the salad so it can sit in the fridge overnight and develop its flavors.

In a large bowl, whisk together the egg white, juice from one of the lemons, olive oil, vinegar, Dijon mustard, Worcestershire sauce, garlic, Parmesan cheese, salt, and pepper. Once everything is thoroughly mixed, add the mayo and give the mixture one final stir. Cover the bowl and place it in the fridge overnight or for at least 2 hours.

YOU CAN MAKE FRIENDS WITH SALAD

Take the kale leaves and drizzle them with the juice from the other lemon so the acid can cook the leaves just a bit. You should only let the leaves sit in the juice for approximately 5 minutes.

In a small pan, cook the bacon over medium heat for approximately 8 minutes. If you're like me, crispy bacon is the only way to go. Either leave the bacon as full strips or cut each slice in half. Remove from the heat and set aside until needed.

And now for the crouton-anchovies thing. Dump all your sardines or smelts in a bowl filled with the flour, and then fry them in a table-top deep-fryer or a pot with the canola oil at 350°F (180°C) for approximately 6 minutes, or until crispy. Using a pastry brush, lightly paint the kale leaves with the salad dressing, and layer the leaves on a plate with the sardines, bacon, and large Parmesan cheese shavings (grated Parm works too). Grill a couple lemons for some added garnish/lemony goodness on the side.

1 egg white

Juice from 2 lemons, divided

¼ cup (60 mL) olive oil

1 tablespoon (15 mL) white vinegar

2 teaspoons (10 mL) grainy Dijon mustard

1 teaspoon (5 mL) Worcestershire sauce

4 cloves garlic

2 tablespoons (30 mL) freshly shaved Parmesan cheese

1 teaspoon (5 mL) kosher salt

1 teaspoon (5 mL) black pepper

3 tablespoons (45 mL) mayonnaise

1 bunch large kale leaves (stems trimmed)

1 package (8 ½ oz/240 g) smoked bacon

30 fresh smelts or sardines

2 cups (500 mL) all-purpose flour

1 cup (250 mL) canola oil

Lemons (optional)

"CHICKEN FRIED" BACON WITH BASIL AIOLI

SERVES 6 TO 10

FIRST CAME THE CHICKEN FRIED CHICKEN. THEN CAME THE CHICKEN FRIED STEAK. AND NOW I PRESENT TO YOU — CHICKEN FRIED BACON! THE ACTUAL COOKING TIME IS SHORT, BUT YOU NEED TO ALLOW AT LEAST 6 HOURS FOR THE PREP, BECAUSE THE BACON NEEDS TO SOAK IN THE BUTTERMILK BEFORE YOU FRY IT. YOUR BUTCHER WILL LOVE YOU THANKS TO ME AND ALL THE SPECIALTY TRIPS THIS BOOK MAKES YOU TAKE. IT'S A SMALL PRICE TO PAY FOR EXCELLENT INGREDIENTS. TRADITIONALLY, CHICKEN FRIED MEANS FRIED IN CHICKEN FAT. FOR THIS WE ARE USING THE OIL BECAUSE IT'S EASIER TO FIND BUT WE ARE CREATING THE SAME FINGER-LICKING FRIED CHICKEN BATTER ... BUT FOR BACON. YUP.

SOAK IT ALL UP

Have your butcher cut you the extra-thick smoked bacon, about ¼-inch thick (0.5 cm) should be thick enough. Cut each thick strip of bacon into three equal portions. Pour the buttermilk into a container, and whisk in six of the eggs. Toss the bacon in the egg mixture and let it soak for at least 6 hours. The longer you soak it, the more tender the bacon will be after you fry it.

DIP IT GOOD!

While the bacon soaks up all the buttermilk, I suggest you prepare the aioli so that you can go straight from frying to eating. Blitz the remaining two eggs in a food processor or blender. Add the garlic, the Parmesan cheese, and the basil. Blitz everything until completely puréed, then add a little bit of salt to taste. Slowly pour in 3 cups (750 mL) of the canola oil, while the machine is running, to thicken up the aioli. Once the aioli has thickened, give it a taste and add a little bit of salt if needed or a little squirt of lemon juice for added flavor. Place it in the fridge until you're ready to use it. ❯❯❯

6 slices extra-thick-cut smoked bacon

4 cups (1 L) buttermilk

8 eggs

6 cloves garlic

4 oz (100 g) freshly grated Parmesan cheese

½ cup (125 mL) fresh basil leaves, stems removed

6 cups (1.5 L) canola oil

2 cups (500 mL) all-purpose flour

1 tablespoon (15 mL) kosher salt

2 tablespoons (30 mL) smoked paprika

1 tablespoon (15 mL) garlic powder

START DIPPING

AND EATING!

>>> CHICKEN FRY THAT BACON

In a bowl, combine the flour, salt, paprika, and garlic powder. Fill a deep saucepan with the remaining canola oil to a depth of about 1 inch (2.5 cm), or use a table-top deep-fryer and bring the temperature of the oil to 340°F (170°C). Place each piece of bacon in the flour individually and fully cover it. Press the flour into the bacon and really pack it tightly. The tighter you press flour into the bacon, the better the batter will stick after it has been fried. Working in batches, drop the floured bacon into the hot oil, and cook for approximately 2 minutes per side, or until each side has browned and the batter has become nice and crispy. Use tongs to remove the bacon from the oil and place it on some paper towel to soak up the excess oil. Lightly salt the fried bacon pieces, and then start dipping and eating! I love giving a little squeeze of fresh lemon juice for a blast of flavor before I start to dip.

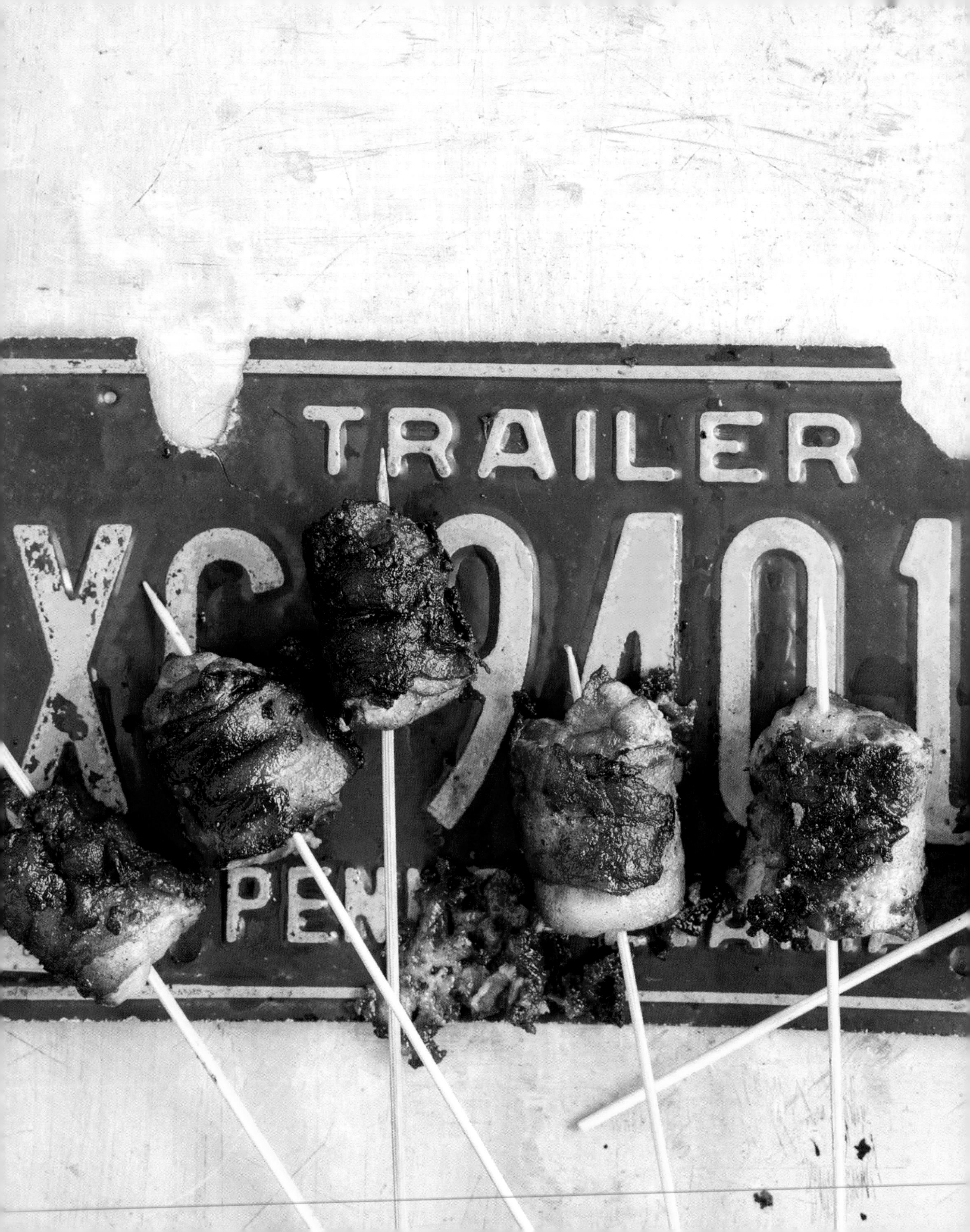
TRAILER

ALABAMA TAILGATERS

A FEW YEARS AGO I DID A POP-UP AT TORONTO'S FESTIVAL OF BEER. I WAS SPONSORED WITH 90 LB (40 KG) OF BACON. KIND OF THE BEST THING EVER. I QUICKLY REMEMBERED A BACON-WRAPPED HOTDOG I HAD AT A TAILGATE PARTY AND STARTED TINKERING AWAY AT THE RECIPE. AND 90 LB OF BACON LATER ...

SERVES 5

BA-BA-BA-BACON!

Cut the slices of bacon two-thirds of the way down and make a T-shape with each slice. Place a slice of beef carpaccio where the two pieces of bacon cross, and lightly season with salt and pepper. Top the beef carpaccio with a little bit of grated cheese, chopped kimchi, and finely chopped cilantro. Fold the two shorter ends of the bacon over the stuffing, and then roll the longer part of bacon until you have a ball of bacon wrapped around the kimchi, cheese, and beef.

BACON AND CHEESY GOODNESS

Preheat the oven to 350°F (180°C). Prepare the Sriracha aioli. In a pan, grill the bacon balls over high heat for 4 to 5 minutes per side. Transfer the grilled bacon balls to a baking sheet, and cook them in the oven for approximately 12 minutes, or until the heat penetrates all the layers of the tailgater (you'll have to taste one to be sure) and the cheese oozes out of each ball with ease. Stick each ball on its own skewer and serve with some Sriracha aioli.

10 slices thin-cut fatty bacon

10 slices beef carpaccio (thinly shaved raw beef)

1 teaspoon (5 mL) kosher salt

1 teaspoon (5 mL) black pepper

¼ cup (60 mL) grated mozzarella cheese

½ cup (125 mL) finely chopped kimchi (see page 118)

1 bunch cilantro, stems removed and finely chopped

½ cup (125 mL) Sriracha aioli (see page 94)

LARD HAVE MERCY, AUSTIN, TEXAS

I LIKE TO THINK I HAVE A PRETTY CLEVER FOOD TRUCK NAME — FIDEL GASTRO'S — A CULINARY SCRIPTURE THAT WAS JUST BORN TO BE A FOOD TRUCK. ONCE IN A WHILE, I COME ACROSS OTHER FOOD TRUCK NAMES THAT JUST STAND OUT. LARD HAVE MERCY ... WELL DONE.

I HAVE TO SAY THAT AUSTIN, TEXAS, IS IN ALL HONESTY ONE OF THE COOLEST NORTH AMERICAN CITIES I'VE EVER VISITED. IT'S SMART, ARTISTIC, CULTURAL, AND TRENDY, AND IT GETS STREET FOOD. LIKE, I MEAN, *REALLY* GETS IT. THERE ARE PROBABLY MORE FOOD TRUCKS AND CARTS THAN THERE ARE RESTAURANTS. THEY HAVE THESE STREET FOOD HUBS ALL OVER THE CITY WHERE MULTIPLE TRUCKS PARK AND SERVE. SO HERE I AM, FIRST TIME IN AUSTIN, AT ONE OF THESE HUBS AND I SEE ABOUT 12 TRUCKS ON THE UNIVERSITY CAMPUS. BBQ HERE, TACOS THERE, AND BAM, ALL OF A SUDDEN I SEE IT ... LARD HAVE MERCY. A TRUCK THAT IS 100% DEVOTED TO BACON. THEY HAD BACON CHEESEBURGERS, BACON SANDWICHES, BACON ON A STICK, BACON-WRAPPED SAUSAGES THAT HAD BACON IN THEM, BACON-WRAPPED CHICKEN LOLLIPOPS. THEY BUILT AN ENTIRE FOOD TRUCK MODEL AROUND THE SENTIMENT I EXPRESSED AT THE BEGINNING OF THE CHAPTER. OH, LARD HAVE MERCY!

I HAVE TO SAY THAT AUSTIN, TEXAS, IS IN ALL HONESTY ONE OF THE COOLEST NORTH AMERICAN CITIES I'VE EVER VISITED. IT'S SMART, ARTISTIC, CULTURAL, AND TRENDY, AND IT GETS STREET FOOD.

BACON JAM

THIS ISN'T SO MUCH A DISH, BUT RATHER A BACON ACCESSORY THAT YOU CAN PAIR WITH ALMOST ANYTHING. CHEESEBURGERS ... WITH BACON JAM. PEANUT BUTTER CUPS ... WITH BACON JAM. FRENCH ONION SOUP ... WITH BACON JAM ... SEE WHERE I'M GOING WITH THIS? AND IT KEEPS FOR QUITE A WHILE. THE FAT CONGEALS WHEN YOU REFRIGERATE IT AND IT CAN LAST FOR MONTHS, SO THERE'S NO NEED TO RUSH THROUGH YOUR BATCH. THAT SAID, ONCE YOU START COOKING WITH BACON JAM, PEOPLE WILL BE HOOKED. JUST AN FYI.

6 lb (3 kg) double-smoked bacon

4 Spanish onions

Canola oil

4 cups (1 L) soy sauce

2 cups (500 mL) brown sugar

MMMMM ... BACON!

Cube the slab of bacon into ½-inch-thick (1 cm) cubes. Some of the pieces will be nice and fatty, and some will be all meat — this is exactly what you want. You can make bacon jam with sliced bacon but it just doesn't come out the same way. Trust me, go to a butcher or deli counter and just order one big slab of double-smoked bacon. Danish double-smoked bacon has been some of the best I've ever used for this recipe. Cook the cubed bacon pieces in a large saucepan (no oil required) over high heat for 5 to 6 minutes, or until the bacon is nice and crisp and all the fat has been sweated out. Turn down the heat to medium-low and use a ladle to spoon some of the bacon grease out of the pan.

BACON: IN JAM FORM.

Cut the onions into 1-inch (2.5 cm) dice and place them in a separate pan with some canola oil. Cook them for approximately 6 minutes, and then add the soy sauce and cook without stirring for an additional 10 minutes, or until the onions are soft and fully cooked. Transfer the onions to the saucepan holding the bacon cubes, and stir well. Add the brown sugar, and keep stirring. Turn down the heat to low, and let it cook for about 2 hours, or until the bacon cubes are fully caramelized. Every 10 minutes or so, give the bacon a good stir and check to see that it's not on the verge of burning. Turn off the heat, and let the mixture cool for approximately 10 minutes. Transfer the cooked bacon to a blender or food processor, and blitz it until it becomes a paste. Put it into a large container and let it cool for approximately 1 hour before you place it in the fridge. As it starts to cool, the fat and the sugar congeal and begin to make your jam. You have successfully jammified bacon. Push yourself as a home cook to see how many different ways you can use it.

Transfer the final product to an airtight container and refrigerate for up to 2 months. This isn't suitable for freezing.

BACON JAM WITH BRUSSELS SPROUTS AND RADICCHIO

SERVES 6 TO 8
AS A SIDE DISH

SO, HERE'S YOUR FIRST BACON JAM TWIST ON AN ITALIAN CLASSIC. I GREW UP EATING BRUSSELS SPROUTS COOKED IN PANCETTA, A CURED ITALIAN BACON OF SORTS. THIS VERSION KICKS IT UP A NOTCH OR TWO BECAUSE YOU CAN GET THE SMOKY BACON FLAVOR INTO EVERY CREVICE OF THE SPROUT.

BRUSSELS NOW WITH MUSCLES

First cut each Brussels sprout into either halves or quarters; halves if you like them a little more firm, and quarters if you prefer them a little softer. Throw the sprouts in a hot pan over high heat with a little bit of olive oil. Cook them for 5 or 6 minutes, or until they start to brown. Once they are browning, add half the radicchio from the full head. Just throw the whole leaves in and give them a toss. Cook the radicchio for approximately 2 minutes, or until it's wilted. It should almost look like purple spinach. Add the bacon jam with a spoon and keep shaking the pan around so that the Brussels sprouts begin to pick up all the flavor off the pan as the jam begins to melt. The warmth of the pan will melt the bacon jam (it takes approximately 2 minutes to fully melt), allowing it to cover the radicchio and the sprouts and giving the dish a nice little charring. Turn off the heat before the sprouts burn from the sugar, and add the remaining radicchio leaves. Squeeze in half of the lemon juice. At this point, you will have some radicchio that is firm and some that is fully cooked in the dish.

Plate everything, and grate the Parmesan cheese over the dish. Top with a final squeeze of fresh lemon, and serve immediately.

12 Brussels sprouts

Olive oil

1 head radicchio lettuce

2 tablespoons (30 mL) Bacon Jam (see page 192)

Juice from 1 lemon, divided

4 oz (100 g) Parmesan cheese

CARBONARA FRIES

SERVES 4 TO 12
(DEPENDS ON HOW MANY
FRIES YOU COOK)

THIS DISH IS THE PERFECT COMBINATION OF POUTINE AND PASTA. IT TAKES THE CONCEPT AND PROCESS OF PASTA CARBONARA AND REPLACES THE PASTA WITH FRENCH FRIES. STREET FOOD GENIUSNESS! I USUALLY USE CAVENDISH DOUBLE-COATED FRIES FOR THIS DISH. I'M NOT SAYING YOU *MUST* USE THESE FRIES, BUT THE EXTRA COATING (WHICH IS UNIQUE TO CAVENDISH) ALLOWS THE CARBONARA SAUCE TO STICK TO THE FRIES INCREDIBLY WELL WITHOUT THEM GETTING SOGGY.

NO PASTA HERE

Heat canola oil in a table-top deep-fryer to 300°F (150°C), or add 2 inches (5 cm) of canola oil in a deep pot and heat it to 300°F (150°C).

If you choose to make your own fries instead of using frozen, I would suggest using russet potatoes. Cut the potatoes to your preferred thickness (skin on or peeled, whichever you prefer) and blanch them in the hot oil for approximately 5 minutes. To make your own version of extra-coated fries, let the fries cool for approximately 20 minutes, and then toss them in flour and fry them fully, with the oil at 375°F (190°C), for another 10 minutes or until crispy golden brown. I prefer to use frozen for this dish, but if you absolutely want to make your own fries for it, now you can!

CARBONARA TIME!

Cut the bacon into ¼-inch (0.5 cm) cubes. Toss them into a skillet (no need for oil) over high heat, and cook for approximately 6 minutes, or until crispy and brown. Whisk the eggs yolks until nice and creamy. Place them in the fridge until needed.

Once the fries and bacon are perfectly crisp, immediately toss them together in a large bowl and slowly add the egg yolks. The heat from the fries and bacon will soak up the yolk. Only add enough yolk to cover the fries, do not drown them and make them soggy. Toss the fries and bacon in some salt as if you were tossing wings in sauce. Plate the fries on a large sharing dish or in individual containers, and grate fresh Parmesan cheese over them. Season with black pepper and a sprinkle of dried Italian chili flakes. Voilà, carbonara fries!

Canola oil

1 large bag (4 lb/2 kg) of frozen fries with double-fry coating or 12 russet potatoes

2 lb (1 kg) slab Danish or double-smoked bacon

6 egg yolks

1 teaspoon (5 mL) kosher salt

4 oz (100 g) fresh Parmesan cheese

1 teaspoon (5 mL) black pepper

1 teaspoon (5 mL) dried chili flakes

LOCKHART'S BBQ, DETROIT, MICHIGAN

DETROIT REALLY IS AN INTERESTING CITY. QUITE OFTEN IT'S CRITICIZED FOR ITS FINANCIAL WOES, AMONG OTHER THINGS, BUT I SAW A TOTALLY DIFFERENT CITY THAN THE ONE THAT SO OFTEN FEATURES IN THE MEDIA. YES, THE CITY DOES HAVE SOME SERIOUS FINANCIALLY RELATED ISSUES — UNEMPLOYMENT, ABANDONED BUILDINGS AND HOMES, A SEVERELY UNDERSTAFFED POLICE FORCE, AND AN INFRASTRUCTURE FOR 4 MILLION PEOPLE BUT A POPULATION OF LESS THAN 800,000, FOR EXAMPLE. YES, DETROIT ISN'T IN THE BEST SHAPE, BUT I DIDN'T SEE A LOST CAUSE, I SAW TREMENDOUS INSPIRATION.

I WAS IN TOWN FOR THE DO IT YOURSELF STREET FAIR — AN EVENT DESIGNED TO HELP PROMOTE AND REBUILD THE CITY OF DETROIT THROUGH THE COLLABORATION OF LOCAL ENTREPRENEURS, CHEFS, ARTISTS, AND MUSICIANS. IT WAS ON THIS TRIP THAT I WAS TOLD TO CHECK OUT LOCKHART'S BBQ AND TO MEET A MAN NAMED BUBBA. BUBBA IS THEIR PIT MASTER. I COULDN'T MAKE THIS SHIT UP EVEN IF I TRIED.

SO, I VENTURE OUT TO LOCKHART'S BBQ TO HAVE SOME OF THE BEST BBQ I'VE EVER HAD, AND IN TRUE PIT MASTER FORM, BUBBA SENT OUT HIS MIXED PLATTER OF NINE DIFFERENT ANIMALS SMOKED TO PERFECTION AND SERVED WITH A SIDE OF WHITE BREAD AND ABOUT 20 SAUCES. INSERT HEAVENLY ANGELS SINGING HERE.

WHEN WE TALKED, HE TOLD ME ABOUT HOW BBQ WAS HIS THIRD CAREER AND THAT HE USED TO WORK AS A MECHANIC FOR ONE OF THE LARGE U.S. AUTOMOTIVE COMPANIES, AND THAT HIS LOVE OF BBQ ACTUALLY SAVED HIM. WE JUST MET, AND HE'S TELLING ME EVERYTHING ABOUT HIS CITY, HIS LIFE, AND HIS FAMILY. I'M HEARING ALL OF THIS WHILE SNACKING ON RIBS WITH SAUCE ALL OVER MY FACE, AND I'M JUST BLOWN AWAY. THE VERY CONVERSATION HE AND I HAD WENT WAY BEYOND BARBECUED MEAT. IT WAS ABOUT LOVING SOMETHING ENOUGH TO NOT GIVE A SHIT IF IT GOES WRONG. IT WAS ABOUT TAKING THIS BACK. BUBBA REPRESENTED THE NEW FACE OF DETROIT.

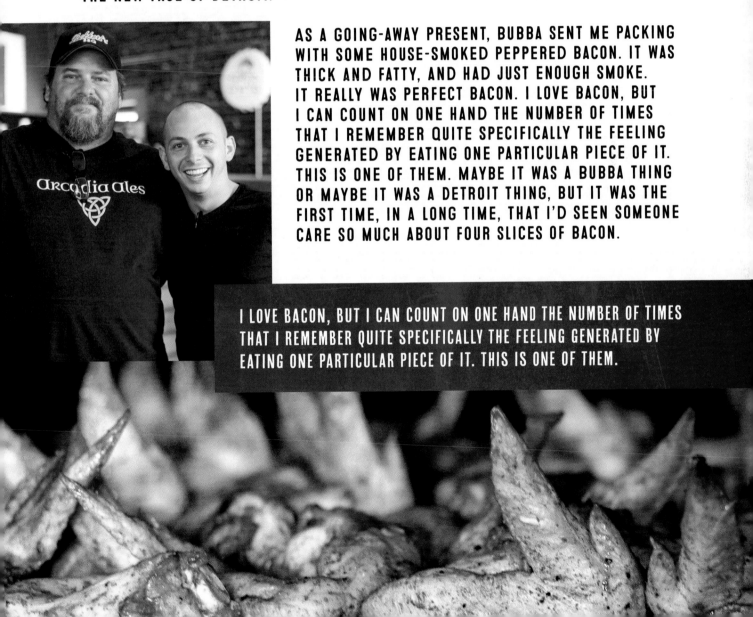

AS A GOING-AWAY PRESENT, BUBBA SENT ME PACKING WITH SOME HOUSE-SMOKED PEPPERED BACON. IT WAS THICK AND FATTY, AND HAD JUST ENOUGH SMOKE. IT REALLY WAS PERFECT BACON. I LOVE BACON, BUT I CAN COUNT ON ONE HAND THE NUMBER OF TIMES THAT I REMEMBER QUITE SPECIFICALLY THE FEELING GENERATED BY EATING ONE PARTICULAR PIECE OF IT. THIS IS ONE OF THEM. MAYBE IT WAS A BUBBA THING OR MAYBE IT WAS A DETROIT THING, BUT IT WAS THE FIRST TIME, IN A LONG TIME, THAT I'D SEEN SOMEONE CARE SO MUCH ABOUT FOUR SLICES OF BACON.

I LOVE BACON, BUT I CAN COUNT ON ONE HAND THE NUMBER OF TIMES THAT I REMEMBER QUITE SPECIFICALLY THE FEELING GENERATED BY EATING ONE PARTICULAR PIECE OF IT. THIS IS ONE OF THEM.

RUM-CANDIED BACON BITES

SERVES 4 TO 6

RUM, CANDY, BACON. RUM, CANDY, BACON. RUM, CANDY, BACON. I REALLY DON'T WHAT ELSE TO SAY ABOUT THIS DISH OTHER THAN RUM, CANDY, BACON. BITE-SIZED PIECES OF PORK BY WAY OF RUM, CANDY, AND BACON. #RUMCANDYBACON.

CANDY COATED

Cut your bacon chunk into ¼-inch (0.5 cm) cubes. Throw it into a hot skillet (no oil required) over high heat and cook for approximately 4 minutes, until the meat browns and gets a little crispy, and some of the fat has cooked off.

Add most of the chocolate hazelnut spread, the brown sugar, and the paprika to the skillet with the bacon. Now at this point, if you decide to go take a phone call or something, you will burn your bacon. Just chill by the pan and candy your bacon! Remember to stir it while you chill, though. As the bacon starts to soak up the spices, the meat will darken and a glaze will form in the pan. Slowly pour in the dark rum, and give the bacon a stir. If you are using a gas or open flame stovetop, take the pan off the heat before you add the rum. Place the skillet back on the heat, if you had to remove it, and cook for 8 to 10 minutes, or until the rum is slightly reduced and all the sugar and paprika are cooked off. If your bacon looks overcooked, it probably is, so make sure to watch it closely while it cooks. If the bacon looks like it could use a little more love, then give it love!

Now you have delicious, dark, candied bacon. Add a little bit of the coarse salt to the bacon, and stir it around, and then add a little more on top. Drizzle with the remaining chocolate hazelnut spread as garnish. Make sure you use coarse salt so that you can see the large crystals stick to the bacon.

2 lb (1 kg) chunk of Danish double-smoked slab bacon

2 tablespoons (30 mL) chocolate hazelnut spread

2 tablespoons (30 mL) brown sugar

1 tablespoon (15 mL) smoked paprika

1 cup (250 mL) dark rum

1 teaspoon (5 mL) coarse salt

STUFF
ON STICKS

IF YOU'VE EVER WONDERED WHAT MAKES A DISH QUINTESSENTIAL STREET FOOD, PUTTING IT ON A STICK IS A GREAT START. STEAK, FISH, PORK, GRILLED, FRIED ... IT DOESN'T REALLY MATTER. JUST PUT IT ON A STICK AND ALL OF A SUDDEN YOUR MENU IS COOLER.

FOOD ON A STICK IS PORTABLE, UTENSIL-FREE FOOD THAT IS GREAT WHEN YOU'RE ON THE RUN. THAT'S PRETTY MUCH CORE TO ALL STREET FOOD. BUT FOR WHATEVER REASON, IF YOU TAKE ANY KIND OF FOOD THAT PEOPLE SAY TASTES GREAT AND YOU FIND A WAY TO PUT THAT EXACT SAME DISH ON A STICK, IT'S LIKE YOU HAVE INVENTED THE WHEEL. I'VE SEEN IT DONE. BEING ABLE TO PRODUCE A STICK-FRIENDLY VERSION OF A DISH HAS NOT ONLY MADE IT STREET FOOD BUT ALSO MADE YOU INCREDIBLY COOL. SO, LET'S GET COOL AND PUT SOME STUFF ON STICKS.

STUFF ON STICKS

PEANUT BUTTER AND JELLY TENDERLOIN YAKITORI

SERVES 2 TO 4

MY NEXT COOKBOOK WILL BE ALL ABOUT DIFFERENT WAYS TO USE THE CLASSIC COMBINATION OF PEANUT BUTTER AND JELLY. I KNOW THAT PEANUT BUTTER IS ONE OF THOSE SENSITIVE INGREDIENTS BECAUSE OF VERY SEVERE ALLERGIES, BUT WHEN AND IF YOU ARE IN A POSITION TO EAT IT, YOU HAVE TO MOVE AWAY FROM BORING LITTLE SANDWICHES AND EXPERIMENT WITH USING OTHER FOOD VESSELS LIKE BEEF ON A STICK TO BRING OUT THE BEST OF THOSE FLAVORS. YOU'LL NEED WOODEN SKEWERS FOR THIS.

IT'S LIKE AN UPSCALE BBQ MEETS A BIRTHDAY PICNIC

Cut the tenderloin into cubes no bigger than 1-inch (2.5 cm) square. Because the steak is round you will never get perfect squares, but who the hell wants a perfect square? Not this guy. Lightly season the tenderloin to taste with salt and pepper. In a bowl, combine the soy sauce, peanut butter, and oyster sauce. In a small bowl, reserve 3 tablespoons (45 mL) of this sauce to brush on the meat later. Using a spoon, work the marinade so the thick peanut butter becomes more of a thinner paste. Toss the tenderloin pieces in the marinade until they are fully covered by the sauce.

PEANUT BUTTER JELLY TIME

Now that we've covered the peanut butter portion of this dish, on to the jelly! It's jelly in the loosest sense of the word, but jelly nonetheless. Throw the cranberries (fresh or frozen) into a small saucepan over high heat and cook for approximately 5 minutes. Add the sugar, the cayenne, and the 1 tablespoon (15 mL) of salt with the Cointreau and 1 cup (250 mL) of water, and turn down the heat to medium-low. Cook, while stirring, for approximately 15 minutes, or until the water is fully reduced and you are left with a thick cranberry sauce — a.k.a. jelly — and the berries are caramelized thanks to the sugar. If you feel like the berries could keep reducing down, add another ½ cup (125 mL) of water and keep rolling with it. ❯❯❯

STUFF YOU NEED

Wooden skewers

1 lb (500 g) beef tenderloin

Kosher salt

Black pepper

¾ cup (180 mL) soy sauce

2 tablespoons (30 mL) smooth peanut butter

1 tablespoon (15 mL) oyster sauce

1 cup (250 mL) fresh or frozen cranberries

½ cup (125 mL) granulated sugar

1 teaspoon (5 mL) cayenne pepper

1 tablespoon (15 mL) kosher salt

2 oz (60 mL) Cointreau (or other orange-flavored liqueur)

2 cloves garlic

1 tablespoon (15 mL) unsalted butter

1 tablespoon (15 mL) sesame seeds

›› › Ideally, this meat should be cooked on a BBQ grill. Heat a BBQ to 450°F (230°C) and grill the meat for 4 minutes on each side. Remove it from the grill, let it rest for about 5 minutes, and then brush on some of the reserved sauce. Watch the meat when it's on the BBQ because the marinade might cause the grill to flare up and burn. Meanwhile, thinly slice the garlic. Melt the butter in a skillet over high heat, and add the sliced garlic. Cook the garlic for approximately 2 minutes. Pour this over the cooked meat.

If a BBQ isn't an option, thinly slice the garlic. Melt the butter in a skillet over high heat, and add the sliced garlic. Cook the garlic for approximately 2 minutes, and then add the marinated tenderloin pieces. Cook the meat for approximately 5 minutes and then brush with the reserved sauce. Cook for an additional 2 to 3 minutes, or until medium-rare. Take the meat out of the pan and thread the cubes onto the skewers. Place the skewers on a plate and top with sesame seeds. Serve with the cranberry jelly on the side.

PEANUT BUTTER JELLY TIME

THINGS GET FRIED, THINGS GET PUT ON STICKS

HOLY KOBE CORN DOGS

STREET FOOD AND CARNIVAL FOOD ARE KIND OF LIKE COUSINS. THINGS GET FRIED, THINGS GET PUT ON STICKS, AND EVERYTHING IS ABOUT FUN AND FLAVOR FIRST. CORN DOGS ARE THE AMBASSADOR OF THIS RELATIONSHIP. NO MATTER WHAT ELSE IS AVAILABLE TO EAT AT A CARNIVAL, KY AND I USUALLY DEFAULT TO AT LEAST ONE HOTDOG WRAPPED IN CORNMEAL BATTER, FRIED, AND PERCHED ON A STICK.

SERVES 6 TO 10

YOU'LL NEED 10 WOODEN SKEWERS FOR THIS. YOU CAN DO THIS RECIPE WITH ANY HOTDOG, BUT IF YOU CAN FIND KOBE BEEF DOGS I HIGHLY RECOMMEND YOU USE THEM. THEY ARE THE TASTIEST HOTDOGS I HAVE EVER HAD, AND THE FLAVOR JUST EXPLODES WHEN YOU BITE INTO THEM.

STUFF YOU NEED

10 wooden skewers

1 cup (250 mL) yellow cornmeal

1 cup (250 mL) all-purpose flour

4 teaspoons (20 mL) baking powder

¼ teaspoon (1 mL) kosher salt

¼ teaspoon (1 mL) black pepper

1 egg

1 cup (250 mL) 2% milk

10 all-beef hotdogs

½ cup (125 mL) yellow mustard

2 tablespoons (30 mL) sambal oelek

SUP, DOG?

First, make your batter. In a large bowl, combine the cornmeal, flour, baking powder, salt, and pepper. Crack in the egg, add the milk, and then mix your batter thoroughly. Skewer the hotdogs with the wooden skewers, and dip them in the batter. Fry them, three at a time, in a pan (not a skillet) with ½ inch (1 cm) of canola oil heated to 350°F (180°C) for approximately 3 minutes on one side. Flip and do 3 minutes on the other side, then rest them on paper towel to soak up the excess oil.

In a bowl, mix the mustard with the sambal. Now you have spicy sambal mustard that has the familiarity of the bright yellow mustard but with a bit of kick.

IF YOUR HEART DESIRES … JUST ADD BACON

You can take this recipe one step further by cooking some strips of bacon to the point where they are cooked but not too crispy to manipulate. Wrap the bacon tightly around the dog and pierce each end of the bacon with the skewer to keep it in place. Batter it and fry it as above. (P.S. You're welcome!)

PERUVIAN MEATBALLS

MEATBALLS AREN'T JUST MEATBALLS. THE ONES I GREW UP EATING AS A LITTLE BOY ARE DIFFERENT FROM THE ONES MADE IN THE FOOD MARKETS OF MEXICO, ARE DIFFERENT FROM THE ONES ENJOYED IN PERU, ARE DIFFERENT FROM THE ONES THAT YOU GET FROM THAT SWEDISH FURNITURE STORE. THE MEATBALL TELLS A STORY. INSIDE ARE ALL THE THINGS THAT BRING THE FLAVORS OF A CULTURE TOGETHER, WHILE OUTSIDE IS THAT FIRST IMPRESSION THE MEATBALL WANTS TO MAKE. WHAT KIND OF MEMORIES OR FEELINGS DOES IT WANT TO EVOKE? MEATBALLS REALLY DO ALLOW A CULTURE AND A COMMUNITY TO SHARE A BIT ABOUT WHO THEY ARE. YOU'LL NEED WOODEN SKEWERS FOR THIS.

THE SAUCE

Preheat the oven to 375°F (190°C). Chop the bell peppers and red onion into small chunks. Toss them into a bowl with the 1 cup (250 mL) of olive oil. Finely chop all six cloves of garlic and add them to the bowl, mixing them around to coat thoroughly. Transfer them to a baking pan, and roast for approximately 12 minutes, or until they are nicely charred and soft. Take them out of the oven, and blitz in a food processor until you have a chunky sauce. Wash the cilantro with its stems still on and chop it. Add the cilantro and Peruvian yellow peppers to the food processor, and give it all a good blitz. Once everything has been blended together, warm a little bit of olive oil in a large saucepan over medium-high heat. Stir in the contents of the blender. Add the tomato sauce, stir in the butter, turn down the heat to low, and let it simmer, uncovered, while you make the meatballs. It shouldn't be perfectly smooth, but we don't want it too chunky either. (I know, I know ...) ❯❯❯

Wooden skewers

2 yellow bell peppers

1 red onion

1 cup (250 mL) olive oil

6 cloves garlic

1 bunch cilantro

1 jar (10 oz/300 g) of ají amarillo peppers (yellow Peruvian peppers) or spicy yellow banana peppers

1 jar (28 oz/796 mL) tomato sauce

½ cup (125 mL) salted butter

1 lb (500 g) fatty ground pork

2 lb (1 kg) ground lamb

1 tablespoon (15 mL) ground cumin

1 tablespoon (15 mL) smoked paprika

1 tablespoon (15 mL) chili flakes

1 tablespoon (15 mL) ground ginger

1 tablespoon (15 mL) kosher salt

1 tablespoon (15 mL) black pepper

½ cup (125 mL) dried breadcrumbs

4 eggs

1 bunch green onions, finely chopped

½ cup (125 mL) queso fresco (fresh cheese), or freshly grated Parmesan

1 bag (6 oz/170 g) chicharrón or pork rinds

››› THE BALLS

Mix the pork and lamb meat in a bowl, making sure the meat is fully mixed together. Add the cumin, paprika, chili flakes, ginger, salt, and pepper. Give it a quick stir and then add the breadcrumbs, eggs, and 1 cup (250 mL) of room-temperature water. Mix well to combine. Form the meat into sixteen meatballs. Throw some more olive oil into a skillet over high heat and sear the balls for approximately 2 minutes, or until they have a nice crusty exterior. Once the meatballs are cooked, add them to the pepper sauce. Simmer the meatballs in the sauce, uncovered, at medium-low heat for approximately 45 minutes to an hour.

Divide the meatballs evenly between the skewers, place them on a serving platter, and generously cover each meatball with sauce. Garnish with green onion, queso fresco, and crumbled chicharrón.

MEATBALLS AREN'T JUST MEATBALLS

LET'S GET COOL AND PUT SOME STUFF ON STICKS

LAMB KEBAB ON A PITA

GREEK AND MEDITERRANEAN CUISINE EMBODY SOME OF THE MOST IMPORTANT STREET FOOD CONCEPTS: MEAT, STICKS, WRAPS, AND FAMILY TRADITION. THIS RECIPE TAKES THE SIMPLE, TRADITIONAL PITA AND MODERNIZES IT WITH FULL FLAVOR ELEMENTS AND GREAT VISUAL APPEAL. I SUGGEST USING FRESHLY GROUND LAMB AND ROASTED GARLIC. THE REST OF THE INGREDIENTS JUST FALL INTO PLACE. YOU'LL NEED LONG METAL SKEWERS FOR THIS.

STUFF YOU NEED

SERVES 4 TO 8

Long metal skewers

1 can (19 oz/540 mL) chickpeas, drained and rinsed

1 cup (250 mL) extra virgin olive oil

6 cloves garlic

Juice from 2 lemons

1 teaspoon (5 mL) tahini

1 teaspoon (5 mL) kosher salt, divided

1 teaspoon (5 mL) black pepper, divided

1 English cucumber, peeled, seeds removed, and roughly chopped

2 cups (500 mL) Greek yogurt

1 cup (250 mL) cream cheese

1 ½ lb (750 g) ground lamb

½ cup (125 mL) finely chopped curly parsley

1 teaspoon (5 mL) ground cumin

1 teaspoon (5 mL) smoked paprika

1 teaspoon (5 mL) crushed fennel seeds

2 zucchinis, skin on and cut into thin strips

8 small pitas

½ cup (125 mL) kalamata olives, diced

HUMMUS (THAT'S ALL I'VE GOT)

Lots of little elements to this dish, so let's get started. First, blitz the can of chickpeas in a blender or food processor with the olive oil. Add two of the garlic cloves, the lemon juice, tahini, and ½ teaspoon (2.5 mL) each of the salt and pepper. Blitz until you have a chunky hummus. When done, transfer to a bowl, cover, and place in the fridge until needed.

Wash out the blender or food processor, and toss in the four remaining garlic cloves, cucumber, Greek yogurt, and cream cheese. Blitz until the cucumber and garlic have fully broken down but you still have a chunky texture. Transfer this tzatziki to a bowl, cover, and place in the fridge until needed.

LAMB ME TENDER

Put the ground lamb in a bowl, and add the parsley, cumin, paprika, fennel seed, and remaining ½ teaspoon (2.5 mL) each of the salt and pepper. Mix the meat thoroughly, using your hands, and form it into eight kefta sausages around the metallic skewers. Make two kefta sausages per skewer.

Preheat the BBQ to 500°F (260°C). Barbecue the meat, with the lid open, for 10 to 12 minutes. Once the meat comes off the grill, throw the thinly cut zucchini and pita bread on the grill for a few minutes just to give them some char flavor. Keep the meat on the skewers.

Build each pita starting with the hummus, then a strip of the zucchini, a skewer of lamb meat, and a topping of tzatziki and diced kalamata olives.

BLACKENED COD TEPPANYAKI

SERVES 2

STUFF YOU NEED

8 skewers or chopsticks

1 fillet (1 lb/500 g) black cod

½ cup (125 mL) soy sauce

2 tablespoons (30 mL) oyster sauce

1 tablespoon (15 mL) honey

1 tablespoon (15 mL) grated ginger

1 green onion, finely chopped

1 tablespoon (15 mL) olive oil

1 lb (500 g) frozen edamame

1 oz (30 mL) whiskey

Juice from 2 limes

2 cloves garlic, thinly sliced

1 teaspoon (5 mL) chili flakes

1 teaspoon (5 mL) kosher salt

1 tablespoon (15 mL) sesame seeds

I REMEMBER BEING A YOUNG KID AND GOING TO MY FIRST TEPPANYAKI GRILL. THERE WERE FLAMING ONIONS, RICE BOWLS BEING THROWN IN THE AIR, AND PROTEINS. MY FAVORITE WAS ALWAYS THE COD. A SWEET AND BUTTERY FISH THAT TASTES AMAZING WHEN MIXED WITH A STICKY BLACKENED SAUCE AND A NICE CHAR OFF A COOKING SURFACE. YOU'LL NEED EIGHT SKEWERS OR EIGHT CHOPSTICKS FOR THIS.

COD BLESS

Cut the black cod into eight evenly sized pieces. In a large bowl, combine the soy sauce, oyster sauce, and honey with the ginger and green onion. In a small bowl, set aside 2 tablespoons (30 mL) of the marinade to add to the fish once it's cooked. Mix everything well, and fully submerge the fish in the marinade. Let the pieces marinate for approximately 1 hour, covered, in the fridge.

Heat the olive oil in a nonstick skillet. Get the oil really hot, and add the marinated fish to the skillet. Because of the sugars, the fish will char almost immediately. Cook for approximately 2 minutes on one side, then flip the fish pieces over and turn down the heat to medium-low. Add the reserved marinade to the skillet. Just drizzle it over the fish. DO NOT SHAKE the pan. Black cod is a buttery fish and will break apart easily. Cook the fish for approximately 5 minutes on the reverse side.

HEEEERE, FISHY, FISHY

While the fish is cooking, prepare the edamame. In a saucepan, boil some salted water over high heat and add the edamame. Cook the edamame for 3 to 4 minutes. Once cooked, drain the edamame and set them to one side until needed.

Once the fish has cooked on both sides, take the skillet off the heat and hit it with the shot of whiskey to deglaze (with the fish still in the skillet). Place the skillet back on the heat for approximately 30 seconds and then gently remove the fish from it. Add the lime juice to the pan, and then toss in the garlic and chili flakes. Cook for approximately 2 minutes and then add the edamame. Toss the edamame around in the pan, and add the salt. Cook for approximately 3 minutes just to let the edamame absorb the flavor in the pan. Sprinkle the sesame seeds over the fish and either skewer the fish with skewers or eat with chopsticks. Serve with the seasoned edamame.

CANDIED MAPLE SCALLOPS

SERVES 6

COOKING WITH ANYTHING SUGAR-BASED ALWAYS NEEDS A LITTLE EXTRA FOCUS FROM THE COOK. THESE ITEMS CAN GO FROM HOT TO BURNT VERY QUICKLY. YOU NEED TO PAY ATTENTION OR ELSE YOU'LL JUST END UP THROWING FOOD OUT, OR EATING SOMETHING YOU DON'T LIKE. IN THIS RECIPE IT KIND OF HELPS THAT WE ARE COOKING THE SUGAR WITH SCALLOPS. I THINK OVERCOOKED SCALLOPS ARE A CRIME AGAINST HUMANITY OF THE OCEAN. LUCKILY, THE SUGAR IS A GREAT INDICATOR OF WHEN TOO MUCH IS TOO MUCH. WHEN YOU HAVE THAT NICE SUGARY CRUST, STOP. IMMEDIATELY. COOK IT ANYMORE AND YOU WILL HAVE A DRY, FLAVORLESS BURNT SCALLOP. YUM?

MAKE STICKY TIME

Mix the maple syrup, pineapple juice, and rum in a bowl, and stir until they become a sweet and potent sauce. In another bowl, combine the flour, salt, pepper, and cinnamon.

Preheat the oven to 400°F (200°C). Use paper towel to dry the scallops. Make sure they are nice and dry, and then toss them in the seasoned flour. Heat the olive oil in a skillet over high heat. Make sure the oil is very hot. Test the temp with a small sprinkle of water. When it bubbles, the oil is hot enough. Turn the pan on its side so you have a pool of oil. This pool is where you're going to do your cooking. Sear two scallops at a time so you don't cool down the oil. Sear them for 1 to 2 minutes per side, or until they have a nice crust. Place the seared scallops on a baking sheet and brush them, top and bottom, with the marinade. Bake them in the oven for approximately 6 minutes. You want them a little undercooked in the center so you're not left with chewy scallops.

A LITTLE BIT OF CURED PORK NEVER HURTS

Take the pancetta, and place it in a hot nonstick pan over high heat. Pour in the rest of the marinade, and cook for approximately 1 minute, stirring. It will burn if you don't stir it constantly. Once the scallops are done, take them out of the oven and skewer them, two per stick, and squeeze lemon juice over them. On a plate, scatter the maple-glazed pancetta over the scallops and garnish with some daikon sprouts.

STUFF YOU NEED

6 wooden skewers

1 cup (250 mL) maple syrup

¼ cup (60 mL) pineapple juice

1 oz (30 mL) dark rum

2 tablespoons (30 mL) all-purpose flour

1 teaspoon (5 mL) kosher salt

1 teaspoon (5 mL) black pepper

1 teaspoon (5 mL) ground cinnamon

12 large seas scallops (fresh, not frozen)

2 tablespoons (30 mL) olive oil

3 pieces thick-cut pancetta, cubed into ½-inch (1 cm) pieces

1 lemon

2 tablespoons (30 mL) daikon sprouts

I'VE BEEN FORTUNATE ENOUGH TO BE A PART OF A LOT OF FOOD EVENTS — MAINLY TORONTO EVENTS, BECAUSE THAT'S WHERE I LIVE, BUT MOST RECENTLY SOME ACROSS CANADA AND THE U.S. NEVER HAVE I SEEN AN EVENT QUITE LIKE THE PHILLY NIGHT MARKET. THIS EVENT HAPPENS FOUR TIMES A YEAR AND IN A DIFFERENT AREA OF THE CITY EACH TIME. THE CITY AND THE EVENT ORGANIZERS WORK TOGETHER TO FIND A NEW PART OF PHILLY THAT THEY WANT TO HIGHLIGHT AND TO HOST THE EVENT. THE EVENT TAKES PLACE ON THE STREETS AND IS SPREAD OVER ABOUT TEN BLOCKS — FIVE INTERSECTING BLOCKS.

THAT ONE BITE CAPTURED THE ESSENCE OF THE PHILLY NIGHT MARKET FOR ME — IT WAS BOLD, INTENSE, AND OVER BEFORE I KNEW IT.

PHILLY NIGHT MARKET, CHINATOWN, PHILADELPHIA

WHEN I WAS THERE, THE EVENT TOOK PLACE IN PHILLY'S CHINATOWN. PICTURE ABOUT 30 FOOD TRUCKS LINING THE STREETS, ABOUT ANOTHER 20 POP-UP FOOD STANDS, AND LIQUOR, CRAFT BEER, AND SIGNATURE JUICE DRINK VENDORS. THERE WERE FOUR DJS COVERING FOUR DIFFERENT SECTIONS, A LIGHT SHOW, AND A PUBLIC KARAOKE STAND. NOT TO MENTION THE LOCAL BARS AND RESTAURANTS IN THE AREA, AND ABOUT 20,000 PEOPLE.

EVERYTHING, AND I MEAN EVERYTHING, DID WELL THAT NIGHT. BARS WERE FULL, ALCOHOL VENDORS WERE ABLE TO SERVE FROM THEIR STREETSIDE TENTS, FOOD TRUCKS AND POP-UPS ALL HAD LINES — AND NOTHING WENT WRONG. IT WAS FREE TO ATTEND, WAS PAID FOR BY THE CITY AND PRIVATE SPONSORSHIP, AND WAS THE RESULT OF AMAZING COLLABORATION. I WAS BLOWN AWAY.

I WORKED THE EVENT, SO I DIDN'T HAVE MUCH TIME TO ACTUALLY EAT MUCH. BUT I HAD ONE BITE FROM THE POP-UP ACROSS THE STREET. SALSA VERDE GRILLED BABY OCTOPUS ON A STICK. THAT ONE BITE CAPTURED THE ESSENCE OF THE PHILLY NIGHT MARKET FOR ME — IT WAS BOLD, INTENSE, AND OVER BEFORE I KNEW IT.

CHARRED OCTOPUS

I'VE HAD MY FAIR SHARE OF OCTOPUS, FROM FOOD TRUCKS, RESTAURANTS, AND FAMILY. SOMETIMES I COULDN'T TAKE MORE THAN ONE BITE, OTHER TIMES I JUST COULDN'T GET ENOUGH. IN EVERY CASE IT HAS NEVER MATTERED WHERE IT WAS EATEN, BUT HOW IT WAS COOKED. CHEWY OCTOPUS IS A GAME OF PATIENCE, WHEREAS PERFECTLY TENDER OCTOPUS IS A TEASE BECAUSE YOU JUST CAN'T EVER SEEM TO GET ENOUGH. THAT SAID, YOU MIGHT WANT TO GET A LITTLE EXTRA FOR THIS RECIPE. YOU'LL NEED WOODEN SKEWERS FOR THIS RECIPE.

SERVES 6 TO 8

ARE YOU SQUIDING ME?

Take the whole octopus and place it in a large pot with enough water so that the water sits just on the highest point of the octopus. Cut all the lemons in half and throw them in the water with their rind on. Bring the water to a boil over high heat. Once the water comes to a boil, turn down the heat to medium-low, and cook the octopus, covered, for approximately 1 hour. The thickest part of the octopus has to be fork tender before it is removed. After an hour, remove the octopus from the hot water and let it cool for approximately 10 minutes. Wash the octopus under cold water to help remove the membrane. Slice the octopus into pieces so you have nice long tentacles to skewer.

Cut the leafy fennel tips off the fennel and place them in water. Cut off and discard the green stems on the fennel and just keep the large white section. Slice it really thinly and put it in a bowl with the rice wine vinegar so the acid cooks the fennel down a bit. Drain the fennel after approximately 30 minutes and lightly season with salt and pepper. Using a cheese grater, zest the oranges and set the zest aside. Remove the pith from the oranges and slice the flesh into ½-inch (1 cm) pieces. Set the orange pieces aside.

Fry the capers in a little bit of olive oil for approximately 5 minutes, or until they become crispy.

TANTALIZING TENTACLES

Paint the octopus tentacles with the hoisin sauce. Add just enough oil to a skillet to cover its bottom, warm over high heat, and cook the octopus for approximately 5 minutes. The meat is already cooked so all you want to do is give the octopus a nice charring on the surface. On a large serving plate, make a bed of fennel, capers, and orange pieces. Skewer the octopus and place the skewers over the salad. Sprinkle sesame seeds over the octopus, and garnish with leafy fennel tips, orange zest, and lime wedges.

STUFF YOU NEED

Wooden skewers

4 lb (2 kg) octopus

6 lemons

2 large bulbs fennel

½ cup (125 mL) rice wine vinegar

Kosher salt

Black pepper

2 large oranges

¼ cup (60 mL) capers

¼ cup (60 mL) all-purpose flour

1 cup (250 mL) hoisin sauce

Olive oil

1 teaspoon (5 mL) sesame seeds

2 limes

MORTADELLA MUSUBI WITH CHILI RAPINI

THIS VERSION OF MUSUBI IS A TAKE ON THE TRADITIONAL HAWAIIAN VERSION, WHICH USES SPAM, SUSHI RICE, AND SEAWEED. MUSUBI IS ACTUALLY A GREAT DISH DESPITE THE BIZARRE FOOD PAIRINGS THAT MAKE IT COMPLETE. THIS VERSION CONTAINS A FEW ITALIAN INGREDIENTS LIKE MORTADELLA AND RAPINI. YOU'LL NEED WOODEN SKEWERS FOR THIS RECIPE. OH, AND A BAMBOO ROLLING MAT IS IDEAL BUT NOT MANDATORY.

KIND OF LIKE SUSHI ... BUT NOT

Before you do anything, soak the rice in slightly less than 4 cups (1 L) of water. Allow double capacity. In simple terms, this means you need to leave enough space in the bowl of water to let the rice double in volume. Rinse the rice in a strainer or colander until the water runs clear. Combine with water in a medium saucepan. Bring to a boil, then turn down the heat to low, cover, and cook for 20 minutes. The rice should be tender and the water should be absorbed. Let cool enough to handle. Add the sesame oil, a splash of rice wine vinegar, and salt to taste. Mix to combine. Set aside at room temperature until needed.

In a saucepan, bring some water to a boil over high heat and add the rapini. Blanche it for approximately 5 minutes, or until the green color intensifies and the leaves are softer. Remove the rapini from the water and cut it into small bits. Finely chop the garlic and the red chili peppers. Heat the olive oil in a skillet over high heat, and add the rapini, chilies, and garlic. Sauté for 5 or 6 minutes. Take the skillet off the heat and let the rapini cool at room temperature. ❯ ❯ ❯

STUFF YOU NEED

Wooden skewers

Bamboo rolling mat (optional)

2 cups (500 mL) Japanese sticky rice

1 tablespoon (15 mL) sesame oil

Rice wine vinegar

Kosher salt

1 bunch rapini

4 cloves garlic

2 red chili peppers

1 tablespoon (15 mL) olive oil

4 slices (each ½-inch/1 cm thick) fatty mortadella

12 sheets seaweed paper

3 eggs

¼ cup (60 mL) corn starch

Canola oil

2 green chili peppers

1 cup (250 mL) soy sauce

››› WHAT THE HELLA IS MORTADELLA?

Mortadella is Italian bologna. But you have to get the fatty kind or else it's not the real thing. It will have big white squares of fat in it. Cut the mortadella slices into 1-inch (2.5 cm) wide strips. Put them in a nonstick pan over high heat, and sear for 2 to 3 minutes per side, or until they have a nice brown exterior.

NOW TO ROLL THE ROLL

Using the bamboo rolling mat (or your hands, but go much slower and more carefully in that case) you are going to roll the musubi just like you would for regular sushi. First, place some sticky rice on a sheet of seaweed, then top it with the mortadella, the rapini, and one last layer of rice. Make sure each layer of rice is as wide as the mortadella. Roll the seaweed as tightly as possible. It will be a little wider than your average sushi roll because of how wide you cut the mortadella. Repeat with the remaining ingredients.

Prepare a slurry with the eggs and corn starch. First whisk the eggs and then mix in the corn starch until you have a loose paste. Cut the rolls in half and batter them in the slurry. Add canola oil to about 1 inch (2.5 cm) deep in a wok or table-top deep-fryer and heat it to 350°F (180°C). Fry the rolls, in batches, for approximately 4 minutes, or until they are crispy and golden brown.

Thinly slice the green chili peppers, place them in a bowl, and add the soy sauce. Skewer each mortadella musubi and dip it in the spicy soy sauce.

AN ITALIAN TAKE ON
A HAWAIIAN DISH

STREET CORN

HERE IN ONTARIO (THE PROVINCE THAT PLAYS HOST TO MY HOMETOWN OF TORONTO) WE HAVE UNBELIEVABLE ACCESS TO FRESH SWEET CORN. UNFORTUNATELY, WE ALSO HAVE THIS THING CALLED WINTER THAT LIMITS THE LIFE EXPECTANCY OF THE CORN, SO WE LIKE TO MAKE THE MOST OF IT. FOR THIS DISH ONLY GET THE WHOLE HUSK CORN, AND TRY YOUR BEST TO BUY IT EITHER DIRECTLY FROM THE FARM OR FROM YOUR LOCAL FARMERS' MARKET. DON'T BUY THE CORN THAT GETS WRAPPED IN PLASTIC PACKING IN GROUPS OF FOUR AND COMES MOSTLY PRE-SHUCKED. YOU WANT NICE FARM-FRESH COBS OF CORN WITH THE HUSK FULLY INTACT. YOU'LL KNOW IT'S THE REAL STUFF BECAUSE OF ITS CORN HANDLE. THIS HANDLE WILL BE THE PSEUDO STICK FOR THIS DISH.

YOU NEED A FEW OTHER THINGS FOR THIS RECIPE TO WORK. THE FIRST BEING A BBQ. YOU CAN DEFINITELY DO THIS EXACT SAME RECIPE IN THE OVEN, BUT TO BE PERFECTLY HONEST, THE CORN JUST COMES OUT SO MUCH BETTER ON THE BBQ.

IT'S NOT TECHNICALLY A STICK, BUT …

Preheat the BBQ to 500°F (260°C). Roast the cobs of corn, husks on, on the BBQ, with the lid open, for approximately 15 minutes. Make sure you turn the corn every 5 minutes or so to ensure the husk doesn't go up in flames. That said, the corn isn't fully roasted until the outer layer of the husk is almost blackened. It's like walking a tightrope.

BUTTER IS BETTER

In a small pot, melt the butter over medium heat and add the lemon juice as the butter melts. Mix it all well to combine. Once the butter is melted, remove it from the heat and cool for approximately 10 minutes to allow the butter to congeal.

Peel the husks back on the cobs of corn and pull off all the silk, but leave the big roasted outer leaves of the corn. Combine the paprika, salt, and pepper in a bowl. Slather the lemon butter on the cobs of corn and grill them for a couple more minutes, with the outer leaves still pulled away from the kernels. Sprinkle the rub all over the roasted corn kernels and grab it by the leafy green husk. Serve with lime wedges as you mow down. Some jalapeño aioli (page 87) would also go very well drizzled over the corn.

6 cobs of farm-fresh corn, husks on

1 lb (500 g) salted butter

Juice from 6 lemons

1 tablespoon (15 mL) smoked paprika

1 tablespoon (15 mL) kosher salt

1 teaspoon (5 mL) black pepper

2 limes

TEMPURA-FRIED FONTINA WITH TOMATO CHILI JAM

DEEP-FRYING CHEESE IS ONE OF THOSE MYSTERIOUS ADVENTURES TO MOST HOME COOKS. THE ASSUMPTION IS THAT IT WILL JUST MELT AND BE BLAHHH. NOT TRUE! GIVE IT THE RIGHT BLANKET OR CRUST AND YOU'LL GET SOMETHING HOT AND CRISPY CONTAINING SOMETHING HOT AND GOOEY. GOOEY IS JUST SO AWESOME. YOU'LL NEED WOODEN SKEWERS FOR THIS.

SERVES 4 TO 6

STUFF YOU NEED

6 wooden skewers

12 Roma tomatoes

1 tablespoon (15 mL) olive oil

1 Spanish onion

10 cloves garlic

4 long red Italian chili peppers

¼ cup (60 mL) soy sauce

¼ cup (60 mL) fish sauce

¾ cup (180 mL) granulated sugar

¾ cup (180 mL) red wine vinegar

Kosher salt

1 box (10 oz/283 g)
  tempura batter mix

1 large piece (5–7 oz/150–200 g)
  Fontina cheese

TOMATO, TOMATO
(THAT ONLY WORKS WHEN YOU READ IT OUT LOUD)

Cut each tomato into four coins and discard the ends. Preheat the oven to 375°F (190°C). Put the tomatoes on a baking sheet and drizzle them with the 1 tablespoon (15 mL) of olive oil. Roast the tomatoes in the oven for approximately 30 minutes, or until soft and fully roasted.

Finely chop the onion and garlic cloves. In a large saucepan over medium-low heat, add a little bit of olive oil, and toss in the onion, garlic, chili peppers, soy sauce, and fish sauce. Stir continuously until the fish sauce is fully incorporated with the rest of the ingredients. Add the roasted tomatoes and all of the cooking juices to the saucepan, and then stir in the sugar and vinegar. Season to taste with salt. Cook the sauce, uncovered, for approximately 45 minutes, or until it reduces to a thicker jam. As it cools, you will notice the sugars thickening it up into a jam-like sauce.

THE BLANKET

Following the instructions on the box, prepare the tempura batter mix. Cut the fontina cheese into twelve pieces. Skewer each piece of cheese and dip them into the tempura batter to coat. In a wok, deep pan, or table-top deep-fryer, heat 1 ½ inches (4 cm) of canola oil to 360°F (185°C) and fully submerge the tempura-battered cheese. Deep-fry in batches of two or three for approximately 3 minutes, or until the batter is nice and crispy.

Place the fried cheese skewers on a serving platter with the tomato jam on the side for dipping.

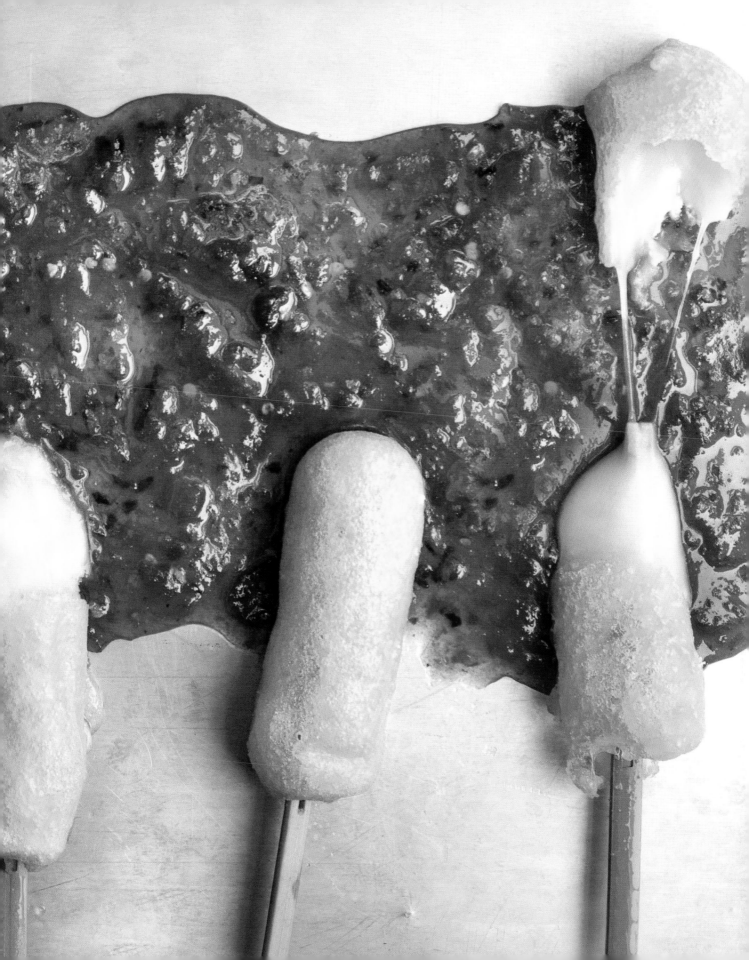

STUFF THAT'S IN BETWEEN BREAKFAST AND LUNCH

ANYONE WHO KNOWS ME WELL KNOWS I'M A SUCKER FOR A GOOD BRUNCH. I'M NOT SURE WHAT I LOVE MORE — COOKING IT, EATING IT, OR DOING BOTH AT 4 P.M. IN MY JAMMIES. AS FAR AS I'M CONCERNED, BRUNCH HAS NO RULES; THE BIGGER AND THE MORE ELABORATE IT IS, THE MORE OF A BRUNCH IT IS.

KY AND I TAKE BRUNCH AT OUR RESTAURANT, LISA MARIE, VERY SERIOUSLY IN AN IMMATURE KIND OF WAY. THE MENU WAS CAREFULLY DESIGNED TO BE EPIC. KIND OF LIKE SAYING, HEY, IF I HAD TO EAT JUST ONE THING TODAY, THIS WOULD BE IT.

(YA BRUNCH!)

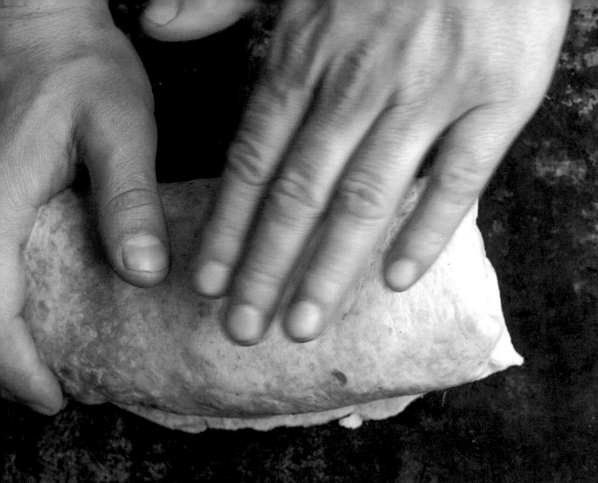

BBQ BRISKET BREAKFAST BURRITO

SERVES 10

THE BURRITO ADHERES TO THE SAME STREET FOOD PRINCIPLE AS PIZZA, MEATBALLS, AND TACOS. IT'S A BLANK CANVAS AND YOU HAVE THE FREEDOM TO PAINT WHATEVER FOOD MASTERPIECE YOU WANT ONTO IT. IT'S INCREDIBLY MOBILE AND THE PERFECT STREET FOOD BECAUSE IT CONTAINS AN ENTIRE MEAL IN ONE MASSIVE TORTILLA. YOUR HANDS ARE LITERALLY HOLDING BRUNCH. #YABRUNCH >>>

2 tablespoons (30 mL) kosher salt

2 tablespoons (30 mL)
  black pepper

2 tablespoons (30 mL)
  cayenne pepper

6 lb (3 kg) beef brisket

6 cups (1.5 L) ketchup, divided

4 cups (1 L) cola

1 cup (250 mL)
  Worcestershire sauce

1 cup (250 mL) short-grain
  white rice

2 green bell peppers

2 large Spanish onions

2 tablespoons (30 mL) olive oil

6 cobs of corn or 2 cans
  (12 oz/341 g each) of corn

2 cans (7 oz/190 g each) white
  beans, drained and rinsed

1 tablespoon (15 mL) molasses

¼ cup (60 mL) red wine vinegar

¼ cup (60 mL) brown sugar

12 eggs

10+ large flour tortillas

1 cup (250 mL) shredded
  cheddar cheese

BBQ WITHOUT THE PIT MASTER, OR THE PIT FOR THAT MATTER

Mix the salt, black pepper, and cayenne pepper together in a bowl. Rub this mixture all over the brisket. In a large bowl, mix three-quarters of the ketchup with the cola and Worcestershire sauce. Preheat the oven to 275°F (135°C). Place the brisket in a roasting pan, and pour the marinade over it. I would actually double this marinade recipe so that you can use it again when you are warming up the brisket. Add 1 cup (250 mL) of water, and then tightly cover the pan with a layer of plastic wrap and a layer of aluminum foil. Place the brisket in the oven and cook for approximately 5 hours, or until the meat just falls apart. Once the brisket is cooked, take it out of the oven and let it rest for approximately 1 hour or so.

Now for everything else burrito-related. Bring 2 cups (500 mL) of water to a boil in a large saucepan. Add the rice, and bring the water back to a boil over high heat. Turn down the heat to medium, cover the saucepan, and let cook until all the water has been absorbed, 15 to 20 minutes. If the rice still has some bite to it, add a little more boiling water and repeat the process until it's cooked.

Thinly slice the bell peppers and onions. Warm the olive oil in a nonstick or cast iron skillet over medium-high heat, and cook the bell peppers and onions for approximately 5 minutes, stirring, or until they darken a bit but still have some crunch. If you have purchased corn on the cob, bring a pot of water to a boil and toss in the shucked cobs. After about 8 minutes in the boiling water the corn should be tender. Remove the corn from the water with tongs and then shave the kernels off the cob into a bowl. Toss with some olive oil or a little bit of butter.

In another pan, pour in the white beans, then add the remaining 1 ½ cups (375 mL) of ketchup, molasses, vinegar, and brown sugar. Mix it all around and cook it over low heat for approximately 30 minutes, or until the beans are good and sticky.

Melt some butter in a pan and begin to scramble the eggs over medium-low heat, stirring, for 8 to 10 minutes, or until the eggs become fluffy. Slice the brisket, widthwise, into pieces that are 1 ¼ to 1 ½ inches (3 to 4 cm) thick. Pour some of the braising liquid from the brisket over the beans. Throw the brisket slices in a skillet over high heat with some of the braising liquid as well and cover the brisket with some of that extra BBQ sauce that you made. Warm the brisket through.

ROLL 'EM UP

Take the tortillas and fill them with rice, cheese, brisket, beans, grilled veg, and corn. Roll them nice and tight. Place the burritos in a clean nonstick skillet, and grill them for approximately 2 minutes on each side over medium heat.

Halfway through this recipe you're probably asking yourself, Matt, why didn't you tell us to make the brisket the day before to save some time? Okay, so this is me telling you that now ... Feel free to make the brisket in advance to save some time.

YOUR HANDS ARE LITERALLY HOLDING BRUNCH

LA BARBECUE AUSTIN, TEXAS

I EVEN HEARD AFTER WE LEFT THAT THERE'S THIS ONLINE SERVICE THAT LETS YOU RENT A BODY TO WAIT IN LINE FOR YOU. WHAT?!? FOR REALS?!?

I THOUGHT I HAD SEEN CRAZY STREET FOOD LINEUPS IN TORONTO — THEN I GOT TO AUSTIN, TEXAS. I WENT TO A BBQ SPOT CALLED LA BARBECUE, AND ... I DON'T REALLY KNOW HOW TO CLASSIFY IT, SINCE IT'S NOT A TRUCK AT ALL BUT THREE SEPARATE TRAILERS, ONE FOR SERVICE AND TWO FOR SMOKING (SMOKING MEAT, I MEAN). I WENT INSIDE THEM, AND ONE TRAILER HAD 50 BRISKETS SMOKING WITH 50 PORK SHOULDERS BENEATH THEM. THE OTHER TRAILER HAD BEEF RIBS, PORK RIBS, AND SAUSAGES. THE SMELL WAS ALL-ENCOMPASSING. AND THEN ... MY WORLD ... WAS BLOWN AWAY. OUR FOOD TRUCK CAN GET REALLY BUSY, SAME GOES FOR OUR RESTAURANT, LISA MARIE. WE HAVE TWO VERY BUSY FOOD BUSINESSES. BUT THEN THERE'S LA BARBECUE BUSY.

HERE WE ARE SETTING UP WITH THE CREW FROM OUR TV SHOW, *REBEL WITHOUT A KITCHEN*, AT ABOUT 9 A.M. AT THE LA BARBECUE TRAILER. BY 11 A.M. THEY HAD A LINEUP 100-PEOPLE DEEP. BY NOON THERE WERE PROBABLY AROUND 200 PEOPLE, AND BY 3 P.M. THEY WERE COMPLETELY SOLD OUT. IT WAS LIKE NOTHING I HAD EVER SEEN BEFORE. AND PEOPLE WERE JUST HAPPY WITH WHATEVER THEY COULD GET THEIR HANDS ON. I EVEN HEARD AFTER WE LEFT THAT THERE'S THIS ONLINE SERVICE THAT LETS YOU RENT A BODY TO WAIT IN LINE FOR YOU. WHAT?!? FOR REALS?!?

la BARBECUE

EST. 2012

I ATE EVERYTHING — BEEF RIBS, PULLED PORK, SAUSAGES — BUT WHAT STOOD OUT WAS THE BRISKET. BRISKET IN TEXAS IS KIND OF A BIG DEAL. IT'S THE BIGGEST THING NEXT TO BEER AND BASEBALL. FROM WHAT I WAS TOLD, YOUR OVERALL BBQ RANKING WAS ULTIMATELY DETERMINED BY YOUR BRISKET. I'VE HAD SOME GOOD BRISKET BEFORE AND I HAVE HAD SOME HORRIBLE BRISKET — SO DRY THAT IT'S LIKE CHEWING ON A MOUSE PAD. WELL, LET ME TELL YOU SOMETHING, YOU HAVE TRULY NEVER REALLY EXPERIENCED BRISKET UNTIL YOU'VE HAD THIS STUFF. THIS WAS THE MOST TENDER, JUICY BRISKET I HAD EVER HAD. IN FACT, THIS WAS THE BEST BBQ I HAD EVER HAD, PERIOD. NOW, I KNOW PEOPLE WILL HECKLE ME AND GIVE ME SHIT FOR THIS CLAIM, BUT HONESTLY? IF YOU CAN SELL OUT OF HUNDREDS AND HUNDREDS OF BBQ GOODS EVERY DAY FROM A PARKING LOT TRAILER THEN YOU KNOW WHAT YOU'RE DOING, AND YOU DEFINITELY DESERVE SOME SORT OF "BEST" RANKING.

AND THEN YOU MEET THE PIT MASTER, JOHN LEWIS, AND IT JUST DOESN'T ADD UP. AFTER I'VE EATEN POUNDS OF THE MOST DELICIOUS BBQ I'VE EVER HAD, OUT COMES THIS SKINNY, CALM DUDE WITH MASSIVE GLASSES. THE TWO IMAGES JUST DON'T FIT. I THOUGHT PIT MASTERS WERE BIG AND LOUD? REGARDLESS, JOHN WAS AND IS THE REAL DEAL. AFTER I ASKED HIM A COUPLE QUESTIONS, I FOUND OUT THAT HE USED TO BE A PASTRY CHEF. ALTHOUGH I WAS TAKEN ABACK BY THIS AT FIRST, IT ACTUALLY MADE QUITE A BIT OF SENSE. BAKING AND PASTRIES ARE ALL ABOUT PRECISION AND SCIENCE, AND I'VE GOT TO SAY THAT PRODUCING BBQ ON THIS KIND OF LEVEL, THIS CONSISTENTLY, AND FOR THIS MANY PEOPLE IS TOTALLY A SCIENCE. FROM CHAMBER HEAT, TO PRODUCT FAT CONTENT, TO SMOKE DISTRIBUTION, TO TIMING AND PROCESS, LA BARBECUE HAS MASTERED THE SMOKY SCIENCE OF TEXAS BBQ.

BENNY AND THE BAGUETTES

I LOVE A GOOD, CLASSIC EGGS BENEDICT. BUT TO BE HONEST, AFTER HAVING HAD IT THE SAME WAY ABOUT 100 TIMES I REALIZED IT WAS DEFINITELY ONE OF THOSE DISHES THAT CAN BE COMPLETELY TRANSFORMED WHILE PAYING RESPECT TO ITS ORIGINAL BRUNCH STATE.

SERVES 6

THE HOLLANDAISE SHUFFLE

Half-fill a saucepan with water and bring it to a simmer. Use some elbow grease to whisk the egg yolks in a bowl with the lemon juice until the yolks double in size. Place the bowl over the water in the saucepan. Do not let the bowl touch the water. If the egg yolks get too hot, they will scramble. In that case you would need to start from scratch. Slowly drizzle in the melted butter, and keep whisking. Once the yolks have thickened again, add the cayenne pepper and salt. Keep the hollandaise in a warm place but not over direct heat while you prep the rest of this dish. It's important to note that this is a 4-hour sauce. If it sits out any longer, you should consider making a new batch.

BA BA BA BENNY AND THE JETSSSSSSS

Bring another saucepan of water to a simmer. Add the vinegar and then crack the eggs into the simmering water. Poach the eggs by creating a little vortex around the egg with a spoon. After 5 or 6 minutes, use a draining spoon to remove the eggs from the water.

Preheat the oven to 350°F (180°C) while the eggs are cooking. Grill the ham in a hot skillet (no oil required) over high heat. Toast the uncut baguette in the oven for approximately 5 minutes, or until toasted to your liking. Cut the baguette into six equal sections, and then slice them to make mini baguette sandwiches by filling it with ham, a poached egg, some hollandaise sauce, and chives. Add some hot sauce if you need to kick it up a notch.

4 egg yolks

Juice from 1 lemon

½ cup (125 mL) melted unsalted butter

½ teaspoon (2 mL) cayenne pepper

½ teaspoon (2 mL) kosher salt

½ cup (125 mL) white vinegar

6 eggs

6–12 slices thick-cut Italian ham

1 rustic baguette

1 bunch chives, finely chopped

BIGGED-UP PANCAKE PORK BURGERS

SERVES 5

COMING UP WITH THIS DISH WAS ACTUALLY A LOT OF FUN. I LOVE PANCAKES. I LOVE SAUSAGE CAKES. I LOVE BURGERS. HMMM, HOW DO WE TAKE ALL THESE ELEMENTS AND MAKE ONE DISH FROM THEM? THE DOUBLE-DECKER PANCAKE PORK BURGER JUST MADE SENSE. EAT IT WITH YOUR HANDS OR WITH A KNIFE AND FORK. USE WHATEVER YOU WANT — JUST MAKE SURE YOU DON'T LEAVE A DROP OF SYRUP BEHIND.

1 ½ cups (375 mL) all-purpose flour

3 ½ teaspoons (17.5 mL) baking powder

2 teaspoons (10 mL) kosher salt, divided

1 teaspoon (5 mL) granulated sugar

1 ¼ cups (310 mL) 2% milk

1 egg

3 tablespoons (45 mL) melted unsalted butter

1 ½ lb (750 g) ground pork

1 teaspoon (5 mL) garlic powder

1 teaspoon (5 mL) all-spice

1 teaspoon (5 mL) black pepper

10 slices American cheddar

1 cup (250 mL) shredded iceberg lettuce

2 Roma tomatoes, thinly sliced

1 cup (250 mL) maple syrup (not pancake syrup!)

PANCAKES ARE ALL GROWN UP NOW

In a large bowl, sift together the flour, baking powder, 1 teaspoon (5 mL) of the salt, and the sugar. Make a center with your fist and pour in the milk, crack in the egg, and add the melted butter. Mix your little heart out until the mixture is smooth. Heat a lightly buttered griddle or skillet over medium-high heat, and pour a small ladleful of batter onto the griddle. Just keep in mind the size of your pancakes because they will be the bun for your burger and you don't want them too big or too small. Cook for approximately 4 minutes on each side, or until brown on both sides. Repeat with the remaining batter (approximately 15 small pancakes).

I LOVE THE SMELL OF PORK IN THE MORNING

For the pork burgers, season the pork with the remaining 1 teaspoon (5 mL) of salt, the garlic powder, all-spice, and pepper. Mix everything well, and use your hands to shape the meat into ten evenly sized patties. Grill the burgers in a skillet with a little bit of vegetable oil over medium-high heat for 3 to 4 minutes per side, or until the juices run clear.

Build a double-decker pancake burger using three pancakes as buns with two patties, cheese on each patty and topped with lettuce and tomato. Pour maple syrup over it all for pure enjoyment.

BRAISED PEAMEAL ON A BUN

AFTER BEING ON THE ROAD ACROSS NORTH AMERICA AND TOTALLY FEASTING ON THE LOCAL STREET FOOD EVERYWHERE I WENT, IT BECAME INCREASINGLY HARDER FOR ME TO FIGURE OUT WHAT TORONTO'S SIGNATURE DISH IS. DESPITE THERE BEING STILL QUITE A BIT OF FOG AROUND IT, I THINK THE PEAMEAL SANDWICH IS TORONTO'S OFFICIALLY UNOFFICIAL DISH. #HOGTOWN. TRY TO BUY THE PEAMEAL THAT COMES IN A LOG FOR THIS.

A CANADIAN TRADITION OF ALL THINGS PIG

So, braising peameal isn't really what people do. And that's why we do it. Take the log of peameal and place it in a deep roasting pan. Preheat the oven to 310°F (155°C). Melt the butter in the microwave. Add the orange juice and half the teriyaki sauce to the bowl of melted butter. Mix well. Pour the buttery orange mixture over the peameal, and tightly cover the pan with a layer of plastic wrap and a layer of aluminum foil. Place the peameal in the oven and cook for 3 to 4 hours, or until the meat just falls apart when you poke it with a fork.

While the peameal braises, thinly slice the onions and slowly cook them in a pan with a little bit of the oil over medium-low heat for approximately 15 minutes, or until they have caramelized.

PULL THEE PIG

When the peameal is ready, break apart all the meat — it will just fall apart the second you stab it with a fork — then cover it again to keep it hot.

Beat three of the eggs and put them in a bowl. Cut each tomato into about six slices. Dredge the tomato slices in the flour, then dip them into the beaten eggs, and then into cornmeal. In a skillet, add the oil to a depth of about ½ inch (1 cm), warm it over high heat, and fry the tomato for approximately 3 minutes, or until the cornmeal is nice and crispy. In a separate skillet, fry the remaining eggs for approximately 6 minutes, or until the whites are cooked but the yolks are still runny.

When everything is ready, place a slice of cheese on the bottom of each bun, then top with peameal bacon and onions. Throw on a fried green tomato slice, and lastly a fried egg. Now, that's a bacon sandwich.

SERVES 12

5 lb (2.3 kg) peameal bacon

1 lb (500 g) salted butter

8 cups (2 L) orange juice

1 bottle (12 oz/355 mL) teriyaki sauce

2 large Spanish onions

1 cup (250 mL) canola oil

15 eggs

2 green tomatoes

1 cup (250 mL) all-purpose flour

1 cup (250 mL) cornmeal

12 buns

12 slices American cheese

HUEVO RANCHERO TOSTADA

NOT ALL BRUNCH ITEMS HAVE TO BE ABSOLUTELY MASSIVE. MOST, SURE, BUT NOT ALL OF THEM. I LOVE THIS DISH BECAUSE IT'S A GREAT EXAMPLE OF HOW NORTH AMERICAN AND LATIN AMERICAN CAN WORK TOGETHER PERFECTLY TO MAKE AN INCREDIBLY TASTY DISH. WHAT I LOVE MOST ABOUT IT IS THAT YOU HAVE HOT, SPICY, SAUCY, CREAMY, AND COOL ALL COMING TOGETHER ON TOP OF ONE CRUNCHY LITTLE TOSTADA SHELL.

SERVES 6 TO 12

THE RANCHERO

In a large bowl, season the ground pork with the cayenne pepper, smoked paprika, 1 teaspoon (5 mL) of the salt, and the pepper. Toss the pork in a large skillet, and brown the meat over high heat for approximately 3 minutes. Finely chop the onion and jalapeño peppers. Once the meat has browned, add the onion, jalapeño peppers, both types of beans, and the canned tomatoes with their juice. Stir everything so all the ingredients are covered with the tomatoes. Add 2 cups (500 mL) of water, the chili powder, and 1 teaspoon (5 mL) of the salt. Let this ranchero sauce cook, uncovered, for approximately 1 hour — keep the heat low so that you do not burn the bottom.

In a bowl, smash up the avocados, and add the Roma tomatoes, cilantro, and lime juice with the remaining ½ teaspoon (2.5 mL) of salt. Give it all a good smashing with your fork but leave it as chunky as you want.

THE HUEVO

When your ranchero sauce is almost complete, start to fry the quail eggs in a small nonstick skillet with a little bit of vegetable oil over medium heat for approximately 3 minutes, or until the whites have cooked. They don't take long to cook but I suggest cooking no more than four at a time, otherwise they will all stick together and some might be overcooked.

Build the tostada by layering each shell with a healthy portion of guacamole, a healthier portion of ranchero sauce, a wee little quail egg, and some crumbled queso fresco.

- 1 lb (500 g) coarsely ground pork
- 1 tablespoon (15 mL) cayenne pepper
- 1 tablespoon (15 mL) smoked paprika
- 2 ½ teaspoons (12.5 mL) kosher salt, divided
- 1 teaspoon (5 mL) black pepper
- 1 Spanish onion, finely chopped
- 2 jalapeño peppers, finely chopped
- 1 can (14 oz/398 mL) black beans, drained and rinsed
- 1 can (14 oz/398 mL) pinto beans, drained and rinsed
- 1 can (26 oz/796 mL) diced tomatoes
- 2 tablespoons (30 mL) chili powder
- 3 ripe avocados
- 2 Roma tomatoes, chopped into small cubes (no seeds please)
- ½ cup (125 mL) finely chopped cilantro
- Juice from 2 limes
- 12 quail eggs
- 12 tostada shells
- ½ cup (125 mL) queso fresco (fresh cheese)

BISON MEATBALL HASH

SERVES 4

HASH DISHES ARE A STAPLE OF AMERICAN BREAKFAST COMFORT FOOD. CARROTS, ONIONS, AND POTATOES ARE WHAT MAKE IT HASH, AND THE REST CAN REALLY BE A COMBINATION OF LEFTOVERS. CORNED BEEF HASH, SHRIMP HASH, AND PULLED PORK HASH ARE ALL VERY POPULAR. IN THIS CASE WE'RE GOING TO ADD GAME MEAT AND GIVE THAT HASH A LITTLE MORE OOMPH TO TAKE IT BEYOND THAT DISH YOU SIMPLY PUT YOUR LEFTOVERS IN. >>>

1 Yukon Gold potato

1 large Spanish onion

1 large carrot

3 large stalks of celery

2 lb (1 kg) ground bison

1 teaspoon (5 mL) cumin

1 teaspoon (5 mL) garlic powder

1 tablespoon (15 mL) smoked paprika

1 teaspoon (5 mL) dried oregano

4 oz (100 g) Parmesan cheese

1 tablespoon (15 mL) olive oil

1 tablespoon (15 mL) butter

1 teaspoon (5 mL) kosher salt

1 teaspoon (5 mL) black pepper

1 ½ cups (375 mL) tomato sauce (see recipe on page 73)

4 eggs

THE MISE EN PLACE (FRENCH FOR "ALL YOUR LITTLE CHOPPED BITS ORGANIZED NEATLY")

Use a cheese grater to shred the potato. Once the entire potato has been shredded, place it in a bowl and fill the bowl with cold water so that the potato doesn't go brown on you. Then finely chop the onion, carrot, and celery, keeping them all separate.

THE BISON BALLS

Place the ground bison meat in a large bowl and season with the cumin, garlic powder, paprika, dried oregano, and about 1 teaspoon (5 mL) of grated Parmesan. Roll the meat into as many ping-pong-ball-sized meatballs as you can. Now you have all your ingredients in place to make some mighty fine bison ball (meatball) hash.

THE HASH

Warm the olive oil in a large frying pan on high heat and sear the meatballs so that they have a nice crispy brown exterior. Once the balls have been seared, toss in the potato, onion, carrot, and celery. Stir it all around really well so that the ingredients soak up all the oil. Then add the butter, salt, pepper, and tomato sauce. Give one last good stir, and turn the heat down to medium-low. Let it simmer in the pan, uncovered, for about 10 minutes.

After about 10 minutes, your sauce will have reduced a bit and gotten nice and hot. Crack the eggs into the hash pan, covering the meat and other ingredients. Allow the eggs to cook in the pan with the other ingredients. If you don't have a large enough pan, break this step into two parts (two eggs in one pan, two in another). After about 5 minutes of cooking, your hash is done. Use a large spoon or spatula to grab all the ingredients and rustic place it on a plate. Grate the remaining Parmesan cheese over the entire dish.

GIVE THAT HASH
A LITTLE MORE
OOMPH

ELVIS IN A JAR

IT'S A WELL-KNOWN FACT THAT ELVIS'S FAVORITE SANDWICH WAS A PEANUT BUTTER, BACON, AND BANANA SANDWICH. NOW, I'VE ALWAYS ADMIRED THE KING. HE WAS DIFFERENT IN A TIME OF STATIC. HE WAS ROCK 'N' ROLL IN A TIME OF CROONERS. KY CAME UP WITH THIS RECIPE, AND IT CONTINUES TO BE ONE OF OUR MOST TALKED-ABOUT DISHES AT OUR RESTAURANT, LISA MARIE. YOU'LL NEED EIGHT (1 CUP/250 ML) MASON JARS FOR THIS. AND THE PEANUT BUTTER SHOULD BE THE SWEETENED KIND.

WELCOME TO THE HEARTBREAK HOTEL OF WHISKING

Where to begin? The zabaglione is the hardest part of this dish, so maybe let's get that out of the way first. Find a large glass or metal bowl and a pot that will fit the bowl snuggly but still be large enough that there is space between the bottom of your bowl and the water in the pot. The water mustn't touch the bottom of the bowl. (You got all that?) Boil the pot of water over high heat, and then turn down the heat to medium-low and allow the water to simmer. Carefully place the bowl in the pot, and mix the egg yolks with the sugar in that bowl. Whisk thoroughly and quickly, never letting the mixture rest. Slowly pour in the Marsala, and remove the bowl from the heat. Continue to whisk. You're looking to make a thick, foamy, velvety, yellow cream. Once you get it like this, first give yourself a pat on the back and then cover the zabaglione before you put it in the fridge. Cut the bananas into small pieces and cook them for approximately 5 minutes in a nonstick pan over medium heat with 1 tablespoon (15 mL) of the maple syrup.

LITTLE LESS CONVERSATION, LITTLE MORE BACON, PLEASE

Preheat the oven to 400°F (200°C). Cut each slice of bacon in half, place the pieces on a baking sheet, and bake for about 8 minutes. Mix the remaining maple syrup with the rum. Remove the bacon from the oven, paint each slice with the maple syrup–rum mixture, and return to the oven to bake for another 4 minutes. Check the bacon. If it isn't crispy enough for your liking, bake it for a few more minutes. Be careful. The bacon can go from undercooked to burnt very quickly. When the bacon comes out super crispy, give it one more brush of maple syrup–rum. Take half the bacon and chop it into small pieces. Keep the remainder as full pieces. ❯ ❯ ❯

STUFF YOU NEED

8 (1 cup/250 mL) mason jars

4 egg yolks
¼ cup (60 mL) granulated sugar
¼ cup (60 mL) Marsala
2 bananas
½ cup (125 mL) maple syrup, divided
8 slices bacon
2 oz (60 mL) dark rum
2 cups (500 mL) whipping cream
1 cup (250 mL) smooth peanut butter
6 eggs
¼ cup (60 mL) milk
8 slices brioche bread
2 tablespoons (30 mL) unsalted butter

> > > Pour the whipping cream into a bowl and use an electric mixer to give it body. After soft peaks form, add the peanut butter to the mixing bowl and continue to mix until you have peanut butter whipped cream. Place it in the fridge, uncovered, right next to that zabaglione.

Last stop! Beat the eggs together in a bowl with the milk to make an egg wash. Cut each slice of brioche bread into quarters, and dip them into the egg wash. Melt a little bit of butter in a nonstick pan over medium heat, and grill the bread, in batches, for approximately 2 minutes on each side, until golden brown.

HOUND DOGS LIKE ALL THINGS BACON AND SYRUP

Build these bad boys in the jars. Take a piece of French toast and use it as the first layer in the jar. Then build up with a layer of the zabaglione, then crumbled candied bacon, followed by banana slices. Top with another piece of French toast. Slather it with peanut butter whipped cream, and finish this kingly dessert off with a nice half-slice of candied bacon in the middle of your masterpiece and sticking out at the top. The zabaglione and the peanut butter whipped cream might need a quick little whip up with a fork or spoon before they go in.

ELVIS'S FAVORITE

SANDWICH IN A JAR

CAREFULLY
DESIGNED TO
BE EPIC

LEFSA

BASICALLY, A LEFSA IS A NORWEGIAN TORTILLA — MADE FROM POTATO. IT HAS TO BE ROLLED PAPER THIN OR ELSE IT JUST DOESN'T WORK. WHAT MAKES IT STAND OUT IS THE OLIVE OIL. WHEN THE RAW LEFSA HITS THAT GRILL THE AROMA OF OLIVE OIL JUST FILLS THE AIR. THEN YOU GET TO STUFF IT WITH ANYTHING YOU LIKE — A NORWEGIAN BURRITO OF SORTS. LEFSA ARE LIKE POTATO FLATBREADS/TORTILLAS (SEE THE VIKING SOUL FOOD STORY ON PAGE 268). AND ALTHOUGH YOU ONLY NEED FOUR INGREDIENTS TO MAKE THEM, YOU NEED A ROLLING PIN AND SOME SORT OF DEVICE TO PICK THEM UP WITHOUT BREAKING THEM WHEN YOU TRANSFER THEM TO A SKILLET FOR COOKING. (I USE A LONG SPATULA.) ALSO, I SUGGEST MAKING THE POTATO DOUGH THE DAY BEFORE YOU PLAN TO EAT THESE.

STUFF YOU NEED

Rolling pin

Long spatula

6 russet potatoes

½–1 cup (125–250 mL) extra virgin olive oil

3–4 cups (750 mL–1 L) all-purpose flour

Kosher salt

LEFSA

First, peel the potatoes, place them in a large saucepan of salted water, and bring the water to a boil. Cook the potatoes until they are really soft. Once they're cooked, transfer the potatoes to a bowl or large container and use a masher to mash them good. Pour in ½ cup (125 mL) of the olive oil, and continue to mash some more. You want a lot of oil. You'll see it start to pool in pockets in the potatoes. Watch carefully so that you can catch them before they start to look dry. Start with ½ cup (125 mL), but have extra on hand in case. Let the potatoes cool in the bowl or container to room temperature, and then give them one final big stir. Transfer the mashed potatoes to a large bowl and place them in the fridge overnight.

The next day, add 1 cup (250 mL) of flour to the bowl of potatoes, working it in with your hands. Cover your table or wooden cutting board with more flour. Take a handful of the potato and put it down on the flour. Then add more flour to the potato, and continue to work it with your hands until the ball looks more like dough than potato. Form the dough into ten evenly sized balls.

Grab your rolling pin and cover it with flour. Roll one piece of dough out super thin. I'm talking paper thin. If you're using a board, move it close to your cooking surface. Use a plug-in griddle pan or a large nonstick skillet and get it on high heat. Gently use your tool (your long spatula, or whatever you decided to use) to get under the lefsa and place it on the hot grill. You don't need to use oil because there's already so much in the potato. You will see the lefsa start to bubble and give off an awesome cooking smell thanks to the olive oil. Allow it to cook for approximately 3 minutes, or until you see it bubble, and then give it one flip on the pan to allow it to cook on the other side. After approximately 2 minutes, remove your lefsa and lightly salt. Repeat with the remaining dough.

Use lefsa immediately or store in an airtight container in the fridge for up to 2 days.

LEFSA WITH SALMON SALAD AND DRUNKEN CRANBERRIES

SERVES 10 TO 12

IN THIS CASE WE ARE STUFFING LEFSA WITH COLD ITEMS SO THAT IT CAN STRADDLE THAT SWEET AND SAVORY PLACE. THE CREAM CHEESE AND THE BEER JAM ARE YOUR MAJOR FLAVOR AND TEXTURE CONTRIBUTORS. THE FISH SALAD IS REALLY JUST THE PROTEIN, SO FEEL FREE TO MIX IT UP HOWEVER YOUR NORWEGIAN HEART DESIRES.

THE SAUCE

It's better if you have the time to make this sauce beforehand so you can refrigerate it and let the sugars congeal. To make your sauce, put the frozen cranberries into a pot, and pour in the beer and maple syrup. Then add 1 cup (250 mL) of water and let it cook at a simmer, uncovered, for approximately 45 minutes over medium heat or until it reduces. Using a spoon, crush the cranberries so that even more flavors unleash into your sauce.

THE SALMON

Preheat the oven to 375°F (190°C) and line two baking sheets with parchment paper. Rub the salmon with 1 tablespoon (15 mL) of the olive oil, thyme, salt, pepper, and juice from one of the lemons. Place the salmon on one of the prepared baking sheets and put it in the oven. Bake the salmon for approximately 20 minutes. Remove the leafy tips from the fennel and place them in a bowl of water to soak until you are ready to use them as garnish. Cut the stems off the fennel and then cube the bulb. Rub the fennel cubes with 1 tablespoon (15 mL) of the olive oil, salt, and pepper. Put this on the other baking sheet and put it in the oven for approximately 20 minutes. When the salmon and fennel are both fully roasted, pull them out of the oven and let them cool to room temperature. ❯❯❯

- 2 cups (500 mL) frozen cranberries
- 1 pint (16 oz/470 mL) dark beer
- ½ cup (125 mL) maple syrup
- 4 lb (2 kg) boneless, skinless salmon fillet
- 1 cup (250 mL) olive oil, divided
- 6 sprigs fresh thyme, stems removed
- Kosher salt
- Black pepper
- Juice from 4 lemons, divided
- 1 whole fennel
- 4 English cucumbers
- 2 red bell peppers
- 1 bunch green onions
- ¼ cup (60 mL) Dijon mustard
- ¼ cup (60 mL) mayonnaise
- 4 cloves garlic
- 1 cup (250 mL) cream cheese
- ¼ cup + 2 tablespoons (100 mL) ricotta cheese
- 10 to 12 lefsa (see page 260)

››› Once cooled, shred the salmon in a bowl, and then finely chop the fennel into small pieces and add it to the bowl. Do the same with the cucumbers, bell peppers, and green onions. Cut the cucumber into three large pieces and then cut each piece lengthwise into quarters. Take your knife and slice the seeds right off the top and then chop your cucumber into small dice. Mix it all together with some Dijon mustard, mayo, juice from two and a half lemons, and salt and pepper to taste.

Crush the garlic. Combine the garlic with the cream cheese, ricotta cheese, and the remaining lemon juice in a blender, and blitz until smooth. Spread the ricotta cream cheese on the lefsa, and top with salmon salad, cranberry sauce, and fennel tips.

SWEET & SAVORY

BRUNCH HAS NO RULES

S'MORE FRENCH TOAST SAMMICHES

SO, YOU ASK, WHAT IS THIS DISH EXACTLY? TAKE THE IDEA OF S'MORES, THEN TAKE FRENCH TOAST … AND TA-DA, WE HAVE OUR DISH. MY FAVORITE CHOCOLATE HAZELNUT SPREAD FOR THIS? NUTELLA. NEED I SAY MORE?

WANT S'MORE?

Cut the loaf of brioche bread into ¼-inch (0.5 cm) slices if it wasn't pre-sliced. Take two slices of bread and spread chocolate hazelnut spread on one slice and marshmallow fluff on the other. Crumble up the graham crackers, and put some on top of one slice. Close it like you would any other sandwich. Beat the eggs in a bowl, and dip the sandwich into the egg.

Melt the butter in a nonstick pan over medium heat, and grill the French toast sandwich for 2 to 3 minutes per side, or until it gets a nice brown color. Transfer the sandwich to a plate, cut it in half, and drizzle with maple syrup. Make as many sandwiches as you can from the jars of chocolate hazelnut spread and marshmallow fluff, but if you're a liberal spreader and like to eat both contents directly from the jars, maybe you'll be lucky to get two.

1 loaf brioche bread

1 jar (13 oz/375 g) chocolate hazelnut spread

1 jar (7 oz/200 g) marshmallow fluff

20 graham crackers

6 eggs

2 tablespoons (30 mL) unsalted butter

¼ cup + 2 tablespoons (100 mL) maple syrup (not pancake syrup)

VIKING SOUL FOOD, PORTLAND, OREGON

PORTLAND, OREGON, IS KIND OF LIKE AUSTIN, TEXAS — LOTS
OF FOOD TRUCKS AND CARTS, AND LOTS OF OPTIONS ... KIND OF.
I MEAN, TACOS AND THAI FOOD ARE PRETTY POPULAR WHEN YOU
ENTER THE MANY, MANY STREET FOOD HUBS THAT PORTLAND HAS
TO OFFER, BUT THEN ALL OF A SUDDEN YOU COME ACROSS THE
VIKING SOUL FOOD CART AND IT'S LIKE YOUR CONFUSION AND
INTRIGUE ARE JUST MASKED BY HUNGER AND WHAT YOU HOPE
ARE VIKING-SIZED PORTIONS OF WHO KNOWS WHAT ANIMAL.

Viking
Soul
Food

CONQUER the GENERIC

"HEY, MATT, WHERE YOU GOING TODAY, DUDE?" "OH, YOU KNOW, JUST GOING FOR A SWIM THEN OUT FOR SOME VIKING SOUL FOOD. YOU IN?" DO YOU KNOW HOW BADASS THAT SOUNDS?

THE CUISINE OF THE VIKING SOUL FOOD CART IS NORWEGIAN AND HAS UNIQUE FLAVOR COMBINATIONS AND CONSISTENCIES. I HAD A LEFSA, WHICH CAN ONLY BE REALLY UNDERSTOOD AS A POTATO TORTILLA. IT WAS FILLED WITH SWEET, BEEFY MEATBALLS, LINGONBERRIES, PURPLE SAUERKRAUT, AND A HALF-GRAVY-HALF-CHEESE WHEY SAUCE. I CAN HONESTLY SAY I HAVE NEVER EATEN ANYTHING LIKE IT. I'M NOT TALKING PORTLAND OR FOOD TRUCK, I MEAN, LIKE *EVER*. AND IT JUST SOUNDED PROFOUND. "HEY, MATT, WHERE YOU GOING TODAY, DUDE?" "OH, YOU KNOW, JUST GOING FOR A SWIM THEN OUT FOR SOME VIKING SOUL FOOD. YOU IN?" DO YOU KNOW HOW BADASS THAT SOUNDS? EATING THE FOOD OF VIKINGS?

IT'S RARE TO MEET SOMEONE WHO YOU CLICK WITH INSTANTLY. I REMEMBER SITTING AT METRO HALL IN TORONTO ABOUT 3 YEARS AGO — I HAD JUST STARTED MY COMPANY AND FELT IT WAS IMPORTANT TO NOT ONLY TRY NEW RECIPES AND NETWORK BUT ALSO EDUCATE MYSELF ABOUT THE GROWING AND EVER-CHANGING RED TAPE THAT TORONTO'S STREET FOOD INDUSTRY IS FACED WITH. THERE WERE MANY SPEAKERS THAT DAY, BUT ONE IN PARTICULAR REALLY GOT KY AND ME INTERESTED IN THE ADVOCACY ELEMENT OF THIS BUSINESS. SHE SPOKE WITH EMPATHY, EXPERIENCE, AUTHORITY, AND COMPASSION. OPTIMISM WAS HER FUEL, AND HELPING OTHERS WAS HER PASSION. WE WERE HOOKED ON MARIANNE MORONEY.

MARIANNE WAS A TRAINED ACTRESS WHO MOVED TO TORONTO AND STARTED VENDING JEWELRY IN 1992. PARKED OUTSIDE OF TORONTO'S MOUNT SINAI HOSPITAL, SHE REALIZED THAT MORE AND MORE PEOPLE WOULD TRY TO ORDER FOOD FROM HER, DESPITE HER ONLY SELLING JEWELRY. SO LIKE ANY OTHER SPITFIRE BUSINESS OWNER SHE ADDED HOTDOGS TO HER LICENCE AND SOLD DOGS

Peameal Bacon
Pulled Pork
Salads

Boar · Elk · Bison
Dogs and Sausages
Quinoa   Soup

lates

608

IN THE WORDS OF MARIANNE, PEACE TOGETHER FOREVER.

MARIANNE MORONEY, PTF FOOD CART, TORONTO

AND SAUSAGES ALONGSIDE THE JEWELRY, WITH A SIDE OF FRESH FRUIT, BERRIES, AND GELATO. LITERALLY SELLING EVERYTHING NOW BUT THE KITCHEN SINK, MARIANNE DID ALL THIS AS THE CITY AROUND HER CONTINUED TO MESS WITH FOOD POLICY.

IN 2011, TORONTO'S INFAMOUSLY FAILED À LA CART PROGRAM FORCED MANY VENDORS OUT OF BUSINESS AND OFF THE STREETS. NOT ONLY WAS MARIANNE FIGHTING FOR THEIR RIGHTS AT CITY HALL, BUT SHE WAS ALSO TRYING TO INNOVATE HER OWN CART. SHE PARTNERED WITH BARBERIAN'S STEAK HOUSE AND SOLD THEIR ROAST BEEF, PULLED PORK, CORNED BEEF, AND PEAMEAL BACON. LATER THAT SAME YEAR SHE STARTED TO PREPARE WILD MEAT SAUSAGES: BOAR, ELK, AND BISON, WITH A SIDE OF BAKED SWEET POTATO.

FROM THERE MARIANNE CREATED THE ONE DISH THAT HAS ALWAYS BEEN A MASSIVE PART OF WHO SHE IS AS A PERSON BUT JUST NEEDED TO FIND ALL THE RIGHT INGREDIENTS TO BRING IT TOGETHER: THE LOVE PLATE. A BAKED SWEET POTATO WITH GAME MEAT SAUSAGE, QUINOA, AND COCONUT AND CRANBERRY SPREADS BECAME HER MOST POPULAR ITEM AND REALLY SUMMED UP WHY PEOPLE LINE UP TO EAT HER FOOD. MARIANNE LOVES PEOPLE. TO BE A REALLY GOOD STREET FOOD VENDOR YOU NEED THIS QUALITY, BECAUSE ALL YOU DO IS INTERACT WITH THEM. SHE KNOWS THEIR NAMES, WHAT THEY ORDER, AND HOW OLD THEIR KIDS ARE. MARIANNE IS JUST ONE OF THOSE PEOPLE WHO CARES SO MUCH ABOUT THE WORLD AROUND HER AND HAS MADE BREAKING INTO THE WORLD OF TORONTO STREET FOOD POSSIBLE. SHE IS THE VERY REASON WHY TRUCKS AND POP-UP EVENTS EXIST TODAY. ANYONE IN TORONTO WHO WANTS TO GET INTO THE STREET FOOD WORLD SHOULD AT SOME POINT WALK OVER TO THE PTF CART AT MOUNT SINAI, MEET MARIANNE, ORDER A LOVE PLATE, AND LEARN FROM THIS AMAZING WOMAN.

IN THE WORDS OF MARIANNE, PEACE TOGETHER FOREVER.

STUFF IN BOWLS AND BOXES

MOST STREET FOOD WAS BORN AND BRED AT NIGHT MARKETS. MOST OF ASIA IS FAR TOO HOT TO VEND FOOD ON THE STREETS DURING THE DAY. THE NIGHTS ARE WHEN PEOPLE COME TOGETHER AND CELEBRATE STREET FOOD. BIG BOWLS, SMALL BITES, NOODLES, STICKS, SOUPS, FRIED FOODS, MEAT, SEAFOOD, AND VEGETABLES ... EVERY SINGLE TYPE OF FOOD THAT WE HAVE COVERED IN THIS COOKBOOK CAN BE TRACED BACK TO THESE NIGHT MARKETS. THE RECENT POPULARIZATION OF THE ASIAN STREET FOOD NIGHT MARKETS IN NORTH AMERICA HAS SEEN THIS TRADITIONAL FOOD CULTURE BECOME NEWLY INTEGRATED WITH LIVE MUSIC, CRAFT BEER, FOOD TRUCKS, AND SO ON. BUT MORE IMPORTANT, IT IS PUSHING THE BOUNDARIES OF WHAT STREET FOOD IS. BOWLS AND BOXES, SOUPS AND NOODLES ARE REPLACING THE TRADITIONAL HAMBURGER, HOTDOG, AND FRENCH FRIES — THESE RECIPES ARE INSPIRED BY THE AGE-OLD TRADITION OF PEOPLE COMING TOGETHER TO SHARE STREET FOOD.

EGG DROP PHO

VIETNAMESE PHO SOUP WAS INTRODUCED TO ME QUITE SOME TIME AGO. WHAT I LOVED ABOUT IT THEN — AND STILL DO TODAY — IS THAT THE COOK MAKES A LOT OF THE MEAL RIGHT IN FRONT OF YOU. AND I LOVE HAVING THE OPTION OF HAVING CRUNCHIER VEGETABLES AND MEDIUM-RARE SHAVED BEEF IN MY SOUP INSTEAD OF THE TRADITIONAL OVERCOOKED BABY FOOD THAT SOME SOUPS SEEM TO BE BASED ON. I ADD A POACHED EGG TO MY VERSION OF THE SOUP PARTLY BECAUSE IT LOOKS GREAT, BUT MORE IMPORTANT, BECAUSE WHEN YOU CRACK INTO THAT EGG IN THE SOUP IT BRINGS THE BROTH FLAVOR TO A WHOLE NEW PLACE.

SERVES 10

PHO, PRONOUNCED *FUH*

Finely chop the onions and toss them into a medium pot with the canola oil over high heat. Add the dried chili flakes. Cook the onions, while stirring, for approximately 2 minutes, or until they are soft. Add in the fish sauce, miso paste, and oyster sauce. Keep stirring the onions and pour in the chicken stock. Add about 2 cups (500 mL) of boiling water to cut the stock and then add the bok choy. Cook the bok choy for approximately 5 minutes, or until tender. While the bok choy cooks, crack one egg right into the broth. Stir the broth around that egg for 4 to 5 minutes, or until it is soft-poached. Soft-poach all the eggs, using the same time frame, remove them from the pot, and place them gently on a paper towel.

YOUR PHO AWAITS

To make your bowls, place a cluster of dry vermicelli noodles (or presoaked noodles if you prefer your noodles soft), some raw beef, bean sprouts, enoki mushrooms, and a poached egg in each. Put the broth from the pot over the contents in the bowls (make sure you grab some of the bok choy and onions). The hot broth will soften the sprouts and mushrooms, and will cook the beef and noodles. Let the hot broth rest for approximately 5 minutes before serving. Quarter the lime and squeeze in the juice. You can even toss the squeezed lime wedges in the soup along with the basil leaves. Break the yolk of the eggs with your spoon, and stir it around before you dig in.

2 large Spanish onions

2 tablespoons (30 mL) canola oil

1 tablespoon (15 mL) dried chili flakes

1 cup (250 mL) fish sauce

1 tablespoon (15 mL) miso paste

1 teaspoon (5 mL) oyster sauce

6 cups (1.5 L) warm chicken stock

2 bunches bok choy, stems removed

4 eggs

1 package (14 oz/400 g) dry vermicelli noodles

8 oz (225 g) shaved raw beef ribeye or beef tenderloin pieces

1 cup (250 mL) bean sprouts

1 cup (250 mL) enoki mushrooms

1 lime

1 cup (250 mL) basil leaves, stems removed

MIAMI BEEF RIBS

SERVES 6 TO 10

MIAMI BEEF RIBS ARE SOMETHING YOU NEED TO GET FROM A QUALITY BUTCHER. THEY ARE THINLY SHAVED BEEF RIBS — THE THINNER THE BETTER, BECAUSE THAT MEANS YOU'RE LITERALLY SEARING THEM AND THEN THEY'RE DONE — THAT GO THROUGH THE BONE INSTEAD OF WITH THE BONE. THEY ARE INCREDIBLY FLAVORFUL AND MAKE A VERY AWESOME BBQ TREAT. IF THE BUTCHER HAS NO CLUE WHAT YOU'RE TALKING ABOUT, THEN STEP AWAY FROM THE COUNTER. THEY DON'T KNOW HOW TO USE A BAND-SAW.

Juice from 4 limes, divided

½ cup (125 mL) soy sauce

3 tablespoons (45 mL) hoisin sauce

1 teaspoon (5 mL) chili paste

1 teaspoon (5 mL) honey

1 teaspoon (5 mL) five-spice powder

20 Miami ribs, 3-bone thin-cut

¼ cup (60 mL) sunflower shoots

BEEF RIBS, BABY

Combine the juice from three of the limes with the soy sauce, hoisin sauce, chili paste, honey, and five-spice powder in a bowl. Mix it thoroughly so that there are no clumps. Put the beef ribs into this sauce, cover, and marinate in the fridge overnight.

If you are using a BBQ, preheat it to 450°F (230°C). Take the saucy ribs and grill them for approximately 3 minutes per side. If BBQ isn't an option, place them in a grill pan, and cook them on the stovetop or under the broiler for approximately 3 minutes per side. Squeeze the remaining lime's juice over the finished beef ribs. Because these are cut so thinly, they don't take long to cook. If anything, the skill in this dish is not overcooking the ribs.

Transfer the ribs to a serving platter, and garnish with sunflower shoots.

PORK RIBLETS

THE WORD "RIBLETS" IS JUST CUTE TO SAY. LITTLE RIBLETS ARE JUST BACK RIBS CUT THROUGH THE BONE DOWN THE MIDDLE OF THE RACK. MOST BUTCHERS WANT TO CUT THE RACK IN THREES, AS CUTTING THEM ANY SMALLER CAN BE A LITTLE DANGEROUS. RIBLETS ARE VERY COMMON IN MOST TYPES OF ASIAN STREET FOOD CUISINE, AND BECAUSE THEY ARE MUCH SMALLER THAN JUST BIG OL' RIBS, THEY ARE EASIER TO EAT ON THE GO AND MAKE LESS MESS.

CUTE LIL' RIBLETS.
JUST WANT TO PINCH THEIR PIGGY CHEEKS.

In a blender or food processor, blitz the ginger, garlic, mint leaves, soy sauce, and chili paste. Then add the whiskey, molasses, honey, cayenne, and turmeric to the blender, and give it another couple hits to combine.

Cut the long strips of riblets into three-bone portions. In a small bowl, mix together the salt and pepper, and then rub it all over the riblets. Place the riblets in a large resealable plastic bag, and pour the marinade over them. Let them sit in the marinade, refrigerated, for 12 to 24 hours.

HERE, RIBBY, RIBBY

The next day, take the ribs out of the plastic bag, reserving the marinade, and grill the ribs in a grill pan with about 1 tablespoon (15 mL) vegetable oil over high heat. Sear them for approximately 5 minutes per side, or until you have a nice sear on the riblets.

In a large saucepan over low heat, place the beer, 1 cup (250 mL) of water, and the reserved marinade. Heat this through, then add the riblets to the saucepan and slow-cook them, uncovered, for approximately 2 hours, or until the meat is soft. You need to bring the liquid to a boil, then turn down the heat to maintain a gentle simmer. Take the riblets out of the sauce, and put them on a plate. Turn the heat up to medium-high, and add the butter. On a serving plate, put the ribs on a bed of lettuce, and then pour the sauce over them. Cut the limes into wedges. Top the riblets with finely chopped Thai chilies and serve lime wedges on the side.

2 tablespoons (30 mL) finely chopped ginger

2 tablespoons (30 mL) finely chopped garlic

12 mint leaves

1 cup (250 mL) soy sauce

1 tablespoon (15 mL) chili paste

2 oz (60 mL) whiskey

1 teaspoon (5 mL) molasses

1 teaspoon (5 mL) honey

1 teaspoon (5 mL) cayenne pepper

½ teaspoon (2.5 mL) ground turmeric

1 rack pork back, ribs cut into riblets

1 tablespoon (15 mL) kosher salt

1 tablespoon (15 mL) black pepper

1 tablespoon (15 mL) vegetable oil

1 pint (16 oz/470 mL) dark beer

1 tablespoon (15 mL) salted butter

1 cup (250 mL) shredded iceberg lettuce

2 limes

4 tablespoons (60 mL) finely chopped Thai chilies

LAMB 'N' RAMEN

SERVES 6

LAMB IS NOT A TRADITIONAL PROTEIN FOR RAMEN. I LOVE THE LAMB AND USE IT HERE BECAUSE THE FAT THAT COOKS OFF THE MEAT GIVES A UNIQUE AND DISTINCT RICHNESS TO THE BROTH. THE LAMB FAT FLAVOR DEVELOPS OVER TIME, SO EVERY DAY YOU LEAVE IT, THE RAMEN IS THAT MUCH BUTTER ... WHOOPS! I MEAN "BETTER." FREUDIAN SLIP.

6 cloves garlic

2 Spanish onions

1 leek

1 cup (250 mL) finely chopped green onions

¼ cup (60 mL) canola oil

2 tablespoons (30 mL) freshly minced ginger

1 tablespoon (15 mL) chili paste

¼ cup (60 mL) soy sauce

¼ cup (60 mL) Marsala

1 cup (250 mL) thinly sliced water chestnuts

1 cup (250 mL) thinly sliced brown mushrooms

1 ½ lb (750 g) ground fatty lamb

1 tablespoon (15 mL) kosher salt

1 teaspoon (5 mL) black pepper

1 teaspoon (5 mL) ground cumin

1 teaspoon (5 mL) ground fennel seeds

2 tablespoons (30 mL) basil paste

2 cups (500 mL) warm beef stock

6 eggs

1 ½ lb (750 g) dry ramen noodles

1 bunch fresh spinach leaves, stems removed

1 cup (250 mL) bean sprouts

JAMMIN' TO THE LAMBIN' RAMEN

Finely chop the garlic, onions, leek, and green onions. In a large pot over high heat, warm the oil, and add the garlic, onions, leek, green onions, and ginger with the chili paste. Sauté for approximately 2 minutes, and then add the soy sauce, Marsala, water chestnuts, and mushrooms. Allow to cook for approximately 5 minutes, and then add 2 cups (500 mL) of water to bring down the temperature of the stock.

While we wait for those flavors to take over the boring ol' water, take the lamb meat and season it with the salt, pepper, cumin, fennel, and basil paste. Work all the ingredients into the meat, and using your hands, form them into little imperfect meatballs about the size of a golf ball. Roll all the balls using the palm of your hand. In a nonstick pan, sear the meatballs, approximately 10 balls at a time. Add the cooked meatballs to the stock every time you finish a batch. Once all the meatballs are in the stock, add the warm beef stock (or, if you can find it, lamb broth). Let the soup simmer, uncovered, for approximately 1 ½ hours.

OKAY, NOW SOUP FOR YOU ...

When the soup is almost ready, boil the eggs in a separate pot of water for about 8 minutes. Carefully remove them from the boiling water and place them in a bowl of ice water. Meanwhile, put the noodles and spinach in the broth. Let the noodles cook in the warm broth, and start to spoon the soup into individual bowls. Peel all the shells off the eggs, and cut each egg in half. Place some bean sprouts and two egg halves in each bowl of soup. Serve immediately.

ZUCCHINI NOODLES WITH THAI FRIED CHICKEN

SERVES 4 TO 8

- 8 skin-on bone-in chicken drumsticks
- 4 cups (1 L) buttermilk
- 2 eggs
- 3 large green zucchinis
- 3 large yellow zucchinis
- ¼ cup + 2 tablespoons (100 mL) rice wine vinegar
- 1 bunch basil
- 1 bunch cilantro
- 2 cloves garlic
- 2 tablespoons (30 mL) freshly grated ginger
- 1 jalapeño pepper
- 1 cup (250 mL) coconut milk
- Juice from 1 lemon
- 1 teaspoon (5 mL) tamarind paste
- 1 cup (250 mL) chickpea flour
- 1 tablespoon (15 mL) ground ginger
- 1 tablespoon (15 mL) garlic powder
- 1 tablespoon (15 mL) kosher salt
- 1 tablespoon (15 mL) black pepper
- ¼ cup + 2 tablespoons (100 mL) crushed peanuts

I'D SAY MY TASTE FOR FRIED CHICKEN HAS REALLY EVOLVED OVER THE PAST COUPLE YEARS. WHAT STARTED OFF AS A FRIED CHICKEN BUFFET-FEST IN BUFFALO HAS REALLY TRANSFORMED INTO EXPERIMENTAL DEEP-FRYING. THE BRINE YOU USE FOR YOUR CHICKEN AND HOW YOU SEASON THE FLOUR REALLY DOES POINT THE SUCCULENT MEAT IN A GENERAL FLAVOR DIRECTION. IN THIS CASE I WANTED THE CHICKEN FLAVOR TO BE BALANCED BY THE COOLING ZUCCHINI NOODLE SAUCE.

THE FRENCH THAI?

French the chicken drumsticks. Frenching means cutting around the skin of the drum just above the meaty drum and pulling back the skin to expose a small piece of the bone. Despite popular belief, it has nothing to do with kissing. If you buy the drumsticks at a butcher's shop, ask them to do it. Your butcher will confirm frenching is not kissing. (I hope.)

In a bowl, mix the buttermilk with the eggs. Add the drumsticks and leave the bowl, covered, in the fridge overnight.

When it comes to making long noodles out of zucchini, the best thing to use is a mandolin. Carefully (and I mean very carefully) run the zucchini lengthwise on the mandolin with a julienne attachment so the noodles come out nice and long. If you want to use your knife, cut the zucchini lengthwise into quarters and then into individual strands. But trust me, if you can do it safely, the mandolin is the way to rock 'n' roll. Don't use a vegetable peeler, though. The shape will be all wrong. Combine the yellow and green noodles in a bowl, add the rice wine vinegar and a little bit of salt (not the 1 tablespoon/15 mL — you use that later), and let the zucchini noodles cook in the acid for approximately 30 minutes.   ❯ ❯ ❯

>>> SAUCE TIME

In a blender, blitz the basil, cilantro, garlic, ginger, jalapeño pepper, coconut milk, lemon juice, and tamarind paste until it's smooth and lump-free. Drain the zucchini noodles, using your hands to press out all the vinegar, and then pat them dry on paper towel. In a bowl, mix the dry zucchini noodles with the coconut basil sauce.

In a separate bowl, combine the chickpea flour with the ground ginger, garlic powder, 1 tablespoon (15 mL) of salt, and the pepper. Take the drumsticks out of the buttermilk bath and dredge them in the flour. Press the flour as hard as possible onto the meat. Prepare a table-top deep-fryer or deep saucepan with 2 inches (5 cm) of oil heated to 330°F (165°C). Fry the drums one or two at a time for 10 to 12 minutes, or until the meat is cooked through. Watch carefully so they don't burn.

Let the fried drums rest on paper towel to absorb any excess oil. In bowls, dress the zucchini noodles with some crushed peanuts and top with the fried drums.

EXPERIMENTAL DEEP-FRYING

BIG BOWLS, SMALL BITES, NOODLES, SEAFOOD, AND VEGETABLES

LOBSTA-ZILLA

AS THE PRICE OF LOBSTER CONTINUES TO DROP, WE SEE IT ON MENUS, BOTH RESTAURANT AND FOOD TRUCKS/CARTS, MORE. I THINK NOW THAT WE HAVE MORE ACCESS TO AMAZING QUALITY LOBSTER, HOW WE USE IT IN OUR CREATIVE STREET FOOD WILL REALLY HELP MAKE IT MORE ACCESSIBLE TO PEOPLE AND TAKE AWAY SOME OF THE MYSTERY AND FEAR.

1 lb (500 g) rice noodles

½ cup (125 mL) white vinegar

2 whole, fresh lobsters (no larger than 1 ½ lb/750 g each)

1 large carrot

1 stalk celery

1 tablespoon (15 mL) olive oil

4 cloves garlic

4 Thai chilies

1 cup (250 mL) bean sprouts

1 egg

¼ cup (60 mL) soy sauce

2 tablespoons (30 mL) hoisin sauce

Kosher salt

Black pepper

1 ½ lemons

1 bunch green onions

½ cup (125 mL) chopped fresh basil, stems removed

THIS IS WHAT HAPPENS WHEN YOU TAKE LOBSTER AND GO KAPOW TO IT

Before you do any cooking, soak the rice noodles in water for approximately 30 minutes, or until they are soft. Then get ready to give your lobsters a vinegar bath. Oh yes!

Prepare an ice bath large enough to hold both lobsters. Boil some water in a large saucepan over high heat and add the white vinegar. The reason for the vinegar? It helps keep the lobster meat from sticking to the shell when you crack it open. Boil the lobsters for approximately 12 minutes. Remove them from the water and put them in the ice bath to stop the cooking. Before boiling live lobsters, you can place them in the freezer for approximately 20 minutes to slightly anesthetize them before cooking.

Chop the carrot into thin coins and slice the celery thinly on an angle. Pull the arms off the lobster, crack the shells, and pull out all the meat. Turn the lobster on its back and crack it down the belly into the tail. Pull the meat out of the tail and clean the belly. You should now have beautiful claw, tail, and arm meat, and a hollowed-out lobster shell. Boil the shell for about another 10 minutes before you use it as a vessel for your noodle dish.

BRINGING THE LOBSTER AND THE ZILLA TOGETHER AT LAST

In a wok or large pan, get the oil super hot. Thinly slice the garlic and finely chop the Thai chilies. Toss the garlic, chilies with their seeds, carrots, celery, and bean sprouts into the hot oil. Tossing the ingredients around in the pan constantly, cook them for approximately 5 minutes, and then add the lobster meat. Beat the egg in a bowl and add it to the wok. Immediately toss in the rice noodles with the soy sauce and the hoisin sauce. It is important to keep the ingredients moving so that they do not scorch and burn. Mix it all around for a couple minutes so that the egg covers the noodles while it cooks. Season to taste with some salt and pepper and then squeeze in the juice from the half lemon.

Fill the lobster cavity with the lobster–zilla filling, top it with sliced green onions and basil, and serve with lemon wedges.

SEARED TUNA RICE ROLLS

THIS DISH IS INCREDIBLY FRESH AND LIGHT. YOU CAN CHANGE THE FISH ANVH. DO NOT — I REPEAT, DO NOT — MAKE THIS DISH WITH NON-SUSHI-GRADE FISH.

SERVES 5 TO 10

1 piece (6 oz/185 g) sushi-grade ahi tuna

Kosher salt

Black pepper

1 cup (250 mL) shredded red cabbage

½ cup (125 mL) apple cider vinegar, divided

1 cup (250 mL) shredded green cabbage

2 red jalapeño peppers

8–10 rice paper wraps

1 cup (250 mL) bean sprouts

1 green apple, skin on if you like, cut into matchsticks

1 cup (250 mL) basil leaves

1 cup (250 mL) cilantro

½ cup (125 mL) Sriracha sauce

½ cup (125 mL) oyster sauce

¼ cup (60 mL) pea shoots

NO SUCH THING AS A BORING TUNA SALAD. ESPECIALLY WHEN IT'S NOT SALAD.

Lightly season the ahi tuna with salt and pepper. In a skillet over high heat, sear the tuna for approximately 1 minute per side, or until seared on both sides. Remove the tuna from the heat, let it rest for approximately 5 minutes, and then slice into sashimi-size portions. (Yeah, that's a real measurement now. It means about the size of your thumb.)

In a bowl, soak the red cabbage with ¼ cup (60 mL) of the apple cider vinegar. In a separate bowl, soak the green cabbage with the remaining apple cider vinegar for approximately 10 minutes. Slice the red jalapeño peppers in half, remove and discard the seeds, and slice the peppers into long thin slivers. Remove both cabbages from the bowls and dry them off with paper towel.

SOAKING IT ALL UP

Soak each rice paper wrap in a bowl of lukewarm water until they go from hard to pliable. Lay them on a flat surface such as a clean countertop or a wooden cutting board.

Place some red and green cabbage on a rice paper wrap, add some beans sprouts, jalapeño, apple, a couple basil leaves, and some cilantro. Based on the length of your tuna and how long or fat you want to make your roll, place one or two pieces of tuna on top of the apple slaw. Roll one side over the filling, then tuck in the sides. Once everything is tightly covered, continue to roll the entire wrap. Pour the Sriracha sauce and oyster sauce into a small dipping bowl. Cut the wraps in half, and serve with the sauce and some pea shoots scattered over top as garnish.

BIBIMBAP BOWL

THE BIBIMBAP — PRONOUNCED *PIBIMBAP* — BOWL IS A KOREAN RICE BOWL FILLED WITH VEG, MEAT OR FISH, AND USUALLY AN EGG OF SOME SORT. THE BEST PART ABOUT THE BOWL IS HOW PERFECTLY UNIFORM IT IS. EVERY INGREDIENT TAKES ON ITS OWN WORLD WITHIN THE BOWL. TRADITIONALLY IT'S SERVED IN A HOT STONE BOWL, BUT IF YOU DON'T HAVE ONE JUST LYING AROUND THE HOUSE, A NORMAL BOWL WILL SUFFICE. PLUS, THE HOT STONE BOWL … KIND OF HARD TO MAKE THAT THING MOBILE WITHOUT BURNING OFF THE PRINTS OF YOUR HAND. ›››

2 carrots

1 English cucumber, skin on, seeds removed

1 daikon radish

1 cup (250 mL) rice wine vinegar

Kosher salt

2 Portobello mushrooms

1 bunch kale

Juice from 1 lemon, divided

4 cups (1 L) calrose or white rice

8 jumbo shrimp, peeled and deveined

2 teaspoons (10 mL) wasabi

1 tablespoon (15 mL) salted butter

2 red or green jalapeño peppers

1 sheet seaweed paper

4 eggs

1 cup (250 mL) finely chopped cilantro

½ cup (125 mL) chili oil

PREP YOUR BOWLS

This is a prep-heavy dish. Just sayin'. It's really good, but prep heavy. Start with your veg, keeping all the different veg separate until it's time to bring them together to be devoured in the bowl. Cut the carrots, cucumber, and daikon radish into matchsticks. Lightly pickle each one in separate bowls with the rice wine vinegar and about 1 tablespoon (15 mL) salt. Clean all the dirt off the Portobello mushrooms, use a spoon to remove the gills underneath the cap, and then remove the stalks. Slice the mushrooms very thinly, and cut the kale into small chunks. Steam them together over boiling water in a pot over high heat for approximately 5 minutes, or until soft but not mushy. Place them in a clean bowl, lightly salt, and add half of the lemon juice over top.

Place the rice in a separate pot containing 8 cups (2 L) of water, and cook the rice, covered, over medium-low heat for approximately 10 minutes, or until the water has been fully absorbed. Remove the saucepan from the heat, transfer the rice to a bowl, and cover it until needed.

Get a nonstick pan super hot over high heat, and toss in the jumbo shrimp (no oil). Sear them for approximately 2 minutes, then add the wasabi and butter. Flip the shrimp in the pan, and allow to cook for 7 to 8 minutes, or until the wasabi covers the shrimp. Take the pan off the heat, and add the remaining lemon juice and salt to taste.

BOWL IT ALL HOME

Thinly slice the jalapeño peppers and discard the seeds. Cut the seaweed into little matchsticks to garnish the bowls. Fry all the eggs, but keep them separate.

Build your bowls by placing the rice down first. Then start to place all the items around the side of the bowl but in groups: carrots, radish, cucumber, mushrooms, kale, and two jumbo shrimp per bowl. Top each bowl with a fried egg, and then garnish with the finely chopped cilantro, thinly sliced jalapeño peppers, and the seaweed. Drizzle chili oil over the entire dish.

THE NIGHTS ARE WHEN PEOPLE COME TOGETHER TO CELEBRATE STREET FOOD

BAPCHA – KOREAN FOOD CART, NYC, NEW YORK

QUITE OFTEN, FOOD CARTS AND TRUCKS JUST NEED TO ADAPT TO THEIR SURROUNDINGS. SOMETIMES YOU BASE A MENU NOT ON WHAT YOU WANT, BUT ON WHAT YOU CAN GET. YOU TAKE INGREDIENTS THAT YOU HAVE ACCESS TO AND YOU MAKE SURE YOU PUT TOGETHER THE ABSOLUTELY BEST DISH POSSIBLE.

JOHN AND JEANNIE LEE OWN THE KOREAN FOOD CART BAPCHA (WHICH LITERALLY MEANS FOOD CART OR RICE CART IN KOREAN). THEIR BEEF MARINADE CONSTANTLY CHANGES — KIWI SWAPPED WITH PINEAPPLE, SWAPPED WITH APPLES, FOR EXAMPLE. ALL OF THIS JUST TO MAKE THEIR INCREDIBLY MOIST GALBI AND BULGOGI BEEF SERVED OVER RICE OR GLASS NOODLES. THE PRINCIPLE IS THAT ACID MAY BE ACID, BUT THE FLAVOR OF EACH FRUIT IS UNIQUE AND BOLD AND BRINGS ITS OWN SET OF CHARACTERISTICS TO THE PRINCIPLES OF KOREAN BBQ.

YOU TAKE INGREDIENTS THAT YOU HAVE ACCESS TO AND YOU MAKE SURE YOU PUT TOGETHER THE ABSOLUTELY BEST DISH POSSIBLE.

KIMCHI STEW

SERVES 4

I ABSOLUTELY LOVE THIS RECIPE. IT HAS INCREDIBLE WARMING POWERS, BOTH FROM THE TEMPERATURE IT'S SERVED AT AND FROM THE HEAT OF THE KIMCHI. BUT WHAT I LOVE MOST ABOUT IT IS THAT THE KIMCHI FLAVORS REALLY DO DEVELOP INTO THE STEW. JUST LIKE A PIECE OF STEWED BEEF, THE SLOW-COOKING STEW BREAKS DOWN THE KIMCHI AND TAKES THOSE INTENSE FLAVORS ON A JOURNEY THROUGH THE ENTIRE DISH. THE MORE RICE YOU ADD, THE THICKER THE STEW; THE LESS RICE, THE MORE SOUPY IT WILL BE.

KIMCHI NOW AS A STEW

Dice the celery, carrot, onion, and leek into small pieces. Warm the canola oil over high heat in a soup pot or large saucepan and sauté the veg, stirring, for approximately 5 minutes, or until they soften. Cut the tomatoes into large chunks and add them to the pot as well. Stir well, and pour in the tomato juice, Worcestershire sauce, horseradish, and then the kimchi. Turn down the heat. Add 3 cups (750 mL) of water, and season to taste with salt. Let the soup simmer slowly, uncovered, over low heat for approximately 1 hour. The tomatoes will break down and thicken the stock, and the spice and flavor from the kimchi will start to work their way through the stock.

NO SOUP FOR YOU ... STEW FOR YOU

Place 4 cups (1 L) of water in a large saucepan, bring to a boil, and add the rice. Cook the rice, covered, for approximately 10 minutes, or until the water has been fully absorbed. If the water has been absorbed but the rice is still hard, add a little more boiling water and cook for a few minutes more. If the rice is done, remove it from the heat. Cut the green onions on the diagonal into thin slices for a garnish. Fry the egg for approximately 5 minutes, but make sure that the yolk is still runny.

Place the rice in large bowls but push most of the rice to one side of each. Pour the kimchi and broth over the rice, and top each with a fried egg, green onions, and Sriracha sauce

4 stalks celery

1 large carrot

1 Spanish onion

1 leek

2 tablespoons (30 mL) canola oil

12 Roma tomatoes

1 cup (250 mL) tomato juice

¼ cup (60 mL) Worcestershire sauce

1 tablespoon (15 mL) horseradish

2 cups (500 mL) Kimchi (page 118)

Kosher salt

2 cups (500 mL) short-grain white or calrose rice

1 bunch green onions

4 eggs

¼ cup (60 mL) Sriracha sauce

ROY CHOI, CHEGO, LOS ANGELES, CA

I WAS IN LA FOR ABOUT FOUR OR FIVE DAYS FILMING *REBEL WITHOUT A KITCHEN*, AND HAD ONE OF THE BEST EXPERIENCES OF MY LIFE. I WAS INVOLVED IN A LARGE FOOD EVENT IN THE CITY, AND I GOT TO MEET THE WHO'S WHO OF THE FOOD AND BEVERAGE WORLD IN LA. EVERYONE WAS ABSOLUTELY AMAZING AND IT ACTUALLY DEBUNKED A LOT OF THE MYTHS I HAD ABOUT LA. THESE WERE SOME GOOD PEOPLE WITH GOOD TALENT. THEY WERE REAL AND GENUINE, AND THEY TRULY BELIEVED IN THE COMMUNITY THAT IS LA'S VIBRANT FOOD SCENE. FOOD TRUCKS, RESTAURANTS, BUTCHERS, FARMERS, BLOGGERS, EVENT PLANNERS, AND JOURNALISTS — THEY'RE ALL SO PASSIONATE ABOUT LA AND WHAT THEY DO THERE. I WAS BLOWN AWAY, AND FOR THE FIRST TIME IN A LONG TIME, I CONSIDERED LA AS A POTENTIAL SITE FOR FUTURE BUSINESS FOR OUR OWN COMPANY.

BUT THEN SOMETHING HAPPENED ON MY SECOND-LAST NIGHT IN THE CITY. WE WERE OUT WITH A COUPLE GUYS WHO WORK ON THE TV SHOW, HAVING A COUPLE BEERS DOWN BY THE HOTEL POOL, AND I GOT QUIET. I WENT FROM SOAKING UP ALL THE INTENSE ENERGY THAT WAS LA TO BEING INCREDIBLY REFLECTIVE. THE NEXT DAY WAS, IN MY OPINION, ONE OF THE BIGGEST MOMENTS OF MY CAREER — RIGHT UP THERE WITH LAUNCHING THE FOOD TRUCK AND THE RESTAURANT, EVEN DOING THIS COOKBOOK AND THE TV SHOW. I WAS ABOUT TO MEET A STREET FOOD ICON, ROY CHOI. IF YOU DON'T KNOW WHO THIS IS, JUST SEARCH ONLINE FOR "LA SON" OR THE "KOGI BEEF TRUCK," AND THEN CONTINUE READING.

I'M SITTING WITH THE CREW OUTSIDE CHEGO, WHICH IS ROY'S STREET-FOOD-IN-BOWLS CONCEPT, AND FOR THE FIRST TIME IN A LONG TIME, I WAS NERVOUS. I CAN HONESTLY SAY I WAS NERVOUS ABOUT MEETING HIM. I HAD PRACTICED THIS DEEP, INTELLECTUAL YET TOPICAL SET OF CONVERSATION NOTES, BUT IN THE BACK OF MY MIND ALL I COULD THINK WAS "THIS IS ROY F'NG CHOI. DUDE! ROY CHOI!" AND MY BIGGEST FEAR WAS THAT I DIDN'T QUITE BELONG THERE. WHO WAS I WHEN IT CAME TO ROY CHOI?

KY WAS INCREDIBLY CALM. IN FACT, WHEN I SAW HOW CALM SHE WAS ABOUT MEETING ROY, I THINK I GOT EVEN MORE NERVOUS, BECAUSE WHEN IT COMES TO OUR DYNAMIC, ONE OF US IS ALWAYS CALM AND THE OTHER IS USUALLY A WRECK. THIS TIME WE BOTH GOT THROUGH IT CALMLY.

ROY AND I MET, WE TALKED, WE ATE KIMCHI AND RICE BOWLS TOGETHER, WE FILMED A LITTLE BIT OF TV, AND EVERYTHING FELT PRETTY GOOD. HE WAS DEEP AND VERY PHILOSOPHICAL ABOUT HIS POSITION ON FOOD OR WHAT IT MEANT TO CREATE FOOD FOR PEOPLE. CULTURALLY, FOOD IS AN EXPRESSION OF WHAT YOU KNOW BEST AND WHAT YOU LOVE THE MOST. HE CALLED IT REFRIGERATOR MEALS — THE STUFF YOU HAVE CLOSE BY FOR YOUR ENTIRE LIFE JUST SITTING IN YOUR FRIDGE AS STAPLES OR LEFTOVERS AND YET EVERY SINGLE TIME YOU PULL IT OUT YOU CAN CREATE SOMETHING UNIQUE EVERY SINGLE TIME. I'M TALKING SOME DEEP FOOD CONVERSATION, WITH A CAMERA IN OUR FACES AND KIMCHI RICE IN MY MOUTH. THE WHOLE THING JUST MADE SO MUCH SENSE FOR LA, AND THE NERVOUSNESS WAS GONE. AFTER ALL OF THIS TALK OF TRADITION AND CULTURE, HE LEANED OVER THE TABLE AND TOOK MY CHOPSTICKS THAT WERE STICKING IN MY RICE, AND HE PLACED THEM ON THE TOP OF MY BOWL JUST OFF TO THE SIDE. I WAS WORRIED I HAD DONE SOMETHING OFFENSIVE. WE KEPT ROLLING BUT NOW I WAS NERVOUS AGAIN BECAUSE I THOUGHT I HAD DONE SOMETHING CULTURALLY WRONG — AND THEN WE GOT UP AND SLAPPED HANDS. WHEN HE LEANED IN FOR THE SLAP HANDS/BRO HUG GOODBYE, HE SAID, "RESPECT, BRO." I WAS CALM AGAIN. EVEN IF JUST FOR A COUPLE MINUTES, I FELT LIKE, YES, I DID BELONG, AND YES, I WAS TALKING TO JUST ANOTHER PASSIONATE DUDE WHO LOVES WHAT HE DOES. I WAS LEFT WITH TWO EMPTY BOWLS AND THE WORD "RESPECT."

FOOD IS AN EXPRESSION OF WHAT YOU KNOW BEST AND WHAT YOU LOVE THE MOST.

THANK YOU...

Wow! I wrote a cookbook. Kind of crazy. At least my English degree is getting used. Well, I guess I should start off by thanking my English degree. Thank you, English degree.

Thank you to Andrea Magyar and everyone at Penguin Canada for this opportunity to make *Street Food Diaries*.

Thank you to Josie Crimi, Scott McNeil, and everyone at General Purpose Pictures. Not only did you make the Penguin connection for us and make our awesome *Rebel* show a reality, but you believed in our ability to actually make these things. I love you guys like really, really distant aunts and uncles. From Sweden.

Thank you to Travel + Escape, The Cottage Life Channel, and Blue Ant Media for helping the Fidel Gastro and *Rebel Without a Kitchen* street food brand grow in new media-rific ways.

Thank you to Caiti McLelland. You are such a cool cookbook editor. I can't even tell how you made my words make sense. Not only did you give constructive notes, but you also gave me some awesome confidence along the way.

Thank you to Dani Houston. I've never seen someone go from admin person to food stylist, and then back to admin person, and then over to a bar to work a shift, and then take on a couple law office shifts, and then back to food styling. You have an amazing work ethic.

Thank you to all the food trucks, food carts, restaurants, and chefs we met with across North America, and talked to, and whose food we devoured while working on this book. Special thanks to Turnstyle Tours, who took Ky and me through New York's street food scene in two straight days.

Thank you to Toronto's vibrant and constantly growing street food community — the food trucks, bloggers, writers, chefs, enthusiasts, foodies, and restaurateurs who make Toronto one of the greatest culinary destinations in the world.

WORK HARD

BE SMART

MARKET

Thank you to the entire Fidel Gastro's/Lisa Marie staff, who have not only stood by us as we brought the company to where it is today, but continue to stand by us as we take it in a whacky direction every new day. Thanks for being there. Had you not, I might not have been able to do this book. Now, get back to work!

Thank you to my business partners, Kyla Zanardi and Dom Finelli. Your constant belief in our ability as a company not only bewilders me but also fuels me to keep pushing harder and faster. Thank you.

Thank you to my friends and family for not giving me a hard time for being essentially invisible for the past few years, and especially since I started writing this book. You have always accepted my excuse of "I'm working" with love and support.

Thank you to my parents for having me ... and for believing in my crazy little idea to quit my job and sell sandwiches off a table. Now that is unconditional love.

One massive, massive thank-you to this book's co-creator and photographer, Kyla Zanardi. You pushed us in all the right directions. You are the only person I could have done this book with. You are so incredibly talented it's not even funny. You are the love of my life, and I could not have done this without you. P.S. I still get the relationship discount on food photography, yes?

And a final thank-you to my late nonno. He was my everything, and not a day goes by that his voice and words don't run through my veins. I miss you, Nonno.

Work hard. Be smart.

INDEX

VIVA LA STREET

FOOD REVOLUCIÓN

ABOUT THE AUTHOR

Matt Basile is the creator of the Toronto-based street food brand Fidel Gastro's, which originated as a pop-up selling street food in underground markets across the city. Matt operates one of Canada's most recognizable food trucks and a street-food-inspired cicchetti bar called Lisa Marie, and he is the host of the reality TV show *Rebel Without a Kitchen*. Matt has teamed up with his partner in business and life, Kyla Zanardi, who is the *Street Food Diaries* photographer. The two have spent their lives together making fun food and photographing it.

🏠 **FIDELGASTRO.CA**   f **FIDEL-GASTROS**

🐦 📷 **@FIDELGASTROS**